Differences Between Bible Versions

(Updated and Expanded Edition)

By

Gary F. Zeolla

EXLIBRIS

Piotra Blumczyńskiego

ISBN: 0-75962-501-8

This book is printed on acid free paper.

1stBooks - rev. 5/2/01

Contents

Chapter

Translation Principles

Greek Text-types

KJV Only-ism

Various Versions

Appendixes

Unless otherwise indicated, all Scripture references in this book are from: *The New King James Version*. Nashville, TN: Thomas Nelson Publishers, 1982. See the Bible Versions List page for other versions referred to.

Unless otherwise indicated, all emphases in quotations throughout this book are added.

Bible Versions List

Below is a list of the Bible versions referred to throughout this book. The abbreviation used for each version is in parenthesis.

21st Century King James Version (KJ21). 21st Century King James Bible Publishers: Gary, SD. 1994.

Amplified Bible (Amp). Grand Rapids, MI: Zondervan, 1965.

Analytical-Literal Translation of the New Testament of the Holy Bible (ALT). Copyright © 1999-2001 by Gary F. Zeolla of Darkness to Light ministry (www.dtl.org).

Contemporary English Version/ Bible for Today's Family (CEV). Nashville: Thomas Nelson, 1991.

Darby, John Nelson. *The English Darby Bible* (DBY). Public Domain, 1890.

English Bible in Basic English (BBE). C.K. Ogden of the Orthological Institute, England: Cambridge Press, 1949, 1964.

God's Word (God's Word) is a copyrighted work of God's Word to the Nations Bible Society. Quotations are used by permission. Copyright 1995 by God's Word to the Nations Bible Society. All rights reserved.

Good News Bible/ Today's English Version (GNB). New York: American Bible Society, 1976.

Goodspeed, Edgar. *New Testament: An American Translation* (Gspd). Chicago: University of Chicago, 1938.

King James Version (KJV). Public domain.

King James Easy Reading Sword Study Bible/ Word of God Bible (KJER). Goodyear, AZ: The Publisher, n.a.

Literal Translation of the Bible (LITV). Copyright 1976 - 2000. Used by permission of the copyright holder, Jay P. Green, Sr.

Modern King James Version (MKJV). Copyright 1962 - 2000. Used by the permission of the copyright holder, Jay P. Green, Sr.

New American Bible for Catholics (NAB). Copyright © 1991,1986,1970. Washington, DC; Confraternity of Christian Doctrine.

New American Standard Bible (NASB or NAS77). La Habra, CA: The Lockman Foundation, 1977.

New American Standard Bible (NAS95). La Habra, CA: The Lockman Foundation, 1995.

New English Translation (NET). Copyright 1999.

New Century Version/ The Everyday Bible (NCV). Dallas: Word Publishing, 1988.

New English Bible (NEB). Cambridge: At the University Press, 1972.

New International Version (NIV). Grand Rapids: Zondervan, 1984.

New Jerusalem Bible, with Deutero-canon. Copyright 1985, Doubleday.

New Living Translation (NLT). Tyndale Charitable Trust. 1996.

New King James Version. Nashville, TN: Thomas Nelson Publishers, 1982.

New Revised Standard Version (NRSV). Grand Rapids: Zondervan, 1990.

Peterson, Eugene. *The Message* (Mesg). Colorado Springs, CO: NavPress, 1993.

Phillips, J.B. *The New Testament in Modern English* (Phi). New York: Macmillian Company, 1960.

Revised Standard Version (RSV). Grand Rapids: Zondervan, 1971.

Revised Webster's Bible (RWB). Public Domain, 1995.

Taylor, Kenneth. *The Living Bible* (LB). Wheaton, IL: Tyndale House Publishers, 1971.

Webster, Noah. *English Webster's Bible* (EWB). Public Domain, 1833.

Weymouth's Translation (Wey). Public Domain, n.a.

World English Bible (WEB). Longmont, CO: Rainbow Missions, Inc., copyright-free.

Wuest, Kenneth. *The New Testament: An Expanded Translation* (Wuest). Grand Rapids: Wm. B. Eerdman's, 1961.

Young, Robert. *Young's Literal Translation* (YLT). Public Domain, 1898.

Preface

The Bible study leader was teaching a lesson based on the parable of the vineyard workers (Matthew 20:1-16). After teaching for almost an hour, he finished with a few comments on the statement in verse 16, "Thus the last shall be first, and the first last." He then started asking for prayer requests.

But a lady at the study interrupted him and asked, "What about the second half of verse 16?" The teacher looked at his Bible and said, "There isn't a second half."

The lady replied, "There is in my Bible! It reads, 'for many be called, but few chosen.'" She continued, "I've been sitting here the whole study waiting to hear your comments on this statement. What does it mean?" By now, the teacher was dumbfounded.

Meanwhile, others in the study were all comparing their Bibles trying to figure out why some of their Bibles had this phrase but others didn't.

At this point, an elderly gentleman chided in, "Jesus is teaching about predestination here—that some are predestined to be saved but others are not. I know this is not what is being taught in the churches today, but it is what I believe because it is what the Bible teaches!"

Then a younger man jumped in and disagreed with him, and a heated debate broke out over the subject of predestination. Meanwhile, the teacher was still sitting there looking dazed. He was totally unprepared for this discussion.

The above incident occurred at a Bible study this writer attended. I have had similar problems while teaching my own studies. There have been times when I have asked someone to read a verse which supported what I was saying. However, when the person read the verse, the way it was worded in his Bible, it didn't quite say what I expected.

At other times, I have been sitting in church while the pastor was reading a passage of Scripture. But when trying to follow along, I have gotten "lost" since my Bible read differently from his.

If the reader has had similar experiences, you know this can all be rather confusing. What is happening here? Why does one Bible version read differently than another? Why do some versions of the Bible contain words, phrases, and even entire verses which others omit?

The answers to these questions are important. And they center mainly around two points: translation principles and Greek text-types. Opposing positions on these and other topics lead to the DIFFERENCES BETWEEN BIBLE VERSIONS.

Translation Principles

Gary Zeolla

Chapter One

My Bible Versions Experiences

I have struggled much over the subject of Bible versions and which Bible to use. Below is an overview of my experiences in dealing with this controversial subject.

Initial Bible Versions Experiences

My experience with the Bible began when my brother gave me a *New International Version* (NIV) of the Bible in March of 1983. I read though it three times before I even became a Christian in the winter of 1986.

But then I purchased an interlinear—*George Berry's Interlinear New Testament* to be exact. The Greek text in it is the *Textus Receptus* (TR). *The King James Version* (KJV) is in the margin. Using this interlinear did two things for me.

First, it introduced me to the question of textual variants. At the bottom of almost every page are textual variant footnotes. They compare the TR to seven other published Greek texts. Now at first sight this looked like a lot. At least one variant on every page of the Bible! It can't be that reliable!

However, as I looked at these variants I found that for the most part they were not that significant. There were some that seemed to matter. But overall, the differences were more "nit-picking" to me than anything else. So my previous studies about the textual integrity of the New Testament were confirmed, not hurt by this information.[1]

Second, I began comparing my NIV to Berry's word-for-word English translation below each Greek word. It did not take very long for me to realize that the NIV simply did not match up with this word-for-word translation.

The preacher of the church I was attending at the time used the *New American Standard Bible* (NASB). So I purchased the NASB version of *Ryrie's Study Bible*. Comparing the NASB with Berry's translation I found that it did match up much more closely than the NIV.

I also purchased Alfred Marshall's *NASB-NIV Parallel New Testament in Greek and English: with Interlinear Translation*. It has the Greek text with word-for-word English translation in the middle column, the NASB in the left-hand column and the NIV on the right.[2]

This book enabled me to easily compare the NASB and the NIV with another word-for-word translation. And once again, the NIV was proving to be less than reliable while the NASB matched up with Marshall's translation rather nicely.

So I switched to the NASB as my primary Bible. Since I like to have a light-weight Bible to carry with me, I later bought a burgundy, leather-back, slim-line NASB. This edition became the Bible that I took to church and Bible studies.

About this time, I also purchased *The Comparative Study Bible* (CSB). This hefty book contained the KJV, NIV, NASB, and *Amplified Bible* in parallel columns. So I could now easily compare four different translations.

I also purchased Jay P. Green's *Hebrew-Greek-English Interlinear Bible*. Along with the original languages for both the Old Testament and the New Testament, it has Green's word-for-word English translation below each Hebrew and Greek word and Strong's concordance numbers above each word. In the margin is *The Literal Translation of the Bible* (LITV for "Literal Version").[3]

So my Bible studies consisted of comparing the four versions in the parallel Bible along with the readings in my various interlinears. I then purchased additional study aids coded to Strong's numbers. With these aids, and Green's interlinear, I had some access to the original languages before even learning Hebrew or Greek.[4]

This study further convinced me that the NIV was not a reliable version. Again, the NIV did not match up with Green's word-for-word translation either.

The Amplified was an interesting version. It claims to express "nuances" of the Greek text. This seemed to be a worthwhile goal. But as I studied it, the "amplifications" seemed rather excessive. In the CSB it always was the longest on each page for each of the versions. And at times the amplifications seemed rather conjectural. It also was very awkward to read. So I could not see using it as my primary Bible.

The KJV compared rather closely with the word-for-word translations in the interlinears. But the Elizabethan English was simply too difficult to read. But then, even the NASB had all those "thee's" and "thou's" in it too. So I was not really satisfied with any the versions in the CSB.

Seminary Experiences

In March 1988 I moved from the Pittsburgh, Pennsylvania area to Denver, Colorado to attend Denver Seminary. I dragged all the above mentioned and many other books with me.[5]

I was especially looking forward to studying Hebrew and Greek at seminary. My Bible experiences so far had already showed me how valuable studying the original languages could be. And I was not disappointed. Learning Hebrew and Greek really helped to "open" the Bible up to me. It also led me to further struggle over the subject of Bible versions.

Greek Studies:
I took Greek first at seminary. A couple of the professors worked on the translation of the NIV. They strongly promoted the "dynamic equivalence" method of translation the NIV uses. The NIV preface explains that this translation principle seeks to express the "thought" or "meaning" of the original authors (p.x).

But I could never seem to accept this theory. It always seemed to me that the purpose of a translation was to simply render in English what God SAID, not to try to express what God MEANT by what he said. The latter was the job of commentators, not translators.

So I guess I agreed with the translation principle that was used in the KJV, "This principle of complete (or formal) equivalence seeks to preserve all of the information in the text, while presenting it in good literary form....Complete equivalence translates fully, in order to provide an English text that is both accurate and readable" (p.xxi).

Our class assignments included translating portions of Scripture. The comments I sometimes received on the translations I handed in were that they were "too literal." But I simply felt very uncomfortable about "changing" God's words to make it easier to understand the "meaning" of a passage.

The Greek text we used at seminary was *The Greek New Testament* by the United Bible Societies. This Greek text is known as the "Critical Text" (CT). It was simply assumed at seminary that the CT was to be preferred to the TR.

But I began to do much studying on my own. And my personal studies showed me that the TR was more reliable than my professors made it out to be. I also read about the "Majority Text" (MT). The arguments in its favor seemed to make quite a bit of sense.[6]

Now at this time I was not yet convinced that the TR or MT were to be preferred to the CT. But they at least deserved a hearing. So I purchased a leather-back, compact *New King James Version* (NKJV). Its textual footnotes enabled me to compare the TR which the NKJV is based on with the CT and the MT.

As I compared these footnotes it became apparent that the TR and MT were very similar. The footnotes indicating a difference between the TR and the MT were few and far between. Only in the Revelation were there many such variants. But even then, the differences generally were not that significant.[7] Most of the significant variants that I had previously noticed by studying Berry's interlinear were between the TR/ MT versus the CT.

In addition, the NKJV followed the same "formal (or complete) equivalence" translation principle that the KJV did. However, the NKJV does not have all those "thee's" and "thou's" in it that I found so awkward in the KJV and NASB. So I very much liked my newest Bible.

Hebrew Studies:

Next I studied Hebrew at seminary. On the first day of class the professor said that learning Hebrew would show how really bad most translations are. In particular, he did not seem to be very fond of the NIV. His comments about it were always somewhat "veiled" given that some of his colleagues had worked on its production. But his displeasure with the NIV came through nevertheless.

As I studied Hebrew I found out that the professor was right. Most translations are rather bad. For instance, it was at this time that the National Council of Churches published the *New Revised Standard Version* (NRSV).

I had read a couple of articles praising this new version before it came out. One thing that intrigued me was that it was to have extensive textual footnotes. So when it was published I purchased a nice "Reference Edition" from the seminary's bookstore.

I took it home and started going through it. I got all the way to the second half of the second verse of the Bible before becoming disappointed. The passage read, "while a wind from God swept over the face of the waters."

I started comparing other versions. In every one of these, except one, this passage was a reference to the Holy Spirit. The only version that rendered the verse in a manner similar to the NRSV was the *New World Translation* (NWT), the "Bible" of Jehovah's Witnesses. This did not sit too well with me.

So with my now limited knowledge of Hebrew I did some studying. For several reasons that I won't pursue here, my studies convinced me that the rendering of the NRSV and NWT were simply unjustified. Moreover, the NKJV seemed to be the most accurate of all the versions I checked, "And the Spirit of God was hovering over the face of the waters."[8]

As I studied the NRSV further, I found many others places where I felt its translations were rather poor, to say the least. Also, as advertised, it did have extensive textual footnotes. But it was based on the CT. And as I continued to study the "textual" question I eventually became convinced that the CT simply was not as reliable as the TR/ MT. So with some anguish I realized that I wasted my money on this new version and put it aside.

On the other hand, as I continued to study Hebrew and to use my new NKJV it did seem to be rather accurate. So the money I spent on it was proving to be money well spent.

Leaving Seminary:

After my experiences at seminary, my new compact NKJV was now my primary Bible. I had abandoned the use of the NASB which I had brought to Denver with me. Also, at this point, I wasn't real thrilled with the CSB anymore. Since three of the four versions in it were based on the CT I really did not use it much. But I lugged it back to Pennsylvania anyways. However, later I ended up giving it away.

Of my three interlinears, Green's *Interlinear Bible* was proving to be the most helpful. The interlinear itself was a great aid in studying the original languages. And the LITV in the margin seemed even more accurate than my NKJV, though a little "stilted" in its wording.

So I packed up all my books and other stuff and headed back to Pennsylvania in December of 1990.[9]

Book Experiences

After returning from seminary to the Pittsburgh area I started Darkness to Light ministry in the summer of 1991. The first issue of *Darkness to Light* newsletter was published in July of

1991. From the start I used the NKJV as the "default" version for the newsletter.

Initial articles in the newsletter centered on the essentials of the "the faith" (see Jude 3). But eventually I knew I would have to write on more "controversial" subjects as well (Acts 20:26,27). Given the amount of time I had spent studying the subject of Bible versions it seemed like a logical topic.

I wrote one article that I was going to use in the newsletter, then another, then another. It quickly became apparent that this was simply too difficult of a subject to be dealt with adequately in a short article or even in a series of articles.

So I collected together the articles I had written, added a couple of more, and decided it would be best to publish them in a book format instead. In the spring of 1994 the first edition of *Differences Between Bible Versions* was published by Brentwood Christian Press.

In the book I expressed my reasons for why I thought "dynamic equivalence" was not an appropriate method for translating the Bible. I also detailed why I thought the CT was not as reliable as the TR/ MT.

I advocated "formal equivalence" in translation and the use of the TR/ MT. I recommended the use of any version that adhered to these two criteria. These included the KJV, NKJV, and LITV, along with the then recently published *Modern King James Version* (MKJV).[10]

The reaction I got to my little (95 page) book surprised me. I thought that I would get a bunch of angry letters from NIV users for saying that their Bible version, as compared to the KJV or NKJV, is a "less dependable rendering of the Word of God."[11]

But instead, what I got was mainly angry letters from "KJV Only" people screaming at me for actually recommending the use of any version other than the KJV. Many of the letter writers even included "tracts" condemning the NKJV.

I had tried to prepare for the "KJV Only" people by including a chapter in my book critiquing just such a tract.[12] But

I was not prepared for the venom that flowed from some of these letters and tracts.

This anger seemed misplaced to me. The differences between the KJV and NKJV simply were not that great, in my mind, to elicit such a response. I wrote an article in my newsletter using these tracts as an example of what I thought was improper "judging" on the part of Christians.[13]

Computing Experiences

In September of 1995 I got my first computer.[14] One of the first programs I purchased was the *Online Bible*. Included on it are the KJV, MKJV, LITV, and many other versions, including the Hebrew and Greek texts. It also has a wealth of other study aids on it.

But "missing" on it were the NKJV and an interlinear. So in November I purchased Biblesoft's *PC Study Bible*. It has both of these, along with the KJV and other versions, and many study aids.

The use of these two programs makes the comparing of Bible versions, along with Bible study in general, very easy. I set the LITV as the "default" version on the former program and the NKJV on the latter. I would constantly have both programs open and go back and forth between them.

I also eventually purchased a handheld PC (H/PC). The first program I bought for it was Laridian's *PocketBible* with the NKJV text.[15] The use of a H/PC with this program on it enables me to have a portable Bible program. In addition, with the permission of Jay P. Green the translator of the LITV, I copied the entire text of the LITV off of the Internet onto my H/PC.[16] So I now carry my H/PC to church and Bible studies rather than a hardcopy version of the Bible.

The use of all this technology only confirmed what my previous studies had showed me: namely, the NIV and similar versions are simply not reliable while the four above mentioned versions are faithful to the original texts.

Once I got used to this computing stuff, I decided to set up a Web site for Darkness to Light (www.dtl.org). It went online in July 1996. Initially posted on the site were all the articles from all the back issues of *Darkness to Light*. Then in December of the same year I added the full text of my first book.

This subject area has proven to be the most popular section on this site. I have received more e-mail on Bible versions than other subject covered. And once again, most of the e-mail I have received has been from "KJV Only" people, or at least, "KJV first" people. I have heard barely a whimper from advocates of the NIV and similar versions.

I have also received some e-mail from advocates of the MKJV and LITV telling me I should be advocating these versions instead of the NKJV. In response, I have basically tried to explain that I think the KJV, NKJV, LITV, and MKJV are all worthwhile versions. If someone thinks one of these is "better" than the others that is fine with me. I use all four.

What really bothers me is, while advocates of these four versions are firing salvos at each other, sales of the NIV and similar versions are skyrocketing.

Conclusion

So after all of the above experiences, where do I now stand in regards to Bible versions? First off, I rarely use versions based on the CT or which use a dynamic equivalence method of translating.

My personal studies have shown me that the CT is not as reliable as the TR/ MT. And when I need help understanding what the God meant by what He said, I consult the many commentaries or other study aids I own in hardcopy format and on the above mentioned Bible programs.

The only times I would ever consult such versions would be to write an article or respond to questions on a particular version or verse in a such a version.

Gary Zeolla

As for my primary Bible, I doubt I will ever switch to the KJV. In my opinion, it is no more accurate than the NKJV, but it is much more difficult for me to read. I never liked Shakespeare in high school and I see no reason to struggle with that kind of English while reading the Bible.

The MKJV is somewhat more accurate than the NKJV. But the difference is not that great. And the MKJV is also somewhat more difficult to read. So I see no reason to switch to it.

The only version I have seriously considered switching to is the LITV. It is definitely more accurate than any of the above versions. But it can be rather stilted in its wording. For my own personal studies I have gotten used to it, but I think it might be too awkward to use on my Web site.

And finally, I recently completed my own translation of the New Testament. It is called the *Analytical-Literal Translation* (ALT).[17] For working on this project, I purchased a new Bible program, *BibleWorks for Windows*[tm]. It is much more oriented towards the original languages than the above two programs.

The ALT is similar to the LITV in that is a very literal version, but the LITV is based on the TR while the ALT uses the MT. I also tried to make it as readable as possible. So I am now, of course, also using the ALT in my own studies and writings. I even copied the files for all the New Testament books onto my H/PC. So I now have the ALT, the NKJV, and the LITV with me whenever I go to church or Bible studies.

Footnotes:
[1] See Chapter Six: "Introduction to Textual Criticism."
[2] The Greek text used in Marshall's interlinear is the 21st edition of Eberhard Nestle's *Noveum Testamentum Graece*, a CT type of text.
[3] Green's interlinear is available in a one volume or four volume format (three for the OT and one for the NT). The newest edition of the NT volume now also has the KJV in the right-hand margin. It is bound in a black, leather cover, all of which makes for a very nice-looking and helpful edition. It is

available from Christian Literature World ~ PO Box 4998 ~ Lafayette, IN 47903 ~ www.chrlitworld.com.

[4] Such study aids are available from Christian Literature World.

[5] "Dragged" is the correct term here. I pulled a rented "trailer" behind my car all the way from the Pittsburgh area to Denver. After three days and 1500 miles, I arrived in Denver in the middle of a snowstorm. Quite a trip!

[6] Some of the books I studied are listed in the bibliographies at the end of the various chapters in this book.

[7] See Chapter Ten: "Significant Textual Variants: TR vs. MT" for detailed discussions of the most significant differences between these two texts.

[8] See Chapter Eighteen: "Two NCC Bible Versions" for a detailed discussion of Genesis 1:2 and the NRSV in general.

[9] This time, rather than "dragging" my books, I mailed them! I packed them all up in about two-dozen boxes, took them to the post office and mailed them back to Pennsylvania. I was then able to drive straight through from Denver to the Pittsburgh area—1500 miles in 32 hours. Quite a trip again!

[10] Both the LITV and MKJV are published by Christian Literature World.

[11] From page 48 in my first book, in a chapter titled "Three Popular Bible Versions" (see Chapter Five).

[12] Critiqued in a chapter originally titled, "Is the KJV Inspired?" In this edition of this book, I have expanded this chapter into an entire section. I wanted to be prepared for the KJV only onslaught this time!

[13] This article was titled, "Judge Not ...." It is now posted on Darkness to Light's Web site at: www.dtl.org/dtl/article/judge-not.htm

[14] Actually, I got my first computer in July of 1995 from a computer "superstore." But there was a problem with the processor that the store never could seem to fix right. So after two months, during which time their repair department had it longer than I did, I returned it. I then bought a new computer from a small, local computer store.

[15] Laridian's *PocketBible* is available from their Web site: www.laridian.com. Along with the NKJV, many other Bible versions and Bible study aids can be purchased for the *PocketBible*.

[16] The LITV is posted on A Voice in a Wilderness's Web site at: www.cet.com/~voice/litv/litv.htm.

[17] The ALT is available from the publisher 1stBooks (www.1stbooks.com) and from conventional and online bookstores.

Bibliography:

Aland, Kurt, et al. *The Greek New Testament. Third Edition, Corrected* (Germany: United Bible Societies, 1983). Note: This Greek text is about the same as that used in Marshall's interlinear.

Berry, George Ricker. *The Interlinear Greek-English New Testament.* Grand Rapids, Mich: Zondervan, n.a.

BibleWorks™ *for Windows*™ Copyright © 1992-1999 *BibleWorks,* L.C.C. Big Fork, MT: Hermeneutika. Programmed by Michael S. Bushell and Michael D. Tan.

Comparative Study Bible; A Parallel Bible. Grand Raids, Mich: Zondervan, 1984.

New International Version of the Holy Bible. Grand Rapids, MI: 1978.

KJV/ NKJV Parallel Reference Bible. Nashville: Thomas Nelson, 1991.

Online Bible. Ontario: Online Bible Foundation and the Woodside Bible Fellowship, 1997.

PC Study Bible. Seattle: Biblesoft, 1996.

Chapter Two
Classifications of Bible Versions:

Part One

Versions of the Bible can be classified according to the translation principle and the Greek text-type utilized. This chapter will describe and evaluate each of these classifications. Also, select versions of the Bible will be classified and commented upon.

Literal—Textus Receptus/ Majority Text

The first translation principle is a literal method. This principle simply believes that EVERY SINGLE WORD in the original Hebrew and Greek texts should be translated. In addition, the grammatical forms of words should also be translated as they are in the original texts. So a noun should be translated as a noun, an adjective as an adjective, etc. Moreover, any words added for clarity should be offset in some way, usually by placing them in italics or brackets.

This type of principle produces the type of English translation that would be seen in an interlinear. An interlinear contains the Hebrew or Greek text, and then in-between each line it includes an exact word for word translation. The only difference between a literal version and an interlinear reading is the interlinear would exactly follow the Hebrew or Greek word order (which differs considerably from English word order), while a literal version will re-arrange the words into proper English order as needed. However, a literal version would still follow the original word order closer than any other translation principle to be discussed.

Otherwise, the only significant deviation from an exact word for word translation in a literal version would be to omit the definite article ("the") when it is not needed in English. Hebrew and especially Greek include the definite article much more often than English does. For instance, proper names in the Greek text very often have the article before them, but to read "the Jesus" repeatedly would simply be too awkward for an English translation. Even interlinears generally do not translate such occurrences of the article.

So a literal translation principle produces a very exact reproduction of what God originally said. And this writer believes this method of translating is the only one which concurs completely with the doctrine of verbal inspiration.

Verbal inspiration, "Is a reference to the doctrine that the Holy Spirit so guided the writers of Scripture that even their choice of words conformed to God's intention" (Erickson, p.178). In other words, not just the thoughts or ideas of the Bible are inspired, but the very words and grammatical forms of words themselves.

That the Biblical authors believed in verbal inspiration is evident. Jesus appealed to the tense of a verb for proof of resurrection and the exact wording of a Psalm to demonstrate His Lordship (Matt 22:31,32, 41-45). Paul pointed out that a word was singular, not plural, to show a prophecy applied to Christ (Gal 3:16; see also Deut 4:2; 1Kings 8:56; Josh 21:43-45; 23:14; Prov 30:5,6; Jer 26:2; John 6:63).

There are currently only three English versions available which adhere to a literal translation principle. Below is a discussion of each.

Young's Literal Translation:
The first literal English translation to be produced was *Young's Literal Translation* (YLT), by Robert Young (1822-1888) who also produced *Young's Analytical Concordance*. YLT was first published in 1862, with a revised edition issued posthumously in 1898.

Given that it was translated in the late 1800's, YLT includes many archaic words. Young also used rather awkward wording and punctuation. So it can be rather difficult to read.

In addition, there is a serious problem with the Old Testament (OT). It concerns a detail of Hebrew grammar known as the "*waw* conversive." Without going into technical details, it will just be said that Young did not believe this construction had any significance whereas most every other translator and Hebrew scholar does. This is not a minor point as it affects the way tenses are rendered throughout the OT in YLT. As such, it basically renders the OT of YLT useless. However, the New Testament (NT) of YLT is a very literal and reliable translation, though not very readable.

YLT is now in the public domain and freely available on many Web sites. The Bibles Online page of Darkness to Light's Web site links to many Web-based Bibles: www.dtl.org/links/christian/bibles.htm. In addition, as of this writing, Baker Book House was still publishing a hardcopy edition of YLT, available from Christian Book Distributors ~ (978-977-5000) ~ www.christianbook.com.

Literal Translation of the Bible:
It was almost a hundred years before another literal translation was produced. In 1976, Jay P. Green published the first edition of his *Literal Translation of the Bible* (LITV, for "Literal Version"). A new edition was most recently released in 2000. The LITV is the marginal reading in *The Interlinear Hebrew–Greek–English Bible*, also by J.P. Green. The LITV is also available separately.

The press release for the LITV claims it is, "...the most accurate translation of the Bible in English." And it is very literal and accurate English translation for both the OT and NT, along with being much more readable than YLT.

The LITV is available from Christian Literature World ~ PO Box 4998 ~ Lafayette, IN ~ Within the USA: (800) 447-9142;

Outside the USA: (765) 447-9143 ~ Fax (765) 449-4870 (www.chrlitworld.com).

Analytical–Literal Translation:

The third and final literal translation is this writer's own *Analytical–Literal Translation of the New Testament of the Holy Bible* (ALT). Now the ALT is only of the NT, so for a literal translation of the OT one would need to consult the LITV. However, the ALT does contain some features which the LITV does not. These features will be discussed later.

The ALT is available directly from the publisher 1stBooks (www.1stbooks.com) and from many conventional and online bookstores.

Greek Text- types:

As for Greek text-type, YLT and the LITV are based on the *Textus Receptus* (TR), while the ALT is based on the Majority Text (MT). Both of these texts are based on the Byzantine textual tradition. The TR and MT are very similar, but there are some differences between them, with a few of these being significant.

However, there are a greater number of differences and more significant differences between either of these two texts and the Critical Text (CT), which is based on the Alexandrian text-type. And it should be noted that there is no literal version available based on the CT.

The complex subject of Greek text-types will be pursued in detail in later chapters. Here it will just be said that this writer believes the MT best reflects the original autographs. Given that my own version is based on the MT, this should be obvious. But, as indicated, the TR is very similar to the MT, so it would also reflect the original texts very accurately. Only the CT differs somewhat from these two and from the originals in this writer's opinion. However, the ALT does include an appendix listing significant variants between these three texts, and it is the only one of these three versions to include textual variants.

Conclusion:

So a literal translation principle produces a very exact reproduction of what God actually said—and everything that God says is important. As Jesus declared, "Man shall not live by bread alone, but on every word going out of the mouth of God" (Matt 4:4; LITV). Given these facts, a literal version is the best kind of version to use for in-depth Bible study. And any one of the above versions, with the exception of the OT of YLT, will give the person who does not know Hebrew or Greek very close access to the original languages.

However, literal versions can be somewhat awkward to read. So they might not be the best kind of version to use for such purposes as personal devotional reading, reading aloud in church services or Bible studies, or even for evangelism. But the next translation principle fills these kinds of needs with still very accurate Bible versions.

Formal Equivalence—Textus Receptus/ Majority Text

The second translation principle to be considered is formal equivalence. In this principle, the original Hebrew or Greek texts are still translated in a WORD FOR WORD fashion.

However, occasionally minor words that would be awkward to read in English are omitted. For instance the word "indeed" occurs quite frequently in the Greek NT (e.g. Acts 17:17,26). But most of the time it is unnecessary and even awkward in English. So formal equivalence versions generally omit it.

Also, the grammatical forms of the original words are not followed as closely as in a literal method, and other minor deviations from a strictly literal translation are utilized to improve the readability of the text. For instance, a literal translation of the opening phrase of John 3:36 is, "The one believing." Now, this writer has used literal translations for so long that this phrase seems natural. But to most readers it is somewhat unnatural, so formal equivalence versions will generally render this phrase as, "He who believes."

The latter is a more natural way of speaking and is perfectly justifiable by the Greek text, which has a substantival participle here (i.e. a verbal noun used as the subject of the sentence). However, it should be noted that the literal translation is "inclusive" (i.e. includes both men and women) while the formal equivalence rendering is masculine (i.e. includes only men). The Greek text itself is inclusive.

In any case, even with such minor changes, the formal equivalence method still produces a version that adheres closely to the doctrine of verbal inspiration, but it does so with versions that would be less awkward to read than literal versions.

King James Version/ New King James Version:

The *King James Version* (KJV) is the best-known version to fall into this category. Along with being a formal equivalence translation, it is also based on the TR. As such, the KJV is a highly reliable version of the Bible. And it rightly remains a very popular Bible version.

But this is not to say the KJV is perfect, infallible, or inspired in and of itself as many "KJV-only" advocates claim. This subject is pursued at length in the section "KJV Only-ism." Here, theologian Gordon Clark will simply be quoted as writing, "...one may say that the *King James* can be improved. A committee attempted this and in 1979, trying to preserve the great good and correct the few deficiencies, published *The New King James Version* (Thomas Nelson, Nashville)" (p.6).

The 1979 date is when the NT of the NKJV was published. The OT was published in 1982. The NKJV also updates the archaic language of the KJV, so it is easier to read than the KJV. The NKJV is based on the same Greek text as the KJV, the TR. However, significant textual variants between the TR, MT, and CT are footnoted. In addition, alternate translations and some explanatory notes are provided in footnotes. The KJV and NKJV are available from just about any conventional or online bookstore.

Modern King James Version:

The *Modern King James Version* (MKJV) is a lesser-known version which is also an updating of the KJV. Jay P. Green, the translator of the LITV, also translated the MKJV. The press release for the MKJV says, "...it is the grand old version in the English of today—period!"

It is true that the MKJV updates the archaic language of the KJV, but the MKJV does make other changes as well. However, these changes tend towards making the text more literal than the KJV (and the NKJV). The MKJV is easier to read than the KJV, but somewhat less readable than the NKJV. The MKJV is also based on the TR. As with the LITV, the MKJV is available from Christian Literature World.

World English Bible:

The World English Bible (WEB) is currently being produced as a Web-based Bible (hence the choice of the acronym). Rainbow Missions Inc. is producing it. The publishers are posting the books of the Bible on the Internet as they go through each stage of the revision. As of this writing, the entire NT, Psalms, and Proverbs were finished and available in hardcopy format. But the rest of the OT still has a ways to go.

The translation philosophy is described on the WEB: FAQ page, "Some people like to use the terms 'formal equivalent' and 'dynamic equivalent.' Neither of these exactly describe what we are doing, since we have borrowed ideas from both, but I suppose that we are closer to formal equivalence than dynamic equivalence." Dynamic equivalence is a translation principle that will be discussed in the next chapter. Here it will just be said that this method is less literal than the formal equivalence method.

In any case, the above is a rather accurate description of the translation method of the WEB. It is mostly a formal equivalence version, but it tends towards dynamic equivalence at places. Also added words are not italicized or bracketed as they are in the above three versions. So its accuracy overall is somewhat less than that of the above three versions but much better than true dynamic equivalence versions. However, the WEB is somewhat more readable than any of the above three.

In addition, the WEB differs from the above three versions in that it is based on the MT rather than the TR. Like the NKJV, the WEB has footnotes indicating textual variants, along alternative translations and explanatory notes.

The WEB NT with Psalms and Proverbs can be ordered directly from the WEB's web site (www.ebible.org) or by mail order from: Rainbow Missions Inc. ~ PO Box 1151 ~ Longmont, CO 80502-1151.

Additional KJV Updates:

In addition to the NKJV and MKJV, there are several additional versions which are updates of the KJV. These are (with their dates of publication): *English Webster's Bible* (by Noah Webster of dictionary fame, EWB; 1833), *The Revised Webster's Bible* (RWB; 1995), *The 21st Century King James Version* (KJ21; 1994), and *The King James Easy Reading Sword Study Bible* (KJER; n.a., also called the *Word of God Bible*).

The first three of these versions make minor changes to the KJV text, while updating some, but not all, of the archaic language of the KJV. The last version, however, makes no changes to the text except to update all of the archaic language. So if someone really likes the KJV and wants it mostly the same, but with some or all of its archaic language updated, then one of these versions would be worthwhile.

Since all four or these versions are basically the KJV, their accuracy would be the same as it. The KJER is the only one that updates all of the KJV's archaic language, so it would be the easiest to read. The KJER also has the unique feature of not only placing the words of Christ in red in the New Testament, but also the words of God in red in the Old Testament as well.

The EWB and RWB are in the public domain and available on various software programs, such as the *Online Bible* or *BibleWorks*™ *for Windows*™. The KJ21 is published by 21st Century King James Bible Publishers ~ Post Office Box 40 ~ 1111 North Coteau Street ~ Gary, SD 57237 ~ 800-225-5521. The KJER is available from Global Evangelism Inc. (www.abible.org) or from The Publisher ~ PO Box 5040 ~ Goodyear, AZ 85338 ~ 877KJBIBLE (877-552-4253) ~ www.swordbible.com.

Conclusion:

All of the versions in this class are very accurate and reliable translations. The MKJV would probably be the most literal of all of them, while the WEB would be the most readable. The NKJV would fall in-between these two versions for both accuracy and readability. The KJV would also be in the middle of these two for accuracy, but it would be more difficult to read than any of the above versions due to its archaic English.

The four KJV updates mentioned last would have the same accuracy level as the KJV, and they would be easier to read than the KJV, but how much so would depend on the degree to which the archaic language of the KJV is updated.

Formal Equivalence—Critical Text

This next classification uses the same translation principle as the last one, formal equivalence. But rather than using the TR or MT, the New Testament is based on the CT. And, as mentioned above, this writer believes the CT is inferior to either the MT or the TR.

However, it should be pointed out, there is no question of the overall integrity of the NT text. These three Greek texts are in substantial agreement. The differences are minor as compared to the great degree of agreement between the three texts.

New American Standard Bible:

The *New American Standard Bible* (NASB) is the most important version in this category. There are actually two editions of the NASB. The first edition was published in 1977 and the updated edition in 1995. The main differences between these versions is the OT of the NAS77 utilized archaic words like "thee" and "thou" while the NAS95 does not.

For a detailed review of the NAS95, see Chapter Sixteen. Here it will just be said, either version of the NASB is a generally reliable translation. But given their reliance on the CT, it is recommended this version only be used alongside a version from category one or two. This is especially important as the NAS77 has very few textual footnotes indicating variants between the TR/ MT and the CT.

One example of a variant which is not footnoted in the NAS77 is Matthew 20:16. This is the variant which caused the confusion at the Bible study mentioned in the "Preface" to this book. Another passage where the second half of the verse is omitted and is not footnoted is Romans 11:6. The same is true for the words, "to repentance" at the end of Matthew 9:13. However, such problems were corrected in the NAS95.

Of these two editions, the NAS77 would be slightly more literal while the NAS95 would be somewhat more readable.

Expanded—Critical Text

The versions in the rest of the classifications are all based on the CT. So comments about the problems with this text-type would apply to the rest of the versions to be discussed. Moreover, different translation principles are now utilized.

"Expanded" is the next translation principle to look at. Its purpose is to express NUANCES of the Greek text often missed in a standard translation.

Attempting to express "nuances" of the Greek text is a worthwhile effort. There are many finer details of Greek grammar that most translations miss. Also, there is very often more than on correct way to translated a Greek word in a particular context. And an expanded type of version would bring out these details.

However, there are potential problems with this principle as well. First, the "expansions" can make the text awkward to read. Moreover, the soundness of the "amplifications" can be questionable or interpretive. So what one could end up with is more of a commentary built into the text, than simply a translation.

Amplified Bible:
The Amplified Bible is the best-known version of this type. And it demonstrates both the potential benefits and the potential problems with this translation method.

A good verse to demonstrate these points is Romans 2:1:
"Therefore, you have no excuse *or* defense *or* justification, O man, whoever you are who judges *and* condemns another. For in posing as judge *and* passing sentence on another you condemn yourself, for you who judge are habitually practicing the very same things.

Now the main good point is the *Amplified Bible* brings out is that "practice" in the last phrase is in the present tense. And this tense in Greek can indicate ongoing activity. And the *Amplified* reading does bring out the possible ongoing nature of the action. It is not that the one judging has done the action once but on a continually basis.

Also note that three times in this verse the *Amplified Bible* has added alternative translations to words. This is helpful in understanding the full import of the text, but with three such amplifications in one verse it leaves the verse rather awkward to read.

An even more dramatic example of awkwardness in the *Amplified Bible* is seen in its rendering of the Beatitudes (Matt

5:3-11). Every occurrence of the word "blessed" (Greek, *makarioi*) in this passage is "expanded" considerably.

For instance, the first Beatitude begins, "Blessed—happy, to be envied, and spiritually prosperous [that is, with life-joy and satisfaction in God's favor and salvation regardless of their outward circumstances]...." This rendering is repeated in each of the following eight Beatitudes, and reading nine such "amplifications" in a row would be rather tedious.

It should also be noted that the *Amplified Bible* misses many finer details of the Greek text. For instance, "Matthew 7:1 reads, "Do no judge *and* criticize *and* condemn others so that you may not be judged *and* criticized *and* condemned yourselves."

Once again, the awkwardness of having three translations twice for the same word should be noted. But more important is the first phrase, "Do not judge...." The Greek text here is a prohibitive, present imperative.

> Greek scholars Dana and Mantey explain the sense of this construction:
> "The present tense is properly used for expressing continued action. A prohibition in the present imperative demands that action then in progress be stopped....Thus a prohibition expressed with the present tense demands the cessation of some act that is already in progress" (pp. 301).

Dana and Mantey then use this very verse as an example and render it as "Stop judging ...." *The Amplified* also fails to bring out other such details of Greek grammar.

And finally, the *Amplified* includes explanatory aids within the text. Some of these are very helpful. For instance, Mark 15:25 says Jesus was crucified "the third hour (about nine o'clock in the morning)." Telling readers that the third hour is 9:00 a.m. is helpful for following the timetable of events.

However, some of these explanatory notes can actually be questionable. For instance, in John 19:14, the *Amplified* has the trial of Jesus occurring at "about the sixth hour—about twelve o'clock noon." However, this creates a conflict with Mark 15:25 as Jesus' trial could not have occurred three hours after He was crucified.

The answer to this dilemma is probably that Mark is following the Jewish method of counting time (which begins at 6:00 am) while John is following the Roman time method (which begins the same as ours, 12:00 midnight). An argument in favor of John using the Roman method is that he was writing after the destruction of Jerusalem in 70 AD, while Mark, along with Matthew and Luke, were writing before that event.

So "the third hour" in Mark would be 9:00 am and so would "the ninth hour" in John. Since the times are approximate ("about"), there is no conflict with both events occurring at the same time. But the important point is, the reader of the *Amplified* would not know this explanation.

Another example of a questionable explanatory note is in Hebrews 1:4. Jesus is said to have inherited "the glorious Name (title)." But is Jesus' "glorious Name" merely a title, or is this a reference to His nature? (see John 17:5). "Name" in Scripture often has this wider meaning.

Nelson's Illustrated Bible Dictionary comments in this regard, "A name somehow represented the nature of the person." Furthermore, "A true understanding of the exalted Jesus is often connected with a statement about His name" (Lockyer, pp.744,755; see for instance, Acts 4:10; 15:26; 19:17; 1Cor 6:11; Phil 2:9; Col 3:17; 2Thes 1:12).

So the *Amplified Bible* is a mixed bag. It is helpful in bringing out some finer details of the Greek text, but it misses many others. Its alternative translations are helpful in understanding the text, but they also leave the text awkward to read. And the explanatory aids can be helpful, but at times they are less than reliable.

Gary Zeolla

Analytical-Literal Translation:
Along with being a literal version, the ALT also has the features of an expanded type of version. Greek grammar is translated in such a way as to bring out nuances of the Greek text. However, the ALT brings out as many details of the Greek grammar as possible.

In addition, the ALT includes alternative translations along with other aids within brackets in the text. However, there are usually only one and never more than two alternative translations for any given word, not a list of them. And every effort was made to ensure the accuracy of all bracketed materials.

Also, versions like the *Amplified Bible* are generally along the lines of a dynamic equivalence version in the "un-amplified" parts while the ALT is a literal translation throughout. Another difference is the *Amplified* is a much older version. It was first published in 1965 and can be somewhat hard to find now. But the ALT was published in 2001 and should be readily available.

Part Two of this discussion will look at two additional classifications of Bible versions.

Bibliography:
See end of Part Two.

Chapter Three
Classifications of Bible Versions:

Part Two

This chapter continues the discussion on the classifications of Bible versions.

Dynamic Equivalence—Critical Text

The next method to be looked at is "dynamic equivalence." This translation principle is the most popular one today with the majority of recent versions of the Bible utilizing it.

The goal of dynamic equivalence is to give a THOUGHT FOR THOUGHT rather than a word for word translation. The purpose is to express the IDEA or MEANING of the text for the reader.

General Comments:
Some general comments will be made on this dynamic equivalence principle of translating before a couple a versions are looked at. First, these versions regularly add words which have no actual backing in the Hebrew or Greek texts. And these added words are never italicized or in any way distinguished from words actually translating original God-breathed words (see 2Tim 3:16).

Conversely, "unimportant" words are often left untranslated. Conjunctions (and, but, then, so, for, therefore), interjections (behold), and sometimes entire phrases deemed to be redundant or in some other way "unnecessary" are frequently omitted.

Furthermore, the grammatical forms of words and phrases are frequently changed, much more often than in formal equivalence versions. In dynamic equivalence versions, pronouns can be changed into nouns, nouns into verbs, two different terms or phrases combined into one, and many other such alterations.

But, it must be asked, are not such additions, omissions, and alterations an implicit denial of verbal inspiration?

J.P. Green describes the situation well:

Sorrowfully, we must report that those representing themselves as translators of the Bible in our day are misconstruing their proper role. They plainly believe it is legitimate to reconstruct the text in order to give the reader of their work what THEY believe is THE MEANING of the text.

In other words, they feel that they are empowered to add to, subtract from, or to ignore portions of the text IF SUCH TREATMENT OF THE TEXT WILL ENABLE THEM TO GIVE THE READER THE MEANING OF THE TEXT.

Question: Whose meaning are they giving? THEIR meaning....Result: The result of the insertion of all this fleshly wisdom is CONFUSION! And a corollary result is the treatment of God's actual words as if they were of secondary importance, and therefore there is a lowering of their import and value in the minds of the adherents of a particular view (p.7; emphases in original).

Furthermore, what about this warning from Revelation 22:18,19?

For I testify to everyone who hears the WORDS of the prophecy of this book: If anyone ADDS to these things, God will add to him the plagues that are written in this book; and if anyone TAKES AWAY from the from the WORDS of the book of this prophecy, God shall take away his part from the Book of Life, from the holy city, and from the things which are written in this book (NKJV).

With these general comments behind, a study will now be made of a couple of popular dynamic equivalence versions.

The Good News Bible:

The first dynamic equivalence Bible version to become popular was the *Good News Bible* (GNB; also known as *Today's English Version*). It was the influence of this version that helped to popularize the dynamic equivalence method of translating. The GNB is not too readily available today, but its historical significance necessitates a look at the version itself to see if the precedence it set in Bible translation is one so many versions today should be imitating.

Gordon Fee writes about this version, "The GNB is an outstanding translation by a single author, Robert G. Bratcher, who regularly consulted with others, and whose expertise in linguistics has brought the concept of dynamic equivalence to translation in a thoroughgoing way" (p.42).

But is this version really an "outstanding translation?" The answer to this question depends on one's opinion of the dynamic equivalence theory of translation. The general comments above brought out several potential problems with this method. Two representative verses from the GNB will now be evaluated which demonstrate some of these points.

An example of this principle's propensity for altering and interpreting the text for its readers can be seen in the GNB in Romans 1:17. The NKJV renders the first part of this verse as, "For in it the righteousness of God is revealed from faith to faith." Meanwhile, the GNB has, "For the gospel reveals how God puts people right with himself; it is through faith from the beginning to the end."

A few comments on the differences between the more literal translation of the NKJV and the "dynamic" rendering of the GNB are in order.

First, "it" has been changed to "the gospel." This is probably what "it" is referring to, but God inspired Paul to write a pronoun, not a noun.

31

Second, it is true the Gospel, "reveals how God puts people right with himself." But, this rewrite misses the emphasis on God's righteousness in this passage. It is because God is righteous, and we are not, that we need the Gospel.

Third, "from faith to faith" (Greek, *ek pisteos eis pistin*) could be one of the statements Peter was referring to when he said that in Paul's epistles, "are some things hard to understand" (2Pet 3:16). There are at least seven possible interpretations of this phrase (Cranfield, p.99). The GNB has chosen from among these and rendered the phrase in such a way that only one of these is possible.

Maybe the GNB's interpretation is correct, maybe it isn't. But one would not know the GNB has in fact already interpreted this difficult phrase for its readers unless a formal version is consulted.

The other verse to be examined is Amos 4:6. Here, God says to the Israelites, "'Also I gave you cleanness of teeth in all your cities. And lack of bread in all your places; Yet you have not returned to Me,' Says the LORD" (NKJV).

But what does God mean by the idiom, "cleanness of teeth?" The NKJV answers this question for its readers with an explanatory footnote. The note reads simply, "Hunger."

Now compare how the GNB renders this verse, "I was the one who brought famine to all your cities, yet you did not come back to me."

Notice that the GNB has combined the idiom, "cleanness of teeth" and the phrase, "lack of bread" into one word, "famine." And in doing so, the GNB has interpreted the meaning of the idiom for its readers.

In this case, the GNB is probably right in its assessment. But even Gordon Fee admits, "There can be dangers in this, however, especially when translators themselves miss the meaning of the idiom, as can be seen in the NIV, GNB, and LB translation of 1Corinthians 7:1" (Fee, p.38).

The example Fee gives of where the GNB (and the NIV and *Living Bible*) "missed the meaning of the idiom" will be discussed in the next chapter. Here, it needs to be noted, the GNB doesn't even provide a literal translation of the idiom in a footnote. So, once again, readers using only the GNB would have no way of knowing a phrase in Amos 4:6 had already been interpreted for them.

And lastly on Amos 4:6 and the GNB, the phrase, "Says the LORD" at the end of the verse is omitted. It must have been deemed too redundant to bother with. But since God inspired Amos to write the phrase, why not translate it?

The type of problems detailed above can be seen in most more modern versions which follow the lead of the GNB in using the dynamic equivalence translation method. A couple of these newer versions will be looked at next.

The New International Version:

The *New International Version* (NIV) is currently a very popular Bible version. It was first published in 1984 and quickly earned the distinction of being the first modern-day translation to out-sell the KJV. It did so through a very aggressive advertising campaign.

For instance, a full-page advertisement in *The Beacon* magazine pictures Jesus teaching several people by a lakeside. One of these people is in silhouette. An arrow points to this person with the words, "You are here." The caption reads, "Reading the NIV is the next best thing to being there." The text underneath declares the NIV to be, "unparalleled in its accuracy." This writer's opinion of this bold claim is presented in Chapter Five: "There Popular Bible Versions."

The ad also claims, "The NIV presents the true meaning of God's Word in a language that is understood today." Of course, "the true meaning" that will be "understood" by reading the NIV is what, "they believe is the meaning of the text."

The only way to decide, "whether these things are so" (see Acts 17:11) is to compare the NIV's rendering with a formal equivalence version. Maybe the NIV's interpretation is correct, maybe it isn't, but a person has no way of deciding if only the

NIV is being read. Again, much more about the NIV will be said in a later chapter.

God's Word:

God's Word is a newer dynamic equivalence version. It was published in 1995. The back cover of the edition of *God's Word* this writer has states, "When you read *God's Word*, you will discover the FULL INTENDED MEANING ... it will mean—as closely as possible—the same to you as it did to those who read or heard it in its original languages of Greek, Hebrew, and Aramaic" (ellipse in original).

Translating the Bible in way that enable readers to "discover the full intended meaning" sounds very commendable. However, there is very often much debate as to what the original "intended meaning" was. If we knew for sure exactly what particular verses meant "to those who read or heard it in its original languages" then many theological debates could be settled. But, unfortunately, this simply is not always the case. And the only way a translation can claim to express the full original intended meaning is by inserting interpretation into the text. This problem will be seen in verses to be looked at. But first, another feature of God's Word needs to be considered.

The Preface to *God's Word* explains an interesting feature of this version:

God's Word avoids using theological terms that have little, if any, meaning for most readers. Instead, this translation uses common, everyday English words that accurately convey the meaning of the original text. In some case traditional words are contained in footnotes the first time they occur in a chapter. Examples of these theological terms include *redemption, justification, repentance, grace,* and *righteousness* (p.xxiv).

Now a word like "justification" would probably be difficult for many today, but it is debatable if words like "repentance" or "grace" actually "have little, if any, meaning for most readers" today. But the most important question is, do the words that *God's Word's* uses to replace these words accurately reflect the meaning of the original words?

Ephesians 2:8,9 will help to illustrate the above points. The verses will be quoted first from the NKJV, then from *God's Word*:

> For by grace you have been saved through faith, and that not of yourselves; *it is* the gift of God, not of works, lest anyone should boast.

> God saved you through faith as an act of kindness. You had nothing to do with it. Being saved is a gift from God. It is not the result of anything you have done, so no one can boast.

It should be obvious that these two versions differ greatly. If nothing else, God's word is considerably longer, having 39 words versus the NKJV's 27. But the important question is: are these added words justified by the Greek text? A look at some of the more important changes will answer this question.

First, the conjunction "For" has been omitted in *God's Word*. But this word is important as it indicates that this verse is related to the preceding one. As Greek scholar A.T. Robertson states, "For by grace (*te gar chariti*). Explanatory reason. 'By the grace' already mentioned in verse 5 and so with the article" (Robertson). The problem here is, by omitting this and other conjunctions, *God's Word* makes it much easier for people to take verses out of context. Conjunctions let readers know that one verse must be interpreted in light of a preceding or following verse.

Second, the first sentence has been restructured. Rather than "you" being the subject of the verb "saved," *God's Word* has made it the predicate noun. In order to have a subject for the verb, "God" is added to the text. And it should be noted that neither this word nor any other added word is italicized to indicate they are added.

Third, "by grace" is rendered "as an act of kindness." Friberg's lexicon defines the Greek word (*charis*) in this context as, "as a relig[ious] t[erm] for God's attitude toward human beings *kindness, grace, favor, helpfulness* (JN 1.16, 17; EP 2.8) (Friberg). So "kindness" is a possible rendering of the Greek word. So this is not inaccurate.

However, there is a separate word for "kindness" in Greek (*chrestotes*) which appears in the previous verse. *God's Word* also renders this word as "kindness." By rendering both the same way, *God's Word* hides the fact that two different words are being used. Moreover, again, it must be asked if "grace" is really a word that people today would not understand?

Fourth, "and that not of yourselves" has been changed to "You had nothing to do with it." Now it is true that the latter is a more natural way of expressing the concept, but none of the words are accurate translations of anything in the Greek text. Moreover, a phrase has been changed to a full sentence.

But most importantly, the word "that" has been changed to "it." So a demonstrative pronoun has been replaced with a personal pronoun. But at least *God's Word* is still using a pronoun. This pronoun is important as it refers back to "something" in the verse, but there is much debate as to what that something is. However, the two versions differ as to whether they make a decision for their readers as to what the antecedent to the pronoun is. This can been seen in the next words.

The NKJV begins the next phrase with "it is" in italics. The italics indicate these words are added. But *God's Word* adds, "Being saved is" without indicating the words are added. The Greek text actually has simply "this." So neither version is really literal here. But the NKJV is closer in using a pronoun to render a pronoun rather than *God's Word's* use of a participle functioning as a noun.

The difference here is this: the NKJV leaves it vague as to exactly what "that" refers to, and hence what the "gift from God" is. Many believe "that" and "the gift" refer back to the verb "saved." But others believe they refer to the noun "faith" or the entire preceding sentence, which includes faith, along with grace and salvation.

In favor of the first view is the word "that" is neuter while the word "grace" is feminine. As A.T. Robertson writes, "And that (*kai touto*). Neuter, not feminine *taute*, and so refers not to *pistis* (feminine) or to *charis* (feminine also), but to the act of being saved by grace conditioned on faith on our part."

However, theologian Gordon Clark, after referring to Robertson's comments writes, "Grammatically, neuter demonstrative pronouns, even in the more precise classical Greek, often refer to feminine nouns, especially to abstract feminine nouns. Hence it is false to say that *touto* cannot mean faith" (Clark, p.73). Moreover, in favor of the second view is that "grace" is the closest possible antecedent to "this."

Now there is an important point to all this technical jargon. This verse could help to answer a very important yet very debated question: Do people generate faith from their own "free wills", or is the very ability to have faith a gift from God? If the antecedent to "that" is "faith" then the latter would be true. Faith itself would be a gift from God. But if the word "that" refers back to being "saved," then this verse does not settle the question one way or another.

So what *God's Word* has done is settle this issue for its readers without letting them know that it has done so. In other words, the theological opinions of the translators have been inserted into the text.

Continuing with comments on this verse, the phrase "not of works" has been changed to the sentence "It is not the result of anything you have done." *God's Word* does express the idea, but the only word actually in the Greek text is "not."

And finally, in the last phrase, the negative "lest" and the pronoun "anyone" has been changed in *God's Word* into the conjunction "so" and a different pronoun. But at least the final verb is rendered in a possible manner.

Gary Zeolla

Going back to the issue of "simplifying" theological terms, in addition to rendering "grace" as "an act of kindness," *God's Word* renders "redemption" as "paid the price" (Col 1:14). The Greek word means in part, "(1) lit[erally] as an action, a buying back of a slave or captive through payment of a ransom; hence, *setting free, release* (HE 11.35); (2) fig[uratively] (a) of rescue fr[om] sin *redemption, deliverance* (RO 3.24)" (Friberg).

The English word "redemption" means, "1. to buy or pay off … 8. to obtain the release or restoration of, as from captivity, by paying a ransom. 9. to deliver from sin and its consequences by means of a sacrifice offered for the sinner" (Webster's). So the translation of "redemption" captures fully both the literal and figurative meanings of the Greek word.

The rendering of "paid the price" does include the idea of money being paid, but it misses the idea of it being a "buying back" of something and of the act being a release from captivity. And it completely misses the figurative meaning of the word.

So the rendering of *God's Word* might be easier to understand, but it misses most of the "intended meaning" of the Greek word, all of which the "original hearers and readers" would have understood. So the simplifications of "theological terms" in *God's Word* can sometimes be accurate, but sometimes they can miss the intended meaning of the original words.

In conclusion, there are some words that are translated accurately, though differently, in *God's Word*, but there are many more words that are left untranslated or replaced by completely different words. And at times its simplifications of theological terms miss the intended meanings of the original words. Moreover, by deviating from the actual words and grammar of the original text, the theological opinions of the translators are inserted into the translation.

Paraphrase—Critical Text

"Paraphrase" is the last principle to be studied. With this method, one author REWORDS the Bible to make it as easy to read and understand as possible. But what a user of such a version will be reading and understanding is the one author's opinion on what a particular verse means. And his opinion can be influenced by his own theological viewpoint.

Moreover, a paraphrase pays little regard to the vocabulary, grammar, and syntax of the original Hebrew and Greek texts. As such, all of the general comments made about the dynamic equivalence class would apply here, only more so.

The Living Bible:

The *Living Bible* (LB) was published in 1971 and became the first paraphrase to become popular. It was written by Kenneth Taylor. It can be rather hard to find today. But since it set the stage for later paraphrases, a quick look at the LB would be helpful in seeing the potential problems with this translation method.

An example of a paraphraser's theological biases infiltrating the text can in seen in Taylor's rendering of the second half of Acts 13:48. This passage in the NKJV reads, "as many as had been appointed to eternal life believed." But the LB says, "as many as wanted eternal life, believed." The perfect passive verb has been changed to a simple past, active verb. This moves the basis of salvation from God's previous "appointment" to human "wants" (compare Eph 1:3-7).

Moreover, by not paying attention to the details of the original text, a paraphrase can miss some important points in a verse. An example of this can be seen in Genesis 19:24.

The NKJV translates this verse, "Then the LORD rained brimstone and fire on Sodom and Gomorrah, from the LORD out of heaven." Be sure to note the two occurrences of "the LORD" (or "Jehovah" - Hebrew, *Yahweh*). The early Church Fathers appealed to this phenomenon as proof for the Deity of Jesus. The first LORD was taken as a reference to the Son and the second as referring to the Father.

Irenaeus (120-203 AD) writes about this verse, "For it points out that the Son, who had also been talking with Abraham, had received power to judge the Sodomites for their wickedness" (Bush, p.80). And it should be noted, in Genesis 18, the Person talking to Abraham is called "the LORD" several times.

But Genesis 19:24 in the LB reads, "Then the LORD rained down fire and flaming tar from heaven upon Sodom and Gomorrah." Notice that only one " LORD " has been translated. So by attempting to "simplify" the Bible, the LB has eliminated this passage from being a proof-text for the Deity of Christ.

A new edition of the *Living Bible* came out in 1996 called the *New Living Translation* (NLT). The translators claim that the NLT is no longer a paraphrase but is now a dynamic equivalence version. It is true that the NLT was produced by a group of translators not just one, so technically it would not be a paraphrase. But as Chapter Eighteen will show, the NLT is not even literal enough to be called a dynamic equivalence version. It is still very much a rewording of the Scriptures.

The Message:

The Message is a much newer paraphrase by Eugene H. Peterson. The NT was published in 1993. The OT is being published in parts as Peterson finishes different potions of it. As of this writing, the Wisdom Books and the Prophets have been published.

The back cover of this writer's edition of the *Message's* NT states, "One of the most striking features of the New Testament is that is was written in the street language of the day. The idiom of the playground and marketplace—not the formal, lofty language of government decrees and historical documents." This is true. The NT was written in the common or *koine* Greek of the day.

The Preface then states:

"This version of the New Testament in a contemporary idiom keeps the language of the Message current and fresh in the same language in which we do our shopping, talk with our friends, worry about world affairs, and teach our children their table manners. The goal is not to render a word-for-word conversion of Greek into English, but rather to convert the tone, the rhythms, the ideas, into the way we actually think and speak (p.7).

This writer agrees that the Bible should be translated using modern-day English. And doing so will produce an accurate and readable version. But what Peterson is talking about is re-writing the New Testament so that it expresses its ideas in the manner in which he thinks these ideas would have been expressed if the New Testament were written today. To do this requires completing ignoring all details if the Greek text and simply re-writing the Bible. And by doing so, there is the very real possibility that ideas foreign to the Bible will be inserted into it.

This re-writing and danger can be seen in Acts 2:18-20. This passage will be quoted first from the NKJV and then from the *Message*. The passage occurs during Peter's speech in the upper room before Pentecost and is referring to Judas.

18 (Now this man purchased a field with the wages of iniquity; and falling headlong, he burst open in the middle and all his entrails gushed out. 19 And it became known to all those dwelling in Jerusalem; so that field is called in their own language, Akel Dama, that is, Field of Blood.) 20 "For it is written in the book of Psalms: 'Let his dwelling place be desolate, And let no one live in it'; and, 'Let another take his office.'"

"As you know, he took the evil bride money and brought a small farm. There he came to a bad end,

41

rupturing his belly and spilling his guts. Everybody in Jerusalem knows this by now; they call the place Murder Meadow. It's exactly what we find written in the Psalms: 'Let his farm become haunted so no one can live there.' And also what was written later: 'Let someone else take over his post.'"

It should be noted that the *Message* does not number the verses, just the chapters. And with how "free" the renderings of the *Message* are, it can sometimes be difficult to know where one verse ends and another begins. But the above is probably what constitutes Acts 1:18-20 from the *Message*.

That said, it should be obvious that there is a big difference here. But then, Peterson specifically says he is not producing a word-for-word translation, so it is not surprising the *Message* differs so much from one that is. But the important question is, has Peterson correctly captured the "ideas" of the passage without inserting ideas foreign to it?

So to comment, the first obvious difference is that the NKJV, as with most other versions, places verses 18 and 19 in parenthesis without quotations marks. This makes the words a comment inserted by Luke for the benefit of Theophilus, to whom the Book of Acts was written (Acts 1:12). And the structure of the Greek text favors this format. The *Message*, however, inserts these words into the mouth of Peter as being addressed to those in the upper room. To do so requires completely re-writing the text.

Second, "the wages of iniquity" has been changed to "the evil bride money." The latter is easier to understand, but it does introduce the idea of a "bribe" rather than simply a "wage."

Third, rather than Judas buying a "field," the *Message* has him buying a "small farm." The latter gives the indication that Judas was a farmer, but there is no indication whatsoever in Scripture as to what Judas' occupation was.

Moreover, the word in question means, "place, spot (MT 26.36); piece of ground, field, place (JN 4.5)" (Friberg). So the word itself does not have the connotation of a farm. So Peterson has inserted a guess as to what Judas' occupation was into the text.

Next, "Field of Blood" has been changed to "Murder Meadow." The latter is rather expressive, but then, so is the former. "Field of Blood" is a rather dramatic and understandable phrase, so there really was no need to "update" it. Moreover, it must be asked, what does "Murder" refer to? Judas committed suicide; he was not murdered. So "Suicide Field" or some such rendering would make more sense. But then, why not just leave it as "Field of Blood?"

But the worst example of an unbiblical idea entering into the text comes in the next sentence. "Let his dwelling place be desolate" has been changed to "Let his farm become haunted so no one can live there." So again, the idea of Judas being a farmer has been inserted into the text. But that's not the worst unbiblical idea in this sentence. That comes with the word "haunted."

The word haunted means, "inhabited or frequented by ghosts: *a haunted castle*" (Webster's). So it would seem in Peterson's world there are ghosts haunting the homes of people who die tragic deaths. It is true this is popular mythology, but it is just that, mythology. In the Bible and thus in the real world, there is no such thing as ghosts!

This is very important. There are many people today who believe in such things as ghosts, and even live in constant fear as a result. But becoming a Christian and believing Biblical teachings should deliver a person from such superstitions. However, the *Message* would not be able to deliver such a person, but would probably help to confirm them in their superstitious and fearful ways.

In conclusion, the *Message* is a very readable and expressive book. However, the *Message* completely ignores the original words and grammar of the text and instead re-writes the Bible. In doing so, it inserts ideas that are foreign to the actual Word of God. In just the one passage above, the *Message* has inserted the ideas of Judas being a farmer, of Judas having been murdered, and worst of all, of the existence of ghosts. As such, the *Message* is not a book one could relay on for help in understanding the Word of God.

Conclusion/ Recommendations

The purpose of translating the Bible is so people who don't know Hebrew or Greek can read what God said for themselves. As such, a translation of the Bible should adhere as closely as possible to the actual God-breathed words. But only versions following either the literal or the formal equivalence translation principles actually do so.

As such, the reading of any of the versions in the first two classifications is highly recommended. Versions in the other classifications should be used as secondary Bibles for comparison purposes only. But even then, a person would be better off comparing two or more of the literal or formal equivalence versions, while checking commentaries and other Bible study aids for difficult passages.

It should also be noted that sometimes a person will find one literal or formal equivalence version difficult to read but another to be very readable. So if the reader has been trying to read one of these versions but is finding it difficult, before settling for reading a less accurate type of version, try reading a different literal or formal equivalence version. You just might find one you do find readable. To aid in selecting a version that will fit your needs, Chapter Twenty-two includes sample passages from Bible versions mentioned in the first two classifications.

The next chapter continues this discussion of translation principles, but in a somewhat different manner. It also mentions several additional Bible versions that were not discussed here.

Bibliography for Chapters Two and Three:
Full biographical details for all the Bible versions mentioned in these chapters are given on the page, "Bible Versions List."

The Beacon. April 1993, inside front cover.

BibleWorks™ for Windows™ Copyright © 1992-1999 *BibleWorks*, L.C.C. Big Fork, MT: Hermeneutika. Programmed by Michael S. Bushell and Michael D. Tan.

Bush, L. Russ, ed. *Classical Readings in Christian Apologetics: A.D. 100 - 1800*. Grand Rapids: Zondervan, 1983.

Clark, Gordon. *Ephesians*. Jefferson, MD: The Trinity Foundation, 1985.

Logical Criticisms of Textual Criticism. Jefferson, MD: The Trinity Foundation, 1986.

Cranfield. C.E.B. *International Critical Commentary: Romans*. Vol.I. Edinburgh: T & T Clark Limited, 1975.

Dana, H.E. and Julius Mantey. *A Manual Grammar of the Greek New Testament*. New York: Macmillan, 1955.

Erickson, Millard. *Concise Dictionary of Christian Theology*. Grand Rapids: Baker Book House, 1986.

Fee, Gordon & Douglas Stuart. *How to Read the Bible for All Its Worth*. Grand Rapids: Zondervan, 1982.

Friberg, Timothy and Barbara. *Analytical Lexicon to the Greek New Testament*. Copyright © 1994. As found on *BibleWorks™ for Windows™*.

Green, J.P. *Christian Literature World*. August/ September 1993.

Lockyer, Herbert. ed. *Nelson's Illustrated Bible Dictionary*. Nashville: Thomas Nelson, 1986.

Robertson, A.T. *Word Pictures in the Greek New Testament*, 1934. As found on *BibleWorks™ for Windows™*.

Webster's Talking Dictionary/ Thesaurus. Licensed property of Parson's Technology, Inc. v. 1.0b. Software Copyright 1996 by Exceller Software Corp. Based on *Random House Webster's College Dictionary*. Copyright 1995 by Random House, Inc.

Chapter Four
Five Different Translation Principles

(Which Method is Best?)

Different versions of the Bible follow one of five different principles for translating the original Hebrew and Greek Scriptures. Which method is best? Before this question can be answered, each principle needs to be explained and evaluated.

Translation Principles and Matthew 2:10

A look at how Matthew 2:10 is rendered in several versions of the Bible will introduce the five main translation principles that can be utilized. At the end of this chapter is a list of the meanings of each Bible version abbreviation.

The Greek text (transliterated into English letters) is presented first. A strict word for word translation (as would be seen in an interlinear) is given underneath.

Idontes   de   ton   astera   echaresan   charan
seeing   And   the   star   they rejoice   joy
megalen   sphodra.
great   exceedingly.

Note how awkward the literal translation is if read straight across.

Literal: EVERY SINGLE WORD of the Greek text is translated.

> YLT: And having seen the star, they rejoiced [with] exceeding great joy,
> LITV: And seeing the star, they rejoiced exceedingly [with] a great joy.

ALT: And having seen the star, they rejoiced exceedingly [with] great joy.

Formal Equivalence: The Greek text is translated as WORD FOR WORD as possible.

KJV: When they saw the star, they rejoiced with exceedingly great joy.

NKJV: When they saw the star, they rejoiced with exceedingly great joy.

MKJV: And seeing the star, they rejoiced with exceedingly great joy.

WEB: When they saw the star, they rejoiced with exceedingly great joy.

KJER: When they saw the star, they rejoiced with exceedingly great joy.

EWB: When they saw the star, they rejoiced with exceeding great joy.

RWB: When they saw the star, they rejoiced with exceeding great joy.

NAS77:   And when they saw the star, they rejoiced exceedingly with great joy.

NAS95:   And when they saw the star, they rejoiced exceedingly with great joy.

Notes: These two principles will be commented on together as all of these versions are very similar in this verse. So to comment, the word order has been altered just enough to make the sentence readable. The vocabulary, grammar and syntax of the original have been retained.

Second, every word has been translated except "and" in several of the formal equivalence versions. But this is a rare example as these versions generally do translate all conjunctions. Third, "with" is the only word added for clarity. The three literal versions indicate it as such, but the formal equivalence versions do not. However, all of the formal equivalence versions (except the WEB) generally do offset added words.

Fourth, "seeing" is a plural, aorist (past tense) participle. YLT and the ALT uses "having seen" to indicate the action of the participle precedes that of the verb (rejoiced) in the second clause. The translation of "when they saw" in most of the formal equivalence versions is due to the translators taking the participle as being used in a temporal sense. Any one of these three renderings is a legitimate translation.

Fifth, the different placement of "exceedingly" is due to a different decision as to whether it should be taken as an adjective modifying "joy" or as an adverb modifying "rejoiced." Either is possible, although as an adverb is most likely. Some of the versions that take it as an adjective use "exceeding" (an adjective) since "exceedingly" is technically an adverb.

Finally, the grammatical structure known as a "cognate accusative" has been retained. A "cognate accusative" means the direct object (joy) is from the same root as the verb (rejoice). This is the Greek language way of emphasizing the action of the verb.

Dynamic Equivalence: Attempts to express the MEANING of the original.

NIV: When they saw the star, they were overjoyed.
NLT: When they saw the star, they were filled with joy!
NET: When they saw the star they shouted joyfully.
NEB: At the sight of the star, they were overjoyed.
NAB: They were overjoyed at seeing the star.
NJB: The sight of the star filled them with delight,
NRSV: When they saw that the star had stopped, they were overwhelmed with joy.
God's: They were overwhelmed with joy to see the star.
NCV: When the wise men saw the star, they were filled with joy.

CEV: They were thrilled and excited to see the star.
GNB: When they saw it, how happy they were, what joy was theirs!

Notes: These versions use more idiomatic English than the "formal" ones. However, it should be noted how very different they are from the literal and formal equivalence versions and even from each other.

To comment, the NIV has combined "great" and "joy" into "overjoyed." Since it left out "rejoiced" it was forced to add "were" in order to have a verb. And the question of whether "exceedingly" is an adjective or an adverb has been "solved" by leaving the word untranslated.

The NLT has combined "great," "joy," and "rejoiced" into the phrase "filled with joy." And again, since "rejoiced" was omitted, "were" was added to have a verb. And again, "exceedingly" was left untranslated. The NET has changed the verb "rejoiced" to the adverb "joyfully" and has added "shouted" to have a verb. But at least it includes in a footnote, "*Grk* 'they rejoiced with very great joy.'"

The NEB has rendered the second half of the verse the same as the NIV. Plus, it has changed "the star" (an accusative) into "of the star" (a genitive). The NAB has reversed the two clauses. Otherwise it is similar to the NEB. The NJB is also similar to the NEB in the first half, but the original verb ("rejoiced") has been replaced with "filled."

The NRSV has added "that...had stopped" without any warrant from the Greek text. Further, "were overwhelmed" has been substituted for "rejoiced exceedingly" and "great" is left untranslated. *God's Word* is the same as the NRSV in the second clause, but it has moved this phrase to being the first clause. It has also changed the opening participle ("seeing") to an infinitive ("to see").

The NCV has changed the pronoun "they" into the noun "wise men." The second clause then has the same changes as the NLT.

The CEV has also reversed the clauses. Moreover, the second clause has been changed into "were thrilled and excited." And like *God's Word*, it has also changed the participle into an infinitive.

The GNB has turned the one sentence into two using a comma splice. This is not even good English let alone a faithful rendering of the Greek text. Further, only five of the twelve words have any true backing in the original.

And finally, all of the above versions might have captured the "meaning" of the cognate accusative, but they have hid the construction itself.

Expanded: One author attempts to bring out NUANCES of the original languages.

> Amp: When they saw the star, they were thrilled with ecstatic joy.
> Wuest: And having seen the star, they rejoiced with great joy, exceedingly.

Notes: The emphasis indicated by the cognate accusative is brought out. And Wuest's translation, in this particular example, is similar to the "formal" ones. But in the *Amplified*, the grammatical construction itself has been hid by substituting "were thrilled" for "rejoiced exceedingly."

Paraphrase: The text is REWORDED by one author to make it as simple as possible.

> Gspd: When they saw the star, they were very glad.
> Wey: When they saw the star, the sight filled them with intense joy.
> Phi: The sight of the star filled them with indescribable joy!
> LB: Their joy knew no bounds!

Mesg: They could hardly contain themselves: They were in the right place!
They had arrived at the right time!

Notes: These renderings are very colorful and colloquial. However, as with the dynamic equivalence versions, they each differ greatly from each other and from more literal versions.

To comment, Goodspeed's "very glad" misses the emphasis on the intensity of the emotion indicated by the cognate accusative construction.

Weymouth, like some of the dynamic equivalence versions, has replaced "rejoiced" with "filled." It has also added the words "the sight." But at least "intense" brings out the idea of the cognate accusative construction.

Phillips, like the NEB, has altered the grammar of the first half. And, "joy" is the only one of the five words in the second half actually translating anything in the Greek text.

The LB has left off the entire first half of the verse. And, again, "joy" is the only one of the five words with any backing in the Greek text.

The rendering of *The Message* is very expressive. However, "they" is the only word actually translating anything in the Greek text. The rest is simply the imaginative writing of Mr. Peterson.

And finally, the grammar and syntax of all of these versions bear very little resemblance to that of the Greek text.

Summary: As indicated, all of the versions under the literal and formal equivalence categories are very similar. When translators simply try to translate the original words literally or as word for word as possible, the only differences will be due to different decisions on grammatical constructions and the exact meanings of words.

But again, be sure to note the vast difference between the wordings of the rest of the versions. The translators have paid little or no regard to the original vocabulary, grammar, syntax, or word order. Thus, each has ended up with very different "translations."

"Every Word of God is Pure"

But does any of the above really matter? Does not this sound like a bunch of "nit-picking?" The reason it matters is the Scriptures themselves are very clear in teaching it is wrong to add to or take away from the very words of God.

Proverbs 30:5,6 declares, "Every word of God is pure; He is a shield to those who put their trust in Him. Do not add to His words, Lest He reprove you, and you be found a liar" (NKJV; see also Deut 4:2; Prov 8:8,9; Jer 23:30,31, 26:2; 1Cor 4:6; Rev 22:18,19).

If "EVERY word of God is pure," does this not include the word "exceedingly?" If so, then why do so many of the above versions, except the literal and formal equivalence ones, consider it of such little importance as to leave it untranslated?

The word "rejoiced" also doesn't fare very well in these versions. Most seem to believe this "pure word of God" needs to be changed. In fact, there is no word in the Greek that is not changed or left out by at least one of these versions.

As for adding words, terms like overjoyed, overwhelmed, thrilled, happy, and glad keep popping up; but none of these are actual translations of any individual Greek words. Sometimes the added words even outnumber the original ones.

And it needs to be pointed out that any words added for clarity in the literal and formal equivalence versions are generally offset in same manner. However, with the other versions there is no attempt made to distinguish between words added for clarity and words actually translating original, God-breathed words (2Tim 3:16).

1Corinthians 7:1

But still, is not the meaning of the text the same in each version? In the example given above this may be true. But this is not always the case.

The above example was chosen to show the differences between translation principles without a doctrinal or ethical controversy muddling the issue. But now a verse will be looked at where the MEANING changes widely between versions.

In 1Corinthians 7:1, Paul writes, "Now concerning the things of which you wrote to me: It is good for a man not to touch a woman" (NKJV). All of the literal and the other "formal" versions translate the second part of the verse similarly, along with the NRSV and NJB.

But what does Paul mean by "It is good for a man not to touch a woman?" The meaning is not clear (cp. 2Pet 3:16). But despite this, the rest of the versions feel free to take a stab at interpreting this statement for their readers.

NIV: It is good for a man not to marry.

NIV fn: It is good for a man not to have sexual relations with a woman.

NLT: Yes, it is good to live a celibate life.

NET: It is good for a man not to have sexual relations with a woman.

NEB: It is a good thing for a man to have nothing to do with women.

NAB: A man is better off having no relations with a woman.

God's: It's good for men not to marry.

NCV: It is good for a man not to marry.

CEV: You asked, "Is it best for people not to marry?"

GNB: A man does well not to marry.

Amp: It is well—(and by that I mean) advantageous, expedient, profitable and wholesome—for a man not to touch a woman (to cohabit with her), but to remain unmarried.

Wuest: It is perfectly proper, honorable, morally befitting for a man to live in strict celibacy.

Gspd: it is an excellent thing for a man to remain unmarried.

Wey: It is well for a man to abstain altogether from marriage.

Phi: It is good for a man to have no physical contact with women.

LB: if you do not marry, it is good.

Mesg: Is it a good thing to have sexual relations?

Which of these interpretations is correct? This writer thinks they are all wrong! I do not believe Paul is advocating celibacy (NIV, NLT, NET, God's, NCV, GNB, Wuest, Gspd, Wey, LB). He most definitely is not telling men "to have nothing to do with women" (NEB, also NAB). Can't I even say "hello?"

That an unmarried man is "not to have sexual relations with a woman" is certainly true (NIV footnote; NET). But does this prohibition only include intercourse? There is a lot an unmarried couple can do without actually "going all the way."

Phillips goes to the opposite extreme and says there should be "no physical contact." Can't I even hold hands?

The *Amplified* tries to combine both renderings from the NIV. Problem is, "to remain unmarried" is not necessarily synonymous with "not...to cohabit." Many in our society (unfortunately) cohabit without being married. And the practice of some "expanded" versions of listing several synonyms for select words or phrases can cause the text to be unnecessarily awkward.

And lastly, both the CEV and *The Message* turn the statement into a question. They are probably interpreting the passage as Paul simply repeating a question the Corinthians had written to him. But when "Now concerning" is used elsewhere, the next statement is generally not rendered as a question (7:25;

8:1; 12:1; 16:1). And the two versions don't agree on what this supposed question was.

Interpretation Not Translation

So what is the correct interpretation of 1Corinthians 7:1? Paul could be teaching it is good for a man to refrain from touching a woman sexually in such a way as to "ignite" his own or her sexual passions (see verse 9). But if they cannot refrain from such activity, they should either get married or break off the relationship (verses 36,37). And this interpretation would have profound implications for single Christians today.

But please note, this whole discussion is on INTERPRETATION NOT TRANSLATION. And this is the point. Most of the versions other than the literal and formal equivalence ones have gone beyond simply translating the Greek text but are actually interpreting it. But interpretation is the job of commentators and teachers, not translators (see Neh 8:8; Eph 4:11).

As J.P. Green (editor of the LITV and MKJV) remarks:

As commentators, they are welcome to express their opinions as to the meaning of a verse or passage, and this in any words they may choose to use. But as translators, they are on holy ground, and any words not explicit or implicit in the God-breathed Scriptures is a despising of God the Spirit's teaching and words (p.301).

Anytime anything is added to the text which involves interpretation rather than translation, it should be clearly indicated as such within the text. For instance, to indicate the above-mentioned possible interpretation, the ALT adds "sexually" to the end of the verse, but it does so in brackets so the reader knows it has been added.

Gary Zeolla

Conclusion

Although the versions other than the literal or formal equivalence versions may be easy to read and understand, there is no way of knowing if one is reading and understanding the words and ideas of God or only those of the translator/interpreters. And since only the words of God are "true and faithful" (Rev 21:5), of the five different translation principles, either literal or formal equivalence is the best method to use for translating the Bible.

Which one of these two is best depends on what the Bible is being used for. For in-depth personal, Bible study, a literal version would be best, but for functions such as personal devotional reading, reading aloud in church services or Bible studies, or evangelism a formal equivalence version would probably be best. But either type of version could be used for any of these functions, and comparing more than one would also be helpful, especially in personal Bible study.

Abbreviations (in order of occurrence):
YLT – Young's *Literal Translation.*
LITV – *Literal Translation of the Bible*.
ALT – *Analytical-Literal Translation*.
KJV – *King James Version*.
NKJV – *New King James Version*.
MKJV – *Modern King James Version*.
WEB – *World English Bible*.
KJER – *King James Easy Reading Sword Study Bible*
EWB – *English Webster's Bible*.
RWB – *Revised Webster Bible*.
NAS77 – *New American Standard Bible* (1977 edition).
NAS95 – *New American Standard Bible* (1995 edition).
NIV – *New International Version*.
NLT – *New Living Translation*.
NEB – *New English Bible*.
NAB – *New American Bible for Catholics*.

NJB – *New Jerusalem Bible.*
NRSV – *New Revised Standard Version.*
God's – *God's Word.*
NCV – *New Century Version.*
CEV – *Contemporary English Version.*
GNB – *Good News Bible* (*Today's English Version*).
Amp – *Amplified Bible.*
Wuest – Wuest, Kenneth, *NT: An Expanded Translation.*
Gspd – Goodspeed, Edgar. *NT: American Translation.*
Wey – *Weymouths' Translation.*
Phi – Phillips, J.B. *The NT in Modern English.*
LB – *The Living Bible,* by Kenneth Taylor.
Mesg – *The Message,* by Eugene Peterson.

Bibliography:

Green, J.P. *Unholy Hands on the Bible.* Vol. II. Lafayette, IN: Sovereign Grace Trust Fund, 1992.

Full biographical details for all the Bible versions mentioned in this chapter are given on the page "Bible Versions List."

Chapter Five
Three Popular Bible Versions

(Similarities and Differences)

For nearly four hundred years, and throughout several revisions of its English form, the *King James Bible* has been deeply revered among the English speaking peoples of the world. The precision of translation for which it is historically renowned, and its majesty of style, have enabled that monumental version of the Word of God to become the mainspring of the religion, language, and legal foundations of our civilization (Parallel, p.xxi).

But despite this legacy of the *King James Version* (KJV), numerous new versions have appeared since the late 1800s. Two of the most popular of these new versions are the *New International Version* (NIV) and the *New King James Version* (NKJV). But what are the similarities and differences between these three popular Bible versions? This chapter will investigate some of the most important of these.

The Translators

The first important similarity between these three versions is the number and quality of the translators. King James I of England commissioned "54 prominent Greek and Hebrew scholars of the Church of England" to work on the version which bears his name. The project began in 1604 and was finished in 1611 (*Parallel*, p.v).

Work on the NIV began in 1968. Over a hundred scholars were involved. The New Testament was first published in 1973 and the complete Bible in 1978 (*Story of the NIV*, p.7).

As for the NKJV, "over 130 scholars, editors, church leaders and Christian laity" were commissioned to work on the project. The work began in 1976. The New Testament was finished in 1979 and the Old Testament in 1982 (*Parallel*, pp.ii, v).

So all three versions were produced by dozens of Christian scholars working together over a period of several years. Further, all of these men were committed to belief in the inspiration and infallibility of the Scriptures.

Martin Luther comments in this regard:

. Translating [the Bible] is certainly not everybody's business, as the mad saints imagine; it requires a genuinely pious, faithful, diligent, God-fearing experienced, practiced heart. Therefore, I hold that a false Christian or a sectarian spirit is unable to give a faithful translation (quoted in Green, p.313; see Rom 8:6-8; 1Cor 2:14,15).

Modern-day English

One noticeable difference between the KJV and modern-day versions like the NIV and NKJV is the elimination of the Elizabethan English (words like "thee" and "thou" and the -eth and -est verb endings). Since people today generally do not utilize these archaic word forms, they are replaced with modern terminology (*Parallel*, p.xxii).

Also, words sometimes change meanings over time. Think, for instance, of the different meaning the statement, "He is gay" has today versus a few decades ago.

As such, modern-day versions update words that have changed meaning since 1611. For example, in Mark 10:14 the KJV has Jesus telling the disciples, "SUFFER the little children to come unto me." This may had made sense in 1611, but today it doesn't. So both the NIV and NKJV have "let" instead of "suffer" in this verse.

However, the NKJV translators did not believe this attitude of updating words should extend to technical terms, "King James doctrinal and theological terms, for example, propitiation, justification, and sanctification, are generally familiar to English speaking people. Such terms have been retained..." (Parallel, p.xxii).

But the NIV translators believed differently. As such, some of the technical terms have been replaced. For instance, the word "propitiation" does not occur in the NIV. It has been replaced by "atoning sacrifice" (Rom 3:25; 1John 2:2; 4:10).

It could be argued whether "propitiation" or "atoning sacrifice" is the more generally understood term today. However, one thing is sure, "propitiation" is the more exact translation of the Greek word (Bauer, p.375).

There are several aspects to the Atonement: ransom, propitiation, forgiveness, reconciliation and redemption. By translating the Greek word as "atoning sacrifice" the NIV blurs these distinctions. Thus the NKJV's practice is more specific.

Incidentally, "propitiation" refers to Jesus' act of taking God the Father's wrath against our sins upon Himself. Forgiveness of sins, reconciliation to God, and redemption from sin occur as a result of the propitiation (Murray, pp.147-156).

Translation Principles

"The King James translators were committed to producing an English Bible that would be a precise translation and by no means a paraphrase or a broadly approximate rendering." The NKJV translators had the same commitment.

"This principle of complete (or formal) equivalence seeks to preserve ALL of the information in the text, while presenting it in good literary form....Complete equivalence translates fully, in order to provide an English text that is both accurate and readable" (*Parallel*, p.xxi).

However, the NIV follows a quite different principle known as dynamic equivalence:

The first concern of the translators has been the accuracy of the translation and its fidelity to the THOUGHT of the biblical writers. They have weighed the significance of the lexical and grammatical details of the Hebrew, Aramaic, and Greek texts. At the same time, they have striven for MORE THAN A WORD FOR WORD TRANSLATION. Because thought patterns and syntax differ from language to language, faithful communication of the MEANING of the writers demands FREQUENT MODIFICATIONS IN SENTENCE STRUCTURE and constant regard for the contextual meanings of words (NIV preface, p.x).

Adhering to these divergent principles leads to several differences between how the KJV and NKJV handle the original text versus how the NIV does.

Words vs. Thoughts: The KJV and NKJV attempt to translate the original text as word for word as possible. But the NIV seeks to be a thought for thought translation.

A simple example of the difference between these two philosophies can be seen in Matthew 11:4. The first part of this verse reads in the KJV, "Jesus answered and said unto them." The NKJV says, "Jesus answered and said to them." So these two are virtually identical. And this type of phrase occurs throughout the Gospels.

Now compare the NIV, "Jesus replied." This rendering is simpler to read and captures the MEANING of text, but it obviously is not a word for word translation of what Matthew, as he "was moved by the Holy Spirit," actually wrote (see 2Pet 1:21).

Moreover, what happens if the meaning of the text is not clear? Burton L. Goddard, a member of the NIV Committee on Bible Translation writes, "Despite their expertise they [the NIV translators] frequently found themselves FAR FROM CERTAIN about the MEANING intended by the Holy Spirit, the primary Author of Scripture."

A good example of where the meaning may be "far from certain" can be seen in the first half of Leviticus 20:17. In the NKJV it reads, "If a man TAKES his sister, his father's daughter or his mother's daughter, and SEES HER NAKEDNESS AND SHE SEES HIS NAKEDNESS, it is a wicked thing." The KJV is virtually identical.

However, take a look at the NIV, "If a man MARRIES his sister, the daughter of either his father or his mother, and THEY HAVE SEXUAL RELATIONS, it is a disgrace."

When Moses WROTE "takes" did he MEAN "marries?" And is it possible to SEE a person's "nakedness" without having "sexual relations" with that person?

The NIV translators were so "certain" they knew the answers to these questions that they inserted their interpretation into the text without any indication they have done so. But the KJV and NKJV allow Bible readers to decide for themselves.

And less anyone thinks this is an unimportant point, there could be some important instruction here for single Christians like myself. This verse may help answer the very pressing question, "How far can I go (sexually) before I get married?"

In the New Testament, Paul commands Christians to treat members of the opposite sex like brothers and sisters (1Tim 5:1,2). Could these passages taken together forbid an unmarried couple from simply SEEING each other's nakedness even if they do not "go all the way?" In the KJV or NKJV this could be. But the NIV hides this possibility.

Untranslated Words: There is a divergence in how interjections and conjunctions are handled between the two principles. A study of Luke 2:10 will show this. Here, an angel says to the shepherds, "Do not be afraid, FOR BEHOLD, I bring you good tidings of great joy which shall be to all people" (NKJV). Again, the KJV is similar.

However, the NIV does not translate "for behold." But does this matter? In the Bible, the interjection "behold" is used for "dramatically calling attention to a spectacular scene, or an event of profound importance" (*Parallel*, p.xxi).

But the NIV does not consider this point to be of sufficient importance as to always translate "behold." Another example in a familiar verse is Isaiah 7:14.

And, as indicated, the conjunction "for" was also left untranslated. This conjunction and others (and, but, etc.) are often not translated in the NIV. But conjunctions have an important purpose. They show there is a relationship between the statement to come and the preceding one and what this relationship entails.

This importance can be seen in Romans 1:16-18. In the KJV and NKJV, each of these three verses begins with "for." However, the NIV only translates one "for" (v.17). As a result, the NIV looses Paul's progression of thought in this passage.

Sometimes the leaving out of words can extend beyond just interjections and conjunctions. At times, the NIV leaves out other words and even entire phrases. This can be clearly seen by studying Joshua 1:8. The KJV has 48 words in this verse; the NKJV has 49 words. But the NIV only has 30 words. Obviously, there is a big difference here!

Added Words: Words added for clarity are handled in dissimilar manners. The KJV and NKJV put such words in italics. However, the NIV translators make no such effort to distinguish between their own words and the God-inspired words of the original.

A simple example of this can be seen in the second half of 1Corinthians 7:9, "for it is better to marry than to burn" (KJV).

Herbert Wolf, one of the NIV translators, comments on this passage, "Most INTERPRETERS feel that 'burn' refers to the flames of passion that can only rightly be satisfied in marriage. To make this clear both the NIV and the NKJV translate the verb, "to burn with passion" (Barker, p.131).

A couple of comments are in order on Wolf's comment. First, note that he freely admits the NIV translators depended on what "interpreters" had to say about a passage to determine how to "translate" it.

Second, it is true the NKJV adds the words "with passion" to its text. Wolf, however, fails to mention an important point: in the NKJV these words are in italics, but in the NIV they are printed in the same type as the rest of the verse.

This difference is important as there are actually two possible ways to take what Paul meant by "to burn" in this passage. Greek scholar Fritz Rienecker comments, "It may mean 'to burn with passion' but may possibly mean 'to burn in Gehenna (hell)' because of falling into fornication" (p.405; see 1Cor 6:9,10; Rev 21:8).

The KJV translators left the question open. The NKJV translators present their opinion, but (by putting the added words in italics) leave it to the reader to disagree. But the translators of the NIV fixed the meaning to only the former since the reader has no way of knowing "with passion" was added.

Altered Sentence Structure: In addition to omitting and adding words, the NIV translators believe it is appropriate to alter the grammatical forms of words and phrases in order to express the meaning of the text.

Herbert Wolf explains the NIV philosophy:
Since no two languages express ideas in the same way, sometimes IT IS NECESSARY TO CHANGE ONE OR MORE GRAMMATICAL FORMS to translate a sentence properly. NOUNS MAY BE TRANSLATED AS VERBS, or perhaps CONJUNCTIONS AS PREPOSITIONS. One of the simplest changes is to COMBINE TWO TERMS that really function as one unit."

Wolf then gives the following examples where the NIV has "changed" the grammatical forms of words and phrases:

Deut 7:9: "the covenant and the love" becomes "his covenant of love."
Isa 1:13: the noun "iniquity" is changed to the adjective, "evil."
Gal 3:2,5: the noun "works" is changed into the verbal noun "observing" – "hearing" becomes "what you heard," and "faith" is now "believing" (Barker, pp.132,133).

But is it true translators may add to, subtract from, and alter the very words of God as they believe "it is necessary?" Please carefully consider the following verses: Deut 4:2; Prov 8:8,9; 30:5,6; Jer 23:30,31; Rev 22:18,19.

And lastly, Wolf writes, "While it may be true that AT TIMES THE NIV TRANSLATORS HAVE BEEN GUILTY OF READING SOMETHING INTO THE TEXT, I would contend that overall this version has achieved a high degree of accuracy by its philosophy of translation" (Barker, p.127).

So the NIV translators have only "at times" inserted their own ideas into the God-inspired Scriptures with all their alterations.

Additional Examples: Lev 20:11; Ps 72:16; Prov 20:1; Eccl 3:10; Isa 8:9; Matt 2:10; 4:23; 8:25; 13:3; 18:7; 55:6-13; Mark 6:51; Luke 1:8,51; 2:1,12; 9:12; 23:44,45; John 2:16; 4:50; 6:65; 8:24; 17:19; Acts 7:54; 17:34; 1Cor 7:1,4; 2Cor 5:16,17; 6:7; Gal 5:16-19; Eph 2:3; 5:16; 6:14; Phil 2:7; Col 2:17-23; 3:15; 1Thes 1:3; 4:4 (cp. 1Pet 3:7); 1John 5:18,19.

Greek Text-Type

The *King James New Testament* was based on the traditional text of the Greek-speaking churches, first published in 1516 and later called the *Textus Receptus* or *Received Text*. Although based on relatively few available manuscripts, these were representative of many more which existed at the time but only became known later (*Parallel*, p.xxiii).

The NKJV is also based on the *Textus Receptus* (TR). The Greek text developed from the "many more" manuscripts which "became known later" is called the Majority Text (MT). The TR and MT are very similar.

However, "Since the 1880s most contemporary translations of the NT [including the NIV] have relied on a relatively few manuscripts discovered chiefly in the late nineteenth and twentieth centuries" (*Parallel*, p.xxiii). The Greek text developed from these manuscripts is called the Critical Text (CT).

These two textual traditions are in substantial agreement, but there are some significant differences. The NKJV footnotes these variants. The textual footnotes in the NIV are not as extensive as in the NKJV. Most editions of the KJV do not have any textual footnotes.

There are debates among Christian scholars as to which text-type best reflects the originals. This subject is covered in detail in the next section of this book.

Here it will just be mentioned how all this relates back to the Bible study mentioned in the "Preface" to this book. The confusion was due to a textual variant. The TR and MT have the controversial phrase in two places in Matthew: in 20:16 and in 22:14. The lady who asked the question was reading the KJV, so the phrase was in her Bible in 20:16.

However, the CT has it only once, in 22:14. It omits the phrase from 20:16 since some manuscripts do not have it in this verse. The teacher was using the NIV, so the phrase was not in his Bible.

Furthermore, neither the NIV nor the KJV footnotes the variant. And everyone at the study, except this writer, was using one of these two versions, hence why no one could figure what was going on.

I, however, was reading from the NKJV, and this version does footnote the variant. But before I got a chance to explain all this, the elderly gentleman chided in and the debate began.

If the teacher had been using the KJV or NKJV, his Bible would have contained the controversial phrase, and he could have prepared for possible questions on it. Moreover, if he was using the NKJV, he would have known about the variant and been able to explain why some Bible versions had it and some did not. In this way, all the confusion could have been avoided.

Conclusion

The KJV is a very reliable and accurate translation of the Scriptures. But, unfortunately, its archaic English leaves it difficult to read for many modern-day readers.

The NIV, conversely, is very readable. But its "dynamic equivalence" style of translating and reliance on the CT makes it a less dependable rendering of the Word of God.

Meanwhile, the NKJV is highly readable AND is extremely accurate. And its textual footnotes are very helpful, especially for Bible teachers.

Wilbur Pickering (Master's degree in theology, Ph.D. in linguistics) declares about the NKJV, "AN EXCELLENT TRANSLATION OF A GOOD GREEK TEXT" (quoted in Green, p.575).

Bibliography:

Barker, Kenneth. ed. *The NIV: The Making of a Contemporary Translation*. Colorado Springs: International Bible Society, 1991.

Bauer, Walter. *Greek-English Lexicon*. 2nd ed. Chicago: University of Chicago Press, 1979.

Green, J.P. ed. *Unholy Hands on the Bible*. Vol. II. Lafayette, IN: Sovereign Grace Trust Fund, 1992.

KJV/ NKJV Parallel Reference Bible. Nashville: Thomas Nelson, 1991.

Murray, John. "Atonement" in *Classic Bible Dictionary*. ed. J.P. Green. Lafayette, IN: Sovereign Grace Trust Fund, 1988.

New International Version of the Holy Bible. Grand Rapids, MI: 1978.

Rienecker, Fritz. *A Linguistic Key to the Greek New Testament*. Trans. and ed. by Cleon Rogers. Grand Rapids, MI: Zondervan, 1980.

Story of the New International Version. Colorado Springs, Co: International Bible Society, n.a.

Greek Text-types

Chapter Six
Introduction to Textual Criticism

"There is more manuscript support for the New Testament than for any other body of ancient literature. Over five thousand Greek, eight thousand Latin, and many more manuscripts in other languages attest the integrity of the New Testament" (*Parallel*, p.xxiii).

Moreover, "No other document of antiquity even begins to approach such numbers and attestation. In comparison, *The Illiad* by Homer is second with only 643 manuscripts that still survive" (McDowell, p.39).

Furthermore, "to be skeptical of the resultant text of the New Testament books is to allow all of classical antiquity to slip into obscurity, for no documents of the ancient period are as well attested biographically as the New Testament" (John W. Montgomery, quoted in McDowell, p.40).

The above quotes demonstrate the textual reliability of the New Testament. However, this does not mean there are not variants between these manuscripts. In fact, "Of the approximately five thousand Greek manuscripts of all or parts of the New Testament that are known today, no two agree exactly in all particulars" (Metzger, p.xxiv).

The process of sifting through these manuscripts and variants is known as TEXTUAL CRITICISM. And, "This is a most important and fascinating branch of study, its object being to determine as exactly as possible from the available evidence the original words of the documents in question" (Bruce, p.19).

The following article will present an introduction to textual criticism, "a most important and fascinating branch of study."

Types of Manuscripts

The first issue to look at is what is meant by "manuscript." A manuscript is simply a handwritten copy of the New Testament (NT) dating to before the invention of the printing press (mid 1400's). These could be copies of the entire NT, portions of it (such as just the Gospels or just the epistles of Paul) or simply fragments of a book of the NT. They are of several types.

Papyri: The earliest manuscripts are known as papyri. They are so called because they were written on papyrus. This material was produced from the papyrus plant. Strips of the plant were laid beside and on top of one another, moistened and pressed together, and cut into the desired size. Generally, these sheets were then arranged into scrolls. But the early Christians, instead, folded them down the center and bound them together into what is known as a "codex."

To date, 88 papyri have been cataloged. These date from the second to the eighth centuries. 41 are from the second to the fourth centuries. The earliest is a fragment of the Gospel of John and dates to about 125 A.D. The fragment contains John 18:31-33,37,38. It is now on display at the John Ryland's Library in Manchester.

The papyri are cataloged in scholarly works by a fancy looking "p" and a superscript number. The John Ryland's fragment is number 52.

In the fourth century, parchment began to be used. This was made from animal hide. The hair and flesh were removed and the hide trimmed to size, polished and smoothed with chalk and pumice stone. Parchment was used until paper became popular in the twelfth century.

Uncials: The uncials are the first kind of manuscript written on parchments. They are so called because the entire text was written in capital Greek letters. About 290 uncials have been recognized. They date from the fourth to the fifteenth centuries.

The two earliest are "Codex Sinaiticus" and "Codex Vaticanus." They are named after monasteries on Mount Sinai and in the Vatican, respectively. Both date from the early fourth century. These are also the earliest complete copies of the Bible known. They are also known as, "Aleph" (the first letter of the Hebrew alphabet) and "Beta" (the second letter of the Greek alphabet), respectively.

Uncials are designated with successive English capital letters and a number, with a "0" as the first digit. For instance, "Beta" is designated by B 03. The next earliest uncial is "Codex Alexandria" from the fifth century and is designated as "A 02." The only exception is "Aleph" which uses the Hebrew letter "Aleph" instead of an English letter.

Minuscules: The next kind of manuscripts is the minuscules. They are so named since they are written in small letters, with capitals only used as in modern day writing. These are also called "cursives" (running) because they are written in running script.

The minuscules date from the ninth to the fifteenth centuries. The earliest is from the year 835 and is located in the St. Petersburg Public Library. There are about 2,800 know minuscules. They are simply numbered consecutively.

In addition to actual texts of the Greek NT, there are three additional sources to be consulted in textual criticism.

Lectionaries: The first additional source is the lectionaries. These contain portions of Scriptures that have been divided up into readings for church services. There are approximately 2,200 known lectionaries. They date from the ninth to the fifteenth centuries and are designated by a fancy "l" with a superscript number.

Patristic Citations: The second additional source is patristic citations. These are quotes of the NT in commentaries and other writings of the Church Fathers (church leaders during the centuries immediately following the Apostles).

The use of these in textual criticism can be difficult since it cannot always be determined if the writer was copying the Biblical quote directly from a text, quoting it from memory, or simply making an allusion to a Scripture verse.

There are dozens of Church Fathers which can be appealed to. Some of the more important are: Clement of Rome (c. 95), Ignatius (d. 117), Tertullian (c. 160-220), Origen (185-254), Clement of Alexandria (before 215), Hyppolytus (d. 235), Irenaeus (c. 250), Ambrose (c. 340-397), Chrysostom (344-407), and Augustine (354-430). Various abbreviations are used to designate these and other Patristic citations.

Early Versions: The last additional source is the early versions. These are translations of the Greek NT into other languages. The most important of these are the early Latin versions. The NT was probably first translated into Latin around 200 A.D. The earliest manuscript of such a version is from the fourth century. 50 manuscripts have been categorized. They are designated by "it" (for *Itala*) with a letter superscript.

Next in importance is the Vulgate. This Latin translation was the work, at least in part, of Jerome (c.345-420). It became the official version of the Roman Catholic Church. This accounts for the over 8,000 copies which exist. The earliest is from the fourth century. These are designated by "Vg" and a letter superscript.

Other languages into which the NT was translated in the early centuries are: Syriac, Coptic, Armenian, Georgian, Ethiopic, Gothic, Arabic and many others. Various abbreviations are used for each language (above information taken from Aland, Text, pp.56,57,75-217, Barker, pp.53-57, and charts in the UBS text).

Text-type Families

So there are thousands of manuscripts from which to determine the text of the NT from. Out of these, "over 85% of the text found in *all* manuscripts is identical" (Robinson and Pierpont, p.xlii; emphasis in original). So again, the text of the NT is very well attested.

However, this still leaves about 15% of the text in which there are variants between the manuscripts. When these variants are compared it becomes apparent that the manuscripts divide into at least two "families."

The most important differences can be seen between textual families, although there are still minor variants between manuscripts within a particular text-type. The first of these textual families is the "Byzantine." It is so named since this is the type of text the Byzantine (Eastern, Greek-speaking) Church has used throughout its existence.

Byzantine type texts comprise the vast majority of the manuscripts. Most of the above mentioned uncials, minuscules, and versions reflect this text-type. These manuscripts are generally "late" (i.e. dating after the fourth century). But some are earlier and a few papyri are also classified here.

The second major textual family is the "Alexandrian" (named after the Egyptian city). Only a handful of manuscripts reflect this type, but most of these are "early" (i.e. the fourth century or before). The above-mentioned Codex Sinaiticus and Codex Vaticanus reflect this type, along with some of the papyri.

Two less important text-types are the "Western" and the "Caesarean." There are disagreements among scholars as to whether these even constitute separate families.

Greek Texts and Bible Versions

There is heated debate as to which of the above two major textual families best reflects the autographs (the original texts actually written by the apostles). And this disagreement has led to the development of two different Greek texts for which to translate the NT from.

The first is the "Majority Text" (MT). It is so named since it is developed with the assumption that, under God's providence, the best reading was preserved in the MAJORITY of the manuscripts. With this principle, the MT inevitably reflects the Byzantine text-type. This writer's *Analytical-Literal Translation*, along with the *World English Bible* are based on the MT.

The *Textus Receptus* (TR) is very similar to the MT. This was the Greek text the monumental *King James Version* of 1611 was translated from. More recently, the *New King James Version* was translated from the TR, along with the *Literal Translation of the Bible* and the *Modern King James Version*.

The other modern-day, Greek text is called the "Critical Text" (CT) since textual CRITICS developed it. B.F. Westcott and F.A. Hort first put forth the principles underlying this text in the late 1800s. These principles include the idea that the text of the NT should be approached like any other ancient book.

As such, according to Westcott and Hort, manuscripts should be "weighed not counted." One major consideration in "weighing" a manuscript is its age, the earlier the better. Given this principle, their Greek text mainly reflected the Alexandrian text-type. The *Revised Version* of 1881 was based on this kind of Greek text.

Today, the 27th edition of the Nestle-Aland Greek text and the fourth edition of the United Bible Societies text are the most recent editions of the CT. These two texts are identical and are similar to the Westcott and Hort text.

The books containing each of these recent texts also contain extensive charts and apparatus for doing textual studies. Whenever textual variants occur, the apparatus at the bottom of the page indicates which manuscripts have which reading by the use of the above mentioned symbols. The charts provide information about the dates and contents of the various manuscripts referred to.

In the footnotes, generally all of the Alexandrian manuscripts are listed, but only a sample of the Byzantine texts are listed as the greater number of these precludes listing them all.

And finally, most modern-day versions are based on the CT. Among these are the *New American Standard Bible*, the *New International Version*, the *New Revised Standard Version*, and the *New Living Translation* (the above information gleaned from many sources).

Textual Variants

As previously mentioned, 15% of the NT text differs between the manuscripts. But for most of these variants it is very easy to determine which reading is a "mistake" and which is correct. As such, the above-mentioned, published Greet texts are very similar in their handling of the variants.

The TR agrees with the MT 99% of the time in its handling of variants, and the CT agrees with the MT 98% of the time (Wallace, p.38). So there is only a 1-2% difference overall between these published Greek texts.

Moreover, the majority of variants among manuscripts and between the above-mentioned, Greek texts are insignificant, "Some variations exist in the spelling of Greek words, in word order, and in similar details. These ordinarily do not show up in translation and do not affect the sense of the text in any way" (*Parallel*, p.xxiii).

Following are examples of these types of variants which can be seen by comparing a version based on the MT (or TR) with one based on the CT. The MT reading will be given first and the CT reading afterwards.

First, in Matthew 13:55 the name of one of Jesus' half-brothers is "Joses" in the MT, but "Joseph" in the CT. The difference is only one letter in the Greek. The MT name ends with a *sigma* (s) while the CT has a *phi* (ph). The sounds are somewhat similar.

Moreover, since Jesus' stepfather was named Joseph, it is easy to see how a scribe could assume one of Jesus' half-brothers would also be named Joseph and misread the word. And slight differences in the spelling of proper nouns account for a large portion of the variants found between NT manuscripts.

Second, a simple case of word order change can be seen in Luke 17:23. In the MT, the false prophets shout, "Look here! or Look there!" But in the CT the shout is, "Look there! or Look here!" Not exactly an earthshaking difference.

And finally, in Acts 1:8, Jesus either commands Christians to be witness "to Me" or "of Me." Again, in Greek, the difference is one letter. Moreover, the Greek words involved are homonyms (*moi* vs. *mou*).

Since the early scribes often read the text as they were copying from it, or the text was dictated to a room full of scribes, the reason for this variant is obvious. Moreover, this writer has often typed the wrong word when there is another which sounds exactly like it. Particularly troublesome has been "there" vs. "their."

Furthermore, most of the textual variants are similar to the above examples. And anyone who has ever done much typing or hand copying can easily understand how such simple mistakes can be made. But when someone else reads the text, the mistake is generally noticed. The same situation occurs with the Greek textual variants. In most cases, which variant is correct is obvious, and both the MT and the CT have the same reading.

Moreover, "Fortunately, if the great number of manuscripts increases the number of errors, it increases proportionally the means of correcting such errors, so that the margin of doubt left in the process of recovering the exact original wording is not so large as might be feared; it is in truth remarkably small" (Bruce, p.19).

So when there are differences between manuscripts, more often than not, the correct reading is easily determined. And even when it is not, the variant is generally insignificant.

However, there are some important variants. And for these the evidence is often divided as to which is the original reading. And often the MT follows one reading and the CT another. And it is because of these that there are the heated debates among scholars as to whether the MT or the CT best reflects the originals.

But in such cases, most modern-day versions will footnote the variant. The footnotes in the NKJV are particular helpful in this regard. In this version, any significant variants between the TR, the MT, and the CT are specifically indicated in its textual footnotes. This writer's *Analytical-Literal Translation* lists variants between these three Greek texts in an appendix.

Conclusion

The reasons for the differences between the Majority Text and the Critical Text are much more complicated than the simple points mentioned above. And trying to decide whether the MT or CT best reflects the autographs is even more complex, although very important. And this is the subject of the next two chapters. Here, it will just be emphasized:

Bible readers may be assured that the most important differences in English New Testaments of today are due, not to manuscript divergence, but to the way in which translators view the task of translation. How literally should the text be rendered? How does the translator view the matter of biblical inspiration?" (*Parallel*, p.xxiii).

And these more important matters are addressed in previous and other chapters in this book.

Bibliography:
Aland, Kurt and Barbara Aland. *The Text of the New Testament.* Grand Rapids: William B. Eerdmans, 1987.

Barker, Kenneth. ed. *The NIV: The Making of a Contemporary Translation.* Colorado Springs: International Bible Society, 1991.

Bruce, F.F. *The New Testament Documents: Are They Reliable?* Downers Grove, IL: InterVarsity Press, 1975.

KJV/ NKJV Parallel Reference Bible. Nashville: Thomas Nelson, 1991.

McDowell, Josh. *Evidence that Demands a Verdict.* San Bernardino, CA: Here's Life Publishers, 1979.

Metzger, Bruce. *A Textual Commentary on the Greek New Testament.* New York: United Bible Societies, 1975.

Robinson, Maurice A. and William G. Pierpont. *The New Testament in the Original Greek According to the Byzantine/ Majority Textform.* Atlanta: Original Word Publishers, 1991.

United Bible Societies. *The Greek New Testament.* ed. by Aland, Kurt. et al. Germany: 1983.

Wallace, Daniel B. "The Majority Text and the Original Text: Are They Identical?" in *Bibliotheca Sacra.* April-June 1991, pp.157-158. Quoted in Bob and Gretchen Passantino. "New Age Bible Versions: A Critical Review." *Cornerstone.* Vol. 23, Issue 104.

Chapter Seven:
The Majority Text vs. The Critical Text

Part One

"It was the CORRUPT BYZANTINE form of text that provided the basis for almost all translations of the New Testament into modern languages down to the nineteenth century."

This quote is from Bruce Metzger's book *A Textual Commentary on the Greek New Testament*. On the same page, he also calls the *Textus Receptus* (TR), which reflects the Byzantine text-type, "disfigured" and "debased" (p.xxiii).

In a similar vein, Kurt Aland considers Greek manuscripts which are "purely or predominately Byzantine" to be "IRRELEVANT for textual criticism."

Furthermore, Aland refers to the Critical Text (CT) as "the modern SCHOLARLY text." This is because it is based mainly on the Alexandrian text-type, which he believes to be "of A VERY SPECIAL QUALITY which should always be considered in establishing the original text." And Aland considers this type of text to be the "Standard text" for our day (Aland, pp.viii,31,155).

In contradiction to this view is that of the Majority Text (MT) proponents. J.P. Green, for instance, claims the CT is based on "a handful of CORRUPTED Egyptian manuscripts." And further, he believes "GNOSTIC HERETICS" produced these manuscripts. Thus, by basing their Greek text on these Alexandrian type texts, the CT scholars are, "RE-INSERTING THESE HERESIES into what they boldly call a 'Holy Bible'" (from press releases for the LITV and MKJV).

These two sets of quotes demonstrate the strong feelings held by proponents of both the CT and the MT. They also show that, for the most part, the CT is based on "Alexandrian" type Greek manuscripts while the MT is based on "Byzantine" type

Greek manuscripts. For more on these text-type "families" and other terms used in this article, see the previous chapter "Introduction to Textual Criticism."

This chapter will examine the most important issues relevant to this heated debate, without utilizing diatribes like the above.

Published Greek Texts

There are two primary published Greek texts representing the CT. The first is The United Bible Societies' *The Greek New Testament* edited by five men, including Kurt Aland and Bruce Metzger who were quoted above. The second is *Novum Testamentum Graece* edited by Eberhard Nestle and Kurt Aland. The fourth edition of the UBS text and the 27th edition of Nestle-Aland's text are now identical.

As with the CT, there are two different published editions of the MT: *The Greek New Testament According to the Byzantine Textform* edited by Maurice A. Robinson and William G. Pierpont and *The Greek New Testament According to the Majority Text* edited by Zane C. Hodges and Arthur L. Farstad. These two MTs are virtually identical. See Chapter Eleven: "Meaning of Majority Text" for further discussion on these two MT texts.

Quotes from some of these editors will be utilized throughout this chapter, along with quotations from additional advocates of both positions.

"Providential Preservation"

The Providential Preservation of the Greek Text of the New Testament is the title of a booklet written by Rev. W. MacLean. This title sums up the first argument for the MT. The claim is that God has "providentially preserved" the Byzantine text-type since it best represents the autographs.

In arguing against this claim, D.A. Carson, another CT supporter, states, "I am suspicious of propositional arguments that rest too much on providence, because divine providence can be variously interpreted" (Carson, p.55).

Carson is correct in saying it can be sometimes difficult to interpret divine providence, but the reasons for the MT claim will be presented and the reader can draw his or her own conclusion.

1) The VAST MAJORITY OF GREEK MANUSCRIPTS reflect the Byzantine text-type.

Robinson and Pierpont write in the Introduction to their MT Greek text, "Of the over 5000 total continuous-text and lectionary manuscripts, 90% or more contain a basically Byzantine Textform" (p.xviii).

And CT proponents readily admit that the Byzantine text-type is predominate in the manuscript evidence. For instance, in reference to the minuscule manuscripts, Aland writes, "...more than 80 percent of the manuscripts contain exclusively the Majority Text." But the Alexandrian is represented in only "almost 10 percent" (Aland, pp.102, 128).

Metzger classifies "most minuscules" as "Byzantine Witnesses" (Metzger, p.xxx). And Carson says about the Byzantine text-type, "There are far more manuscripts extant in this tradition than in the other three combined [Alexandrian, Western and Caesarean]" (Carson, p.26).

And finally, a flyer distributed by the publishers of the NASB (a CT based version) states in reference to the TR and Erasmus' Greek NT (which is similar to the TR), "...95% of the known Greek NT manuscripts of the Greek NT are closer to these than to the Greek text behind most modern English translations" (MacRae).

2) Byzantine texts were MORE WIDELY DISTRIBUTED AND ACCEPTED than those reflecting an Alexandrian text-type.

Hodges and Farstad write in the "Introduction" to their Greek text in reference to the two above-mentioned published CTs:

Although eclectic, both rely heavily on a relatively small number of ancient manuscripts that derive mainly from Egypt.... The text which results from dependence on such manuscripts as these may fairly be described as Egyptian. Its existence in early times outside of Egypt is unproven....

On the other hand, the witnesses to the Majority Text come from all over the ancient world. Their very number suggests that they represent a long and widespread chain of manuscript tradition (p.ix).

Robinson and Pierpont write similarly:

The "Byzantine" Textform (otherwise called the "Majority" or "Traditional Text") predominated throughout the greatest period of manual copying of the Greek New Testament manuscripts—a span of over 1000 years (ca. AD 350 to AD 1516). It was without question the dominate text used both liturgically and popularly by the Greek-speaking Christian community (p.xviii).

Again, the CT people acknowledge this domination of the Byzantine texts. Aland says about the "Koine Text" (which he considers to be the precursor to the Byzantine text-type) that it, "...became widely disseminated even in the fourth century," and it became "the dominant text of the Byzantine church."

Meanwhile, the church in Egypt, "led an independent life" from the rest of the church, and, "From the fourth century it had a well defined text (known as the Alexandrian text type) because the administration of the Alexandrian patriarchs was effectively centralized."

So the Alexandrian text was used primarily in Egypt. But despite this, Aland states even the Egyptian text was later subjected to the "corrosive effects" of the Byzantine text-type (Aland, pp.65,56).

But note, nowhere does he say the Alexandrian text had a "corrosive effect" on the Byzantine. So scribes in the Egyptian church eventually tried to bring their text into conformity with the Byzantine text, but the reverse did not happen.

Metzger says the Byzantine text was "distributed widely throughout the Byzantine empire." Moreover, "...during the period from the sixth or seventh century down to the invention of printing with movable type (A.D. 1450-56), the Byzantine form of text was generally regarded as *the* authoritative form of text and was the one most widely circulated and accepted" (emphasis in original, Metzger, p.xx).

3) EARLY TRANSLATIONS OF THE NT into other languages in the early centuries can often have a mixed text, or it can be difficult to determine the kind of text they were based on. But they do generally contain a Byzantine text-type, at least in part.

According to Aland, these include the following (with dates of original translation in parentheses): the Syriac Peshitta (c.400), the Syriac Harkelensis (616), the Palestinian Syriac Version (c.400), the Armenian version (c.400), the Gothic version (c.341), and the Old Church Slavonic version (c.850).

As for the most important early version, the Latin Vulgate, Carson claims this version was based on "a western textual tradition" (Carson, p.56). But Aland refutes this idea and states, "... the consensus today favors the view that Jerome used a contemporary manuscript of the early Koine type [the precursor, according to Aland, to the Byzantine text-type]" (Aland, pp.181-210).

As for the Old Latin versions on which the Vulgate was based, Robinson and Pierpont write that they are, "...a veritable hodgepodge of readings created by individualistic scribes...with no characteristically-prevailing 'majority' text, whether Byzantine or any other" (p.xxix).

Gary Zeolla

So the Old Latin versions, along with the early versions in general, can be somewhat of a mixed bag (due possibly to what Robinson and Pierpont call "the 'human factor' affecting translation into another language" along with scribal alterations; p.xxix). But the early versions do tend to favor the Byzantine Text-type.

4) Remember the quote by Metzger which opened this chapter?—"It was the corrupt Byzantine form of text that provided the basis for almost all TRANSLATIONS OF THE NEW TESTAMENT INTO MODERN LANGUAGES down to the nineteenth century."

It was Erasmus' Greek Testament, "...that Martin Luther and William Tyndale used as the basis of their translations of the New Testament into German (1522) and into English (1525)" (Metzger, pp. xxi-xxiii).

Moreover, every English translation after Tyndale, until 1881, followed the Byzantine text-type. This, or course, included the monumental *King James Version*. Further, "Even though the *Revised Version* of 1881 was intended to replace the KJV, it failed to do so" (Green, MKJV press release).

And, despite numerous new versions which were published following the *Revised Version*, it was not until the *New International Version* (first published in 1978) that a Bible version based on the CT surpassed the sales of the KJV.

John Robbins sums up the situation if the CT scholars are correct, "For nineteen hundred years the church had limped along with defective Bibles, but modern scholarship has greatly improved the Bibles we read" (preface to Clark, p.v).

Denial of Providence

There are two basic arguments used by CT people to try to evade the force of above information. The first is to deny the whole concept of the providence of God operating in the transmission of the NT texts.

For instance, Westcott and Hort promoted the idea that the text of the Bible should be treated like any other ancient book. And Aland says he disagrees with the MT supporters because they, "...oppose all the laws of philology [linguistics] which apply just as much to the New Testament as to all other documents of antiquity" (Aland, p.19).

But, "The Textual Criticism of Westcott and Hort, and their cohorts, cannot be defended from the Bible." Moreover, "It does not matter to them whether the Bible's testimony to itself is denied..." (Green, *Unholy*, Vol.I, p.11). And what is "the Bible's testimony to itself" in this regard?

Psalm 12:6,7 declares:
THE WORDS OF THE LORD ARE PURE WORDS: as silver tried in a furnace of earth, purified seven times. Thou shalt keep them, O LORD, THOU SHALT PRESERVE THEM from this generation for ever" (KJV; see also Matt 5:18; 24:35; Luke 16:17).

"Lateness" of Byzantine Text-Type

The second argument of the CT scholars is to claim that the Byzantine text-type originated "late" (i.e. after the third century). Carson writes, "There is no unambiguous evidence that the Byzantine text-type was known before the middle of the fourth century."

On the other hand, the CT people point to several second and third century papyri which reflect the Alexandrian text-type (Metzger, p.xxix). However, Robinson and Pierpont state that only one of these papyri (#75) is predominately Alexandrian. Of the remaining papyri, they state that each, "...possesses a good degree of 'mixture' between Alexandrian and Western readings (with some 'distinctively Byzantine' readings thrown in for good measure)" (pp.xxvi,xxvii).

Harry Sturz discusses these "distinctively Byzantine" readings in his book, *The Byzantine Text-Type and New*

Testament Textual Criticism. First, he writes, "Although the reasoning of Westcott and Hort seemed sound at the time they wrote, discoveries since then have undermined the confident appraisal that characteristically Syrian [Byzantine] readings are necessarily late" (p.55).

The most important of these discoveries was several Egyptian papyri. Sturz lists "150 distinctively Byzantine readings" found in these papyri. Included in his list are papyri numbers 13, 45, 46, 47, 49, 59, 66, 72, 74, and even #75 (pp. 61, 145-159).

Green explains the importance of these discoveries, "For example, the Chester Beatty Papyri [#45,46,47] contained sixty-five readings which had been ejected from the Bible by the critics. And Papyrus Bodmer II [P66], of the second century, actually was found to contain thirteen percent of all the so called late readings of the critic despised Majority Text" (*Interlinear*, p.xi).

Sturz brings up another very important point about these papyri, "They attest the early existence of readings in the Eastern part of the Roman empire in which the Byzantine and the properly (i.e. geographically) Western witnesses agree and at the same time are opposed by the Alexandrian" (p.70).

In other words, some early "Western" texts agree with the Byzantine tradition where it differs from the Alexandrian. Sturz lists 170 of these types of readings (pp.160-174).

Robinson and Pierpont refer to these kinds of readings as "dually-aligned." They also use this term to refer to readings where the Alexandrian and Byzantine manuscripts agree, but they differ from the Western. They then note that in such cases of dually aligned readings, the Alexandrian-Byzantine combinations are termed by modern critics as "Alexandrian" and the Western-Byzantine readings are termed "Western."

They then write:

> From the present perspective, the Byzantine-Alexandrian and Byzantine-Western alignments are

merely those autograph readings of the Byzantine Textform from which the Alexandrian or Western manuscripts did NOT deviate—a very different picture. Thus, the Alexandrian manuscripts are themselves far more "Byzantine" than they have been given credit for, if only their readings are first considered from a Byzantine-priority perspective (p.xxxv; emphasis in original).

So even in textual criticism, the problem of presuppositions cannot be ignored. If one starts with the assumption that the Byzantine text is "corrupt" then dually aligned readings will automatically be consider to be anything but Byzantine. But if one assumes the Byzantine text is superior then dually aligned readings will be considered Byzantine.

Sturz concludes, "In view of the above, it is concluded that the papyri supply valid evidence that distinctively Byzantine readings were not created in the fourth century but were already in existence before the end of the second century and that, because of this, Byzantine readings merit serious consideration" (p.69).

Now the above is referring to specific readings in the papyri. The papyri do still favor an Alexandrian-Western type of text overall. However, Robinson and Pierpont state in this regard, "Any bold assertion that the point is settled, since no predominately Byzantine manuscripts of the second century have yet to be discovered, certainly seems to beg the question from an argument based on silence" (p.xxvii).

And Sturz asks the question, "What about Byzantine readings which occur in parts of the New Testament where there are no papyri, *as yet*, to confirm them?" (p.64, emphasis in original). The problem is that even with the most recent discoveries, the papyri data is still rather sparse.

Next, a word needs to be said about the preservation and location of the early papyri. Aland says all but one of these early papyri, "...are from Egypt where the hot, dry sands preserved the papyri through the centuries." Meanwhile, in Asia Minor and Greece (eastern areas), "...the climate in these regions has been unfavorable to the preservation of any papyri from the early period" (pp.59,67).

Hodges and Farstad write similarly in this regard, "Egypt, almost alone, offers climatic conditions highly favorable to the preservation of very ancient manuscripts" (p.ix).

So it is not surprising many early papyri have been found which reflect the Alexandrian text since this text existed in Egypt. But even some of these Egyptian papyri, as mentioned above, contain Byzantine and even Western readings.

Meanwhile, papyri used in the east would not have survived due to the unfavorable climatic conditions. So what text was used in these regions in the second and third centuries cannot be determined by specific manuscript evidence.

However, what is known is all of the autographs, except two, were sent to eastern churches. The only exceptions are Romans and Mark, which were sent to Rome. But NONE were sent to Egyptian churches (Green, *Unholy*, Vol.II, p.613).

Moreover, starting in the fourth century, parchment began to be used. This material is much more durable than papyri (Aland, p.76). This, along with the cessation of persecution, accounts for why the number of known manuscripts begins to increase starting with the fourth century. And the vast majority of these later manuscripts reflect the Byzantine text.

In sum, the east held the autographs. In the second and third centuries, Byzantine AND Alexandrian readings existed in Egypt. And from the fourth century on the east utilized the Byzantine text.

Furthermore, papyri has, "...a useful library life of several decades" (Aland, p.75). So the east could still appeal to the autographs, or at least direct copies of them, well into the second century. Meanwhile, Egypt only had copies of copies.

So, if the CT people are correct, despite this advantage, the east, sometime during the second or third centuries and for some unknown reason, abandoned the best text-type in favor of an inferior one. But the Egyptian churches were able to retain the text which reflected the autographs, despite the fact they never saw them.

Lastly in this section, it should be mentioned that Sturz, who is quoted at length in this chapter, is NOT a supporter of the MT. He takes a middle position in this debate. He simply believes, "...the Byzantine text should be recognized as having an important and useful place in textual criticism because it is an independent witness to an early form of the New Testament text" (p.23).

Compare this attitude with the quote from Aland in the introduction to this chapter. He declared the Byzantine text to be "irrelevant for textual criticism."

Byzantine Readings in the Church Fathers

CT advocates will sometimes claim the writings of the Church Fathers do not contain "distinctively Byzantine" readings in them. However, Sturz writes, "... contrary to the statements of WH [Westcott and Hort] and their followers, quotations from early Fathers *have* been found in support of Byzantine readings" (p.78; emphasis in original).

But such readings are dismissed by CT supporters in one of two ways. First, "It is contended that the texts of the Fathers had been assimilated (changed or conformed) to the Byzantine norm by Byzantine scribes as they compiled the manuscripts of the Fathers" (Sturz, p.78).

Though it is possible that such assimilation occurred to some degree, all Byzantine readings in the Church Fathers cannot be so easily dismissed in this way. Sturz lists eighteen Byzantine readings in the Church Fathers that have also been found in the papyri. Sturz writes in this regard, "It should be recognized in these readings which are proven by the papyri, such patristic support appears authentic (i.e. non-assimilated)" (p.79).

And again, if additional papyri were to be found, it is possible that other dismissed Byzantine readings in the Fathers would also have manuscript support. As Sturz states, "it is an argument from silence" to say the Byzantine readings in the Church Fathers did not exist in the early centuries (p.80).

Second, a similar situation is seen in the writings of the Church Fathers as in the papyri in regards to dually aligned readings. If a reading is Byzantine-Alexandrian aligned it is declared Alexandrian by CT scholars and Byzantine-Western alignments will be called Western.

However, if one assumes a Byzantine priority, "Many dually-aligned Alexandrian or Western readings which 'typify' and categorize the text of various Fathers will suddenly be seen to have been Byzantine all along" (Robinson and Pierpont, p.xxxiii).

Lastly, Robinson and Pierpont point out, "Fathers often paraphrase, quote faultily from memory or deliberately alter a quotation to make a point" (p.xxxiii). So dependence on the Church Fathers in textual criticism is precarious at best.

Origin of the Byzantine Text-type

How did the Byzantine Text-type originate and become so predominate in the manuscript evidence? Since CT advocates claim it did not exist in the earliest centuries, they need to provide a plausible theory as to its origin and proliferation.

Carson writes, "The theory advanced by B.F. Westcott and F.J.A. Hort to account for these facts is that the Byzantine text was formed as a conflation [revision] between A.D. 250 and 350" (pp.44,45). Metzger reiterates this idea when he states about the Byzantine text-type, "This conflated text, produced perhaps at Antioch in Syria, was taken to Constantinople, whence it was distributed widely throughout the Byzantine Empire" (p.xx).

However, Sturz writes in this regard, "HISTORY IS COMPLETELY SILENT with regard to any revision of the Byzantine text. Furthermore, "There is NOT A SHRED OF HISTORICAL EVIDENCE that such a recension was made" (pp.122,126). It is for this reason that most CT scholars have abandoned this idea today, though some such as Carson and Metzger still seem to reiterate it.

Secondly, as was hinted at previously in quotes by Aland, some CT scholars try to separate the Byzantine text from the Koine Text. The claim is that the former "evolved" from the later. In other words, a true Byzantine Text did not exist in the earliest centuries, only its precursor the Koine text did. Instead, the Byzantine text was the product of revisionists working with Koine type texts.

However, there appears to be some confusion here as not all CT scholars see a two-stage development. Metzger, for instance, simply gives "Koine" and "Byzantine" as two of several synonymous names for the text type (along with: Syrian, Ecclesiastical, and Antiochian, p.xx).

Metzger does, however, give some indication of an "evolution" within the Koine/ Byzantine text-type. He writes in this regard, "The framers of this text sought to smooth away any harshness of language, to combine two or more divergent readings into one expanded reading (called conflation), and to harmonize divergent passages" (p.xx).

Metzger's claims about the style and development of the Byzantine manuscripts will be looked at later. But here, it needs to be noted that Metzger is asserting the Byzantine text evolved over time by deliberate alterations of scribes.

As for the proliferation of the Byzantine text-type over the Alexandrian, CT scholars will sometimes point to political and historical events to explain it.

For instance, CT advocate Edward W. Goodrick writes: "It is no coincidence that most Greek manuscripts come from Byzantium and most Latin versions in manuscript form from Western Europe. This is because all the other Christian centers fell to Islam early, but Byzantium fell late and Western Europe, except Spain, never fell" (p.55).

In addition, CT scholars will sometimes indicate the predominance of the Byzantine text is also due to the "copying revolution" that occurred in the ninth to tenth centuries. At that time, scribes began to use miniscule (small letters) in copying rather than the previously used uncial (all capital letters). Minuscule print does not take up as much space as uncial print and is less time consuming to write. So less parchment would be needed to copy the entire Bible. Hence copies of manuscripts could be made much quicker and cheaper. And the vast majority of these miniscule manuscripts are Byzantine in type.

Robinson and Pierpont presented an alternate textual transmission theory as to the origin and reasons for predominance of the Byzantine text in the Introduction to their Greek text. But later, Robinson published a paper about the detailed studies he did on the textual variants in the adultery story (John 7:53-8:11). This study caused Robinson to revise his theory.

In the Preface to Robinson and Pierpont's text, Wm. David McBrayer wrote:

Robinson and Pierpont offer a solid case for Byzantine priority and a viable theory of textual transmission. The overwhelming spread and dominance of the Byzantine text suggests this conclusion: during the period of persecution of the church, various "local" text types arose as a result of regional copying and recopying of the original text.

Once Christianity was sanctioned under Constantine, improved communication between the churches resulted in a gradual expansion of the practice of cross-correction of the local text manuscripts which basically restored the autograph Textform and weeded out scribal alterations. This Textform would overcome the influence of "local texts" and finally become the dominate text of the Greek-speaking world. Only a common pre-existing archetype would have permitted order to have come out of chaos. This "universal archetype" could only be the common text underlying ALL local text forms; namely, the original autographs themselves (p.xi; emphasis in original).

In other words, the theory was that very early, "localized" texts would have developed with textual mistakes being copied within that area. But later, copies of texts from a variety of areas would be compared. So gradually, the localized readings would be "weeded out" while readings common to all areas would be reproduced. However, with his extensive work on the adultery story, Robinson realized there was not a "weeding out" process.

He writes in his paper:

There is no Byzantine Text of the PA [*Pericope Adulterae*], even though the mass of Byzantine era MSS [manuscripts] contain the PA in the traditional location without question or comment regarding either its canonicity or authority. The same MSS which generally contain a Byzantine consensus text throughout the gospels nevertheless divide significantly within the text of the PA. ... the text of the PA is probably the key to understanding the history of gospel MSS transmission....

Cross-comparison and correction should have been rampant and extensive within this portion of text due to the wide variety of textual patterns and readings existing therein; instead, correction occurred sporadically, and rarely in a thoroughgoing manner....

Certainly, all the types of PA text are distinct, and reflect a long line of transmission and preservation in their separate integrities. But what does this say about the behavior of the same MSS when they contain a near-common preservation of the remaining text of John? Apparently several things: (a) scribes were basically faithful to their task (this was granted previously); (b) they basically preserved for the most part that which had been presented to them in the exemplars they were copying without major change or mixture occurring from comparison with other exemplars; (c) the lines of transmission generally were not intermingled or altered in any significant degree by scribal activity during (at least) the vellum era (pp.11-13).

Moreover, Robinson identified at least 10 "streams" of textual tradition within the adultery story, confirmed by differences within the adultery story. So each of these transmissional streams are witnesses to separate, much earlier manuscripts. What this means is this: CT scholars can no longer lump together the mass of later Byzantine manuscripts into one "witness" by saying they are just copies of a single earlier manuscript.

Robinson concludes in this regard, "The 10 or so 'text-type" lines of transmission remain independent and must necessarily extend back to a point long before their separate stabilizations occurred—a point which seems buried (as Colwell and Scrivener suggested) deep within the second century" (p.13).

However, despite being so different within the adultery story, these Byzantine manuscripts are very similar in all other parts of the Gospels and in the NT in general. And this uniformity would best be explained by these different streams all originating very early in the transmission of the text. So even though most the Byzantine manuscripts are comparatively "late" they are witnesses to much earlier manuscripts.

Another important implication of these facts is that the earliest manuscripts may not be the best. The variants in the adultery story show that most transcriptional errors occurred in the earliest centuries, but that the texts remained relatively stable thereafter. And even Aland acknowledges, "Practically all the substantive variants in the texts of the New Testament are from the second century …" (p.290).

As for the "copying revolution" being the reason for the predominance of the Byzantine text, Robinson and Pierpont point out:

...scribes apparently destroyed uncial exemplars as they converted the Greek text into the then-standard miniscule format. Thus, the apparently unrelated mass of later minuscules may in fact stem from the long-lost uncial sources far older than the date of the minuscules containing them. This in itself adds a significant weight to the testimony of the minuscules mass, especially those copied in the ninth and tenth centuries, at the height of the copying revolution (p.xl).

Lastly, as for historical and political reasons being behind the predominance of the Byzantine text, these cannot be discounted. However, two points need to be said.

First, the quote from Goodrick above continues by saying, "Neither is it a coincidence that practically all the earliest manuscripts are from Egypt, for that is the only civilization center where the climate inhibits their decay" (p.55).

This point has already been mentioned, but it needs to be emphasized that if CT scholars try to say it is simply due to external reasons outside the control of scribes that the mass of minuscules reflect the Byzantine text, then it could also be said it is simply due to such external reasons that the early papyri reflect the Alexandrian or Western texts.

Lastly, the providence of God could also again be appealed to. Historical and political currents do not just happen—they are under the control of God (Dan 2:21). So it could be God was watching over the area of the world with the most reliable manuscripts so that those manuscripts were copied.

Given all of the above, the mass of minuscules, and their overwhelming testimony to the Byzantine text, cannot be so easily dismissed as CT scholars try to do.

This discussion will be continued in the next chapter.

Gary Zeolla

Bibliography:
See end of next chapter.

Chapter Eight:
The Majority Text vs. The Critical Text

Part Two

This discussion is continued from the previous chapter.

Gnostic Corruptions

Gordon Fee, a CT supporter, claims, "For the New Testament, the better external evidence was preserved in Egypt" (p.32). But is this claim true? Discussed previously were some reasons why manuscripts discovered in Egypt do not necessarily "better" reflect the autographs. In addition, a look at the religious situation in Egypt in the early centuries will be instructive.

Kurt Aland writes, "EGYPT was distinguished from the other provinces of the Church, so far as we can judge, by the EARLY DOMINANCE OF GNOSTICISM; this was not broken until about A.D. 200...although undoubtedly not only the Gnostic but also the broader church was represented there throughout the whole period [of the second through fourth centuries]" (p.59). This situation is significant since the Alexandrian text is primarily supported by manuscripts from Egypt.

Moreover, several Church Fathers wrote about the problem of Gnostics and other heretics altering the Scriptures in an effort to bring them into conformity with their false beliefs. Harry Sturz gives quotations from the writings of the following Church Fathers in this regard: Dionysius (c.170), Irenaeus (c.178), Tertullian (c.200), Clement of Alexandria (c.194), and Origin (c.225; Sturz, pp.115-118).

A particularly interesting passage was written around 230 AD by a now unknown writer. It was preserved by Eusebius in his *Ecclesiastical History*.

This ancient Christian said about heretics:

THEY HAVE TAMPERED WITH THE DIVINE SCRIPTURES WITHOUT FEAR; they have set aside the rule of primitive faith; THEY HAVE NOT KNOWN CHRIST....For anyone who will collect their several copies together and compare them, one with another, will discover MARKED DISCREPANCIES. For instance, Ascelpaides' copies do not agree with those of Theodotus and you can get possession of them, because their disciples have vied in copying THEIR SEVERAL CORRECTIONS (AS THEY CALL THEM), THAT IS DISFIGUREMENTS....

Nor is it likely that they themselves are ignorant of the audacity of this offense. For either THEY DO NOT BELIEVE THAT THE DIVINE SCRIPTURES WERE SPOKEN BY THE HOLY SPIRIT, AND, THEREFORE ARE UNBELIEVERS; or they consider themselves wiser than the Holy Spirit, and what is that but devil possession?

For they cannot deny that the audacious act is their own, since the copies have been written in their own hand; and since they received no such Scriptures from their instructors, THEY ARE UNABLE TO SHOW ANY COPIES WHENCE THEY HAVE TRANSCRIBED THEM, and absolutely DENIED THE LAW AND THE PROPHETS. Thus under the cover of a lawless and impious teaching THEY HAVE SUNK TO THE LOWEST DEPTHS OF PERDITION (Sturz, pp.118,119).

This passage mentions several pertinent points. First, it is those who "have not known Christ" and who "do not believe that the divine Scriptures were spoken by the Holy Spirit" who have "tampered with the divine Scriptures." And this non-belief in the inspiration of the Scriptures shows they are "unbelievers."

Further, they have "denied the law and the prophets" and "have sunk to the lowest depths of perdition."

This implies true Christians are those who "know Christ" and who believe the Scriptures were "spoken by the Holy Spirit." Moreover, Christians were NOT in the habit of "correcting" the Scriptures since they believed the commands and warnings of "the law and the prophets" (see Deut 4:2; 12:32; Prov 30:5,6; Jer 23:30,31; 26:2).

Second, Theodotus was, "a second century heretic" (Moyer, p.398). So heretics were already producing corrupted manuscripts very early. As such, "...it is not true that the earliest manuscripts must be the best" (Clark, p.33).

Third, the heretics are "unable to show any copies whence they have transcribed them." This implies early Christians knew the history of the transmission of manuscripts, how to distinguish faithful from corrupted copies, and thus, which ones to copy.

But despite these points, "That the numerical superiority of the Byzantine text might have been do to its early widespread acceptance of that type as being closest to the autographs does not seem to impress them [the CT scholars]" (Clark, p.32).

Now it is true Egypt is not the only area in which heretics operated. There were heretics other than Gnostics in other areas who also produced corrupt manuscripts.

But Robinson and Pierpont write in this regard:
Heretical tampering did occur, as witnessed by the work of Tatian and Marcion, but the church as a whole, and especially its leaders and theologians, were keen watchdogs against such deliberately-perverted manuscripts. It is not without significance that today we know of Marcion's heretical text only from citations in the Church Fathers, and the heretic Tatian's Diatessaron is seen in but one Greek manuscript fragment, despite its early widespread popularity among the orthodox" (p.xxxvii).

So the earliest scribes did "weed out" heretically, corrupted manuscripts and only copied known reliable ones. As such, if a reading is only found in one or very few manuscripts, especially from only one area, it could be because scribes knew it was corrupt and did not copy it. But readings found in the vast majority of manuscripts are more likely original because the scribes were reproducing known reliable manuscripts.

So in addition to the providence of God, on the human level, the vast superiority of the Byzantine text-type in the manuscript evidence could be do to Christian scribes simply knowing which manuscripts were the best ones to copy and which ones needed to be avoided.

Aleph and Beta

The above ancient writer was quoted as saying the manuscripts the heretics produced had "marked discrepancies" between them. This problem can be seen in the two uncials, Aleph and Beta (also know as Codex Sinaiticus and Codex Vanticanus, respectively).

Aleph and Beta are the manuscripts which the textual note in earlier editions of the NIV is referring to when it says "The two most reliable early manuscripts do not have Mark 16:9-20."

And the CT scholars in general agree Aleph and Beta are among "the most reliable manuscripts." A few years ago, this writer studied textual criticism in seminary. A professor who ascribed to the CT taught the class. He taught us that IF Aleph and Beta agree, then that is the reading to follow.

What he didn't teach us was that that "if" is a very big "if." As J.P. Green writes, "...there can scarcely be found three verses in a row which are the same in Aleph and Beta...in fact there are more than 3,000 differences between them in the Gospels of the New Testament alone" (*Unholy*, Vol.II, p.321).

Now it should be noted that, "No two Byzantine manuscripts are exactly alike" (Robinson and Pierpont, p.xviii). But 3,000 differences in the Gospels alone is excessive, in this writer's mind, for what is supposed to be two of the most reliable manuscripts.

In this regard, I can remember very clearly one time in my seminary class when the professor said it would be difficult to decide which reading was correct on a particular variant because Aleph and Beta disagreed. But if excessive importance were not placed on these manuscripts by my professor, then Aleph and Beta disagreeing would not cause such a difficulty.

Another problem with these manuscripts is they both have "correcting" hands on them. Aleph has several "correcting" hands on it while Beta has a couple. In other words, later scribes made changes in the manuscripts. Most likely, they were trying to bring them in conformity with other manuscripts they had which they considered to be more reliable.

Now again, most manuscripts have some correcting hands on them. But some CT advocates try to say such corrections on Aleph are a plus. Goodrick writes, "The magnificent fourth century manuscript Codex Sinaiticus demonstrates its importance by the fact that it had more than eight proofreaders" (p.53).

However, despite this supposed importance, eventually, Aleph was discarded. It was forgotten for centuries until Constantin von Tischendorf discovered it in the late 1800s and proclaimed it "the critical standard for establishing the text." Aland claims, "Pride of discover was not the only factor here". (pp.11-14).

Tischendorf then made thousands of changes in his previously published Greek New Testament to bring it into conformity with Aleph. And the CT scholars have followed in his footsteps of relying heavily on Aleph (Clark, p.32).

So the early scribes tried to "fix" Aleph by bringing it into conformity with Byzantine texts and eventually discarded it (because they realized it was a hopeless case?). But today's CT scholars are doing the exact opposite!

Moreover, both of these manuscripts have origins near Egypt. Above it was mentioned that Gnostics "dominated" Egypt in early Church history. So it is possible these two Uncials were influenced by heretical corruptions.

But despite these problems, the CT scholars still believe these two Uncials are among the most reliable manuscripts. The reason for this is they are the two earliest, complete manuscripts. Both date to the early 300s. However, remember, with the possibility of early scribal mistakes and heretical corruptions, "...it is not true that the earliest manuscripts must be the best" (Clark, p.33).

Furthermore, Aleph and Beta are only the earliest COMPLETE manuscripts. By "complete" is meant they contain all, or at least almost all, of the 27 books of the NT. But there are many papyri containing portions of the NT which predate these two Uncials.

And, "The Papyri, contrary to what is being taught, are not in any of them a replica of the Vaticanus (B) or Aleph manuscripts, but vary some 50% or more from these so-called 'best manuscripts'" (Green, *Best*, p.538).

So overall, these two Uncials simply do NOT deserve the extreme reliance CT scholars place upon them. As MT advocate James F. Davis writes, "If as [H.C.] Hoskier has noted, Aleph and Beta disagree in the Gospels more than 3,000 times, and Sinaiticus has been noted as exhibiting excessive omission, one has to ask the question: How reliable are they?" (p.3).

And MacLeean writes, "… these manuscripts survived only because they were full of mistakes and little used" (p.38).

"Weighed Rather than Counted"

To evade the vast numerical superiority of the Byzantine manuscripts, CT scholars will try to "lump" them together so that they are in effect only one witness rather than many.

Metzger explains this point as one of his criteria in evaluating manuscript evidence:

The genealogical relationship of texts and families of witnesses. Mere numbers of witnesses supporting a given variant reading do not necessarily prove the superiority of that reading. For example, if in a given sentence reading *x* is supported by twenty manuscripts and reading *y* by only one manuscript, the relative numerical support favoring *x* counts for nothing if all twenty manuscripts should be discovered to be copies made from a single manuscript, no longer extant, whose scribe first introduced that particular variant reading.

Metzger summarizes this point by saying "Witnesses are to be weighed rather than counted" (p.xxvi). However, as was previously discussed, Robinson's studies on the adultery story shows that the manuscripts underlying the passage represented at least ten different "streams" of textual transmission. So the texts underlying the Gospel of John cannot be "lumped" together as just being copies of copies.

Moreover, Hodges and Farstad write:

Any reading overwhelmingly attested by the manuscript tradition is more likely to be the original than its rival(s). This observation arises from the very nature of manuscript transmission. In any tradition where there are not major disruptions in the transmissional history, the individual reading which has the earliest beginning is the one most likely to survive in a majority of documents. And the earliest reading of all is the original one....

It should be kept in mind that by the time the major extant papyrus texts were copied, the New Testament was well over a century old. A reading attested by such a witness, and found only in a small number of other manuscripts, is not at all likely to be a survival from the autograph. On the contrary, it is probably only an idiosyncrasy of a narrow strand of the tradition" (pp.xi-xii).

In addition, Clark writes:

If a score or two score manuscripts have a single ancestor, it implies that a score or two score copyists believed that ancestor to be faithful to the autographs. But if a manuscript has not a numerous progeny ... one may suspect that the early scribes doubted its value. Possibly the early Christians knew that Beta was corrupt, while the later heretics were less interested in wasting time copying their own altered text.

Furthermore, the argument that pits weight against number, if it were to have much force, would require a far more extensive knowledge of manuscript genealogies than anyone now has. Even in the case of the Byzantine text alone, while the manuscripts are basically similar, a true genealogy has never been completed (p.15).

Robinson and Pierpont add:

An important consideration is that, except for a few small "family" relationships which have been established, the bulk of the Byzantine-era documents are not closely-related in any genealogical sense. A presumption, therefore, is toward their relative INDEPENDENCE from each other rather than their dependence upon one another. This makes the Byzantine majority of manuscripts highly individualistic witnesses which cannot be summarily lumped together as one "mere" text-type, to be played off against other competing text-types (p.xix; emphasis in original).

So "number" most definitely does matter as one criterion in determining the text.

"Transcriptional Probabilities"

In addition to the external evidence of the manuscripts, CT scholars also utilize what they call the "Internal Evidence" of "Transcriptional Probabilities."

Metzger outlines these "Transcriptional Probabilities"
1. In general, the MORE DIFFICULT READING is to be preferred....
2. In general the SHORTER READING is to be preferred....
3. Since scribes would frequently bring DIVERGENT PASSAGES INTO HARMONY with one another, in parallel passages....that reading which involves VERBAL DISSIDENCE is usually to be preferred to one which is verbally concordant.
4. Scribes would sometimes: a) REPLACE an unfamiliar word with a more familiar synonym. b) ALTER a less refined grammatical form or less elegant expression IN ACCORD WITH CONTEMPORARY ATTICIZING PREFERENCES; or c) ADD pronouns, conjunctions, and expletives TO MAKE A SMOOTHER TEXT (pp. xxvi, xvii).

Metzger's description of the Byzantine text-type further illustrates these ideas. He was previously quoted as saying, "It is characterized by lucidity and completeness. The FRAMERS of this text sought to SMOOTH AWAY ANY HARSHNESS OF LANGUAGE, to COMBINE TWO OR MORE DIVERGENT READINGS into one expanded reading (called conflation), and to harmonize divergent parallel passages."

Several comments on these "probabilities" and this description of the Byzantine text-type are in order:

1) Metzger's claim about "framers" has already been discussed under "Origin of Byzantine Text" above.

2) The assumption seems to be Christian scribes were in the habit of deliberately altering the text in order to "improve" it. But Robinson's study of the adultery story demonstrates this was not the case. Furthermore, in his book, Metzger never mentions the possibility of a variant being the result of a heretic writing a corrupted manuscript. But the previous extended quote and other statements of the Church Fathers show that heretics were in the habit of producing corrupted manuscripts.

3) It is claimed, "the shorter reading is to be preferred." The reason for this is the assumption that a scribe, if he had two manuscripts before him with two different readings, would combine them.

   But Clark relates in this regard, "Having suffered at the hands of typists, I cannot accept this criteria. They more often omit words and phrases than make additions. The critics will reply: The typist copies only one manuscript; those who copied manuscripts have several copies in front of them. Did they? Maybe sometimes. Maybe not. Who knows?" (pp.16, 23).

   Furthermore, Robinson and Pierpont write, "Conflation is not exclusive to the Byzantine-era manuscripts; the scribes of Alexandrian and Western manuscripts conflate as much or more than what has been imputed to Byzantine-era scribal habits" (pp.xxiii, xxiv). So supposed conflation of two readings into one cannot be used as an argument against Byzantine texts per se.

4) Two additional assumption running through these quotes need to be addressed. First, it is assumed the autographs were written in a difficult style of Greek, one with "verbal

dissidence." But later (Byzantine) scribes would "smooth away any harshness of language."

Second, it is assumed the NT originally had "divergent passages" which were "harmonized" by scribes to eliminate the supposed contradictions.

So the CT scholars seem to assume the autographs were written in a difficult language style and had contradictions in them, but Christian scribes later tried to "fix" these problems. But, as Gordon Clark writes, "No evidence supports this conjecture." Moreover, "Indeed, there is no evidence that any copyist assimilated anything to anything. The critic's argument is mainly unsupported speculation" (pp. 34, 28).

But there are two other possibilities. First, these problems could simply be due to accidental, scribal mistakes. As Clark writes about a scribe, "But it is also possible, for a number of reasons—fatigue, brilliance [bad lighting?], the mispronunciation of a reader—that he changed an easy reading into something more difficult" (p.16).

The other possibility is maybe the heretics, who were known to write corrupted manuscripts, purposely tried to introduce contradictions into the Scriptures and make them difficult to read. Metzger never mentions this possibility. But this scenario concurs better with the known historical facts than the one posed by the CT people.

Davis elaborates:

The Byzantine text is said by its most ardent critics to be smooth and complete Koine Greek and harmonious in the Gospels as an argument against its character. One has to ask the question of why it is assumed that the apostles and other NT writers could not have written in smooth complete Koine Greek, and that their accounts could not have had very close consistency with each other?

When along with the Alexandrian testimony, the NA [Nestle-Aland] and UBS texts omit the phrase "who is in heaven" from the text of John 3:13 describing it as a "later Christological development," one has to ask the question of why the apostle John, reporting what Jesus said could not have had a high view of Christology.

When, along with the Alexandrian testimony, the NA and UBS texts omit "yet" from the text of John 7:8 (tending to portray Jesus as not telling the truth) describe it as introduced to "alleviate inconsistency," one has to ask the question on why John couldn't have written portraying Jesus' statements as consistent with what he did.

When the Alexandrian texts introduce Amos and Asaph as Judean kings, one has to ask the question of why Matthew a Jew himself couldn't have written the historically correct reading of Asa and Amon (Matt 1:7,10). Character and reliability appear to be in the eye of the beholder! (p.3).

In line with the above, Metzger says, "textual criticism is AN ART as well as a science" (p.xxxi). Given the attitudes of the CT people and these subjective rules, Clark declares, "THERE MAY BE RHYME TO ALL THIS, BUT THERE IS NO REASON" (p.45).

Majority Text Criteria

So what criteria does MT scholarship utilize? As the name implies, MT scholarship puts an emphasis on the reading found in the vast majority of the manuscripts. However, this is not the sole criterion that is utilized.

As Robinson and Pierpont write about their Greek text, "... no stemmatic approach is utilized in this edition, nor is 'Number' a sole or necessary criterion" (p.xli). And further, "No procedures are utilized which rely upon mere numerical 'nose-counting,' nor are hypothetical stemmatic or genealogical principles employed. The leading criteria for textual selection have been [John] Burgon's seven canons of textual criticism, carefully applied ..." (p.liii).

Burgon's "seven canons of textual criticism" (or as he called them "The Seven Notes of Truth") are:
1. Antiquity, or Primitiveness.
2. Consent of Witnesses, or Number.
3. Variety of Evidence, or Catholicity [i.e. geographical distribution].
4. Respectability of Witnesses, or Weight.
5. Continuity, or Unbroken Tradition.
6. Evidence of the Entire passage, or Context.
7. Internal Considerations, or Reasonableness (*UnHoly*, Vol. I, p.15).

Most of these points have been addressed in these chapters in one fashion or another. But a few observations would be helpful here.

Looking these "canons" over, it can be seen there is some overlap between MT and CT criteria. However, MT scholars will put more of an emphasis on "Number" and less of an emphasis on "Antiquity" than CT scholars for reasons articulated above. Related to this point, MT scholars consider the Byzantine manuscripts to have more "Respectability" than the Alexandrian manuscripts whereas CT scholars "respect" Aleph and Beta and the Egyptian papyri more.

Also, MT scholars start with different presuppositions. As indicated above, they begin with the presupposition that the NT was originally written in a smooth style without divergent passages whereas CT scholars assume later scribes "smoothed" over the text to make it more readable and consistent. So the scholars would differ as to what is the most "Reasonable" reading in a particular context.

Conclusion

John Burgon mentioned above lived in the late 1800's. The Greek text he was defending was the *Textus Receptus* while the text he was writing against were those by Tischendorf and by Westcott and Hort. Today's MT is in the tradition of the *Textus Receptus* and today's CT in the tradition of Tischendorf and Westcott-Hort. However, today's texts are not identical to these earlier texts. In fact, the two sides have moved closer together over the years.

Farstad writes in the "Introduction" to the *NKJV Interlinear*, "The Majority Text is similar to the *Textus Receptus*, but it corrects those readings which have little or (occasionally) no support in the Greek manuscript tradition." And further, "Those readings in the *Textus Receptus* which have weak support are indicated in the textual notes as being opposed by both Critical and Majority Texts" (pp. x, ix). So in some places, today's MT is closer to the CT than the TR was.

Meanwhile, Robinson and Pierpont relate, "… all Greek New Testament editions since Westcott-Hort have increasingly adopted Byzantine readings to replace those advocated by Westcott and Hort" (p.xxiv). The primary reason CT editions have adopted more Byzantine readings is due to the "distinctively Byzantine readings" found in the early papyri, as was discussed previously.

So how much of a difference is there now between these three published Greek texts?

Daniel B. Wallace writes in this regard:

There are approximately 300,000 textual variants among New Testament manuscripts. The Majority Text differs from the Textus Receptus in almost 2,000 places. So the agreement is better than 99 percent. But the Majority Text differs from the modern critical text in only about 6,500 places. In other words the two texts agree almost 98 percent of the time. Not only that, but the vast majority of these differences are so minor that they neither show up in translation nor affect exegesis. Consequently the majority text and modern critical texts are very much alike, in both quality and quantity (p.38).

A couple of comments are in order. First, "300,000 textual variants among New Testament manuscripts" may sound like a lot. But this number is so high since there are such a great number of manuscripts to compare—more than 5,000. And in these thousands of manuscripts are seen a great number of "singular readings" as Robinson and Pierpont call them (p.xxxi). These are readings that appear in only one manuscript and are obvious mistakes. So they would not be reproduced in any published Greek text.

The ease at which such mistakes can be eliminated is shown by the extreme agreement in textual decisions in the three cited texts. A 1-2% difference between them is very small indeed. And of those differences that are seen, as Wallace points out, the vast majority of these are very insignificant. The point is, the overall textual integrity of the NT is NOT called into question by this debate.

However, despite this narrowing of the differences between the two sides, there still remain some important differences between the MT and CT that continue to fuel this heated debate. Some of these variants are discussed in the next chapter.

Bibliography for Chapters Seven and Eight:
Aland, Kurt & Barbara Aland. *The Text of the New Testament.* Grand Rapids: William B. Eerdmans, 1987.

Carson, D.A. *The King James Version Debate.* Grand Rapids: Baker Book House, 1979.

Clark, Gordon. *Logical Criticisms of Textual Criticism.* Jefferson, MD: The Trinity Foundation, 1986.

Davis, James F. "*Galilaia* or *Ioudaia* in Luke 4:44." Dallas, TX: The Majority Text Society, n.a.

Farstad, Arthur L. et.al. *The NKJV Greek-English Interlinear New Testament*. Nashville, TN: Thomas Nelson, 1994.

Fee, Gordon and Douglas Stuart. *How to Read the Bible for All Its Worth*. Grand Rapids, Zondervan, 1982.

Goodrick, Edward, W. *Is My Bible the Inspired Word of God?* Portland, OR: Multnomah, 1988.

Green, J.P. *Best Books in Print*. Lafayette, IN: Sovereign Grace Trust Fund, 1993.

The Interlinear Greek-English New Testament. Lafayette, IN: Sovereign Grace Publishers, 1996.

Press releases for The Literal Translation of Bible (LITV) and *The Modern King James Version* (MKJV).

Unholy Hands on the Bible. 2 Volumes. Lafayette, IN: Sovereign Grace Trust Fund, 1990, 1992.

Hodges, Zane C. and Arthur L. Farstad. *The Greek New Testament According to the Majority Text*. Nashville: Thomas Nelson, 1985.

Lightfoot, J.B. & J.R. Harmer. *The Apostolic Fathers*. Grand Rapids: Baker Book House, 1988.

MacLean, W. *Providential Preservation of Greek Text of New Testament*. Gisborne, N.Z.: Westminster Standard, 1977.

MacRae, Allan & Robert Newman. "Facts on the Textus Receptus & KJV." Hatfield, PA: Biblical School, 1975.

Metzger, Bruce. *A Textual Commentary on the Greek New Testament*. New York: United Bible Societies, 1975.

Moyer, Elgin. *The Biographical Dictionary of the Church*. Chicago: Moody Press, 1982.

Robinson. Maurice A. "Preliminary Observations regarding the *Pericope Adulterae* based upon Fresh Collations of nearly all Continuous-Text Manuscripts and over One Hundred Lectionaries." 1998, distributed by The Majority Text Society ~ PO Box 141289 ~ Dallas, TX 75214-1289.

Robinson, Maurice A. and William G. Pierpont. *The New Testament in the Original Greek According to the Byzantine/ Majority Textform*. Atlanta: Original Word Publishers, 1991.

Sturz, Harry. *The Byzantine Text-Type and New Testament Textual Criticism*. Nashville: Thomas Nelson, 1984.

Wallace, Daniel B. "The Majority Text and the Original Text: Are They Identical?" in *Bibliotheca Sacra*. April-June 1991, pp.157-158. Quoted in Bob and Gretchen Passantino. "New Age Bible Versions: A Critical Review." *Cornerstone*. Vol. 23, Issue 104.

Chapter Nine
Significant Textual Variants:
MT vs. CT

This chapter will investigate some of the significant variants which fuel the heated debate between supporters of the Majority Text (MT) and of the Critical Text (CT). A few less significant variants will also be looked at which illustrate points mentioned in the previous chapters. The verses will be quoted from the *New King James Version* with disputed parts in capitals.

For the textual evidence, two sources will be referred to: The textual apparatus of the United Bible Societies' (UBS) *Greek New Testament* (CT proponents) and J.P. Green's book *The Gnostics, the New Versions, and the Deity of Christ* (MT proponent).

Notes: The UBS apparatus refers to Greek manuscripts written in small letters as "minuscules" while Green calls them "cursives." For more on the types of manuscripts mentioned see Chapter Six: "Introduction to Textual Criticism."

The *Textus Receptus* (TR) is very similar to, but not identical with, the MT. In all of the variants discussed in this article, the TR and MT have the same reading. So the abbreviation TR/ MT will be used. For a discussion of variants between the TR and the MT, see the next chapter.

Matthew 5:22:
"But I say to you that whoever is angry with his brother WITHOUT A CAUSE shall be in danger of the judgment."

Is it always wrong to get angry, or is there such a thing as "righteous anger?" Without the words, "without a cause" the former would be true. Problem is, this would cause Jesus to be a sinner (see Mark 3:5). It would also introduce a contradiction into the Bible (compare Eph 4:26).

The words "without a cause" translate the one Greek word *eike*. The TR/ MT includes this word but the CT does not. But what is the reason for the CT omitting it?

Metzger writes, "Although the reading with *eike* is widespread from the second century onwards, it is much more likely that the word was added by copyists in order to soften the rigor of the precept, than omitted as unnecessary" (p.13).

Ralph Earle, a member of the NIV Committee on Bible Translation, writes similarly, "It is understandable how a later scribe might add this modifier to soften the rigor of the warning" (Barker, p.56).

A couple of comments are needed on these statements. First, both men assume the omission of the word was deliberate. But is it not possible a copyist simply made a mistake and missed the word?

Second, if the variant arose due to a deliberate alteration, both assume the word was added. But could it not be just as likely that a heretic omitted the word when copying the text in order to introduce the above-mentioned problems into the Scriptures?

So what is the manuscript evidence? The only manuscripts which omit it are one papyri (p67), Aleph, Beta, one minuscule (2174), the Vulgate, an Ethiopic version, and several western Church Fathers. Most of these have Egyptian origins, where the Gnostics were active in the early centuries.

Meanwhile, what is the evidence for including the word? The first manuscript listed in the UBS apparatus is Aleph! Well actually, it is Aleph "corrected." The issue of the various correcting hands on Aleph was discussed in the previous chapter.

Besides Aleph "corrected," the UBS apparatus lists seven other uncials which include *eike*, along with 35 minuscules, all the Byzantine lectionaries, 12 copies of the Old Latin Version, 10 copies of versions in other languages and several western and eastern Church Fathers.

Wilbur N. Pickering lists the evidence as follows: Without *eike*: "two Egyptian uncial MSS., B and Aleph, one papyrus (p67) and 2 cursives (01*, 045))." With the word: "all others including D, E, K, L, M, S, V, W, 037, 038, 041, 042, 0233, f1,13, 33, Italian, Syriac and Coptic versions" (quoted in Green, *Gnostics*, p.106).

This variant demonstrates a "formula" often used by the CT people: Aleph + Beta + very little other manuscript evidence + their own subjective "rules" = the best reading. This pattern is followed even if the vast majority of manuscript evidence and the known historic facts are on the other side.

Matthew 6:13:

And do not lead us into temptation, but deliver us from the evil one. FOR YOURS IS THE KINGDOM AND THE POWER AND THE GLORY FOREVER. AMEN.

The CT omits the doxology at the end of the Lord's Prayer. Metzger gives three main reasons why it does so. First, the doxology is omitted in many Alexandrian and Western texts.

Second, in the manuscripts which contain the doxology, there are minor variants between them. Third, he believes these two points, "...SUGGESTS that an ascription usually in threefold form, was composed (PERHAPS on the basis of 1Chr 29:11-13) in order to adapt the Prayer FOR LITURGICAL USE in the early church" (pp.16,17).

Each of these points will be commented on. First, all of the Byzantine texts have the doxology in some form. Metzger, of course, doesn't consider this to be of any importance though since, as mentioned in the introduction to the Chapter Seven, he considers the Byzantine text-type to be "corrupt" and "disfigured" (p.xxiii). However, the previous two chapters demonstrated that this attitude is not justified.

In fact, it is the exact reverse that could be true. Remember, the heretics, especially Gnostics, were very active in the west and were known to produce corrupted manuscripts. And most of these heretics didn't believe the Christian God was worthy of "the kingdom and the power and the glory forever."

Second, it is true there are minor variants between some of manuscripts and other early Christian writings which contain the phrase. For instance, *The Didache*, written about 100 AD, at the end of the Lord's Prayer has the words, "for thine is the power and the glory for ever and ever" (Lightfoot, p.232).

But it does not follow logically that minor variants like this prove the doxology is not original. In a three-fold formula like this, it would be easy for a scribe to omit one of the ascriptions.

And third, as Metzger generally does, rather than accepting the reason for a variant is simply an accidental mistake on the part of a scribe, he "suggests" a reason why "perhaps" a Christian scribe would have deliberately altered the text.

But, as was discussed previously, Christians were not in the habit of altering the Scriptures, only the heretics were. As Gordon Clark comments, "One may therefore suspect that 'liturgical additions' are not liturgical additions after all" (p.35).

Matthew 11:19:
"But wisdom is justified by her CHILDREN."

The significance of this variant lies in its illustration of the CT people's methods. The question is, should the last word be "children" or "works?" Metzger comments, "The Committee regarded the reading *teknon* (children)...as originated in scribal harmonization with the Lukan parallel (7:35)" (p.30). In other words, the CT people assume a scribe changed the word so the verse would be similar to Luke 7:35.

But, as Clark was quoted previously, "there is no evidence that any copyist assimilated anything to anything" (p.28).

As for the manuscripts, the UBS apparatus lists "works" as used in Aleph, Beta, W, and six versions. "Children" appears in, here we go again, Beta! Again, this is Beta "corrected." Just like Aleph, a couple of scribes tried to "fix" Beta, as was discussed previously.

In addition to Beta "corrected" – "children" is listed as being in eight other uncials, 20 minuscules, the Byzantine lectionaries, 10 copies of the Old Latin, the Vulgate, nine copies of other early versions, seven Church Fathers, and many other Byzantine manuscripts too numerous to list individually in the UBS apparatus. So once again, the "formula" mentioned above is used to determine the CT reading.

Matthew 20:16:
"So the last shall be first, and the first last. FOR MANY ARE CALLED BUT FEW CHOSEN."

This is the variant which caused the confusion at the Bible study discussed in the "Preface" to this book. The TR/ MT includes the second half of this verse, but the CT does not. It must first be mentioned, the question here is not, is this controversial phrase genuine? The CT and TR/ MT both include it in Matthew 22:14. The question is simply does it occur once or twice in Matthew?

Metzger explains why the CT omits it in Matt 20:16, "Although it is JUST POSSIBLE that the words fell out of the text through homoeoteleuton...it is MUCH MORE LIKELY that copyists incorporated them here from 22:14, where they terminate another parable" (p.51).

First, "homoeoteleuton" refers to a copyist missing a word or entire phrase because the last word or letters of the last word of a passage are identical to the ending of the next. The copyist would read the end of the first passage, move his head to write and when returning to look at the original manuscript, focus on the ending of the next passage and thus miss everything in-between.

For instance, in this verse, the Greek word "last" is *eschatoi* and the word "chosen" is *eklektoi*. Notice that both words end with *toi*. So Metzger is saying, the copyist could have written *eschatoi* and when returning to the original, picked up the *toi* at the end of *eklektoi* and started writing from there. In this way, the controversial phrase would be missed.

This may sound a little complicated, but, as mentioned previously, anyone who has done much typing or hand copying has probably made a similar mistake at one time or another.

But, of course, despite it being "just possible" that the variant originated by such a scribal mistake, Metzger goes on to hypothesize that a scribe deliberately inserted this phrase. But why this is "much more likely" is never really explained. That both passages are parables is not much of a reason for a Christian scribe to alter the Scriptures.

As for the manuscript evidence, Metzger says "most witnesses" include the phrase. These include basically all of the Byzantine texts, whereas eleven Alexandrian texts omit it (Metzger, p.51).

Mark 1:1:
    The beginning of the Gospel of Jesus Christ, THE SON OF GOD.

The significance of this variant is again in the demonstration of the CT scholars' methods. Do the words, "the Son of God" belong in the text? This is a difficult question for the CT people since this is one of the many places where their "two most reliable manuscripts" conflict. Beta contains the phrase, but Aleph does not.

Metzger first admits that the phrase's absence "may be due to oversight in copying." But, again, this simple explanation is not sufficient for Metzger, so he continues, "On the other hand, there was always a temptation (to which copyists often succumbed) to expand titles and quasi-titles of books" (p.73).

The problem is finally "solved" by enclosing the words in brackets. Brackets are put around words in the UBS text, "whose presence or position is regarded as disputed" (UBS, p.xlvii).

But is the evidence really so divided? In addition to Aleph, the only other Greek manuscripts which the UBS apparatus lists as omitting the phrase are a ninth century uncial (Theta) and an eleventh century minuscule (#28). Otherwise, only two versions and eight Fathers omit it.

As Clark observes, "*The New American Standard* [1977 edition] surely exaggerates when in its margin it says that 'MANY manuscripts omit the Son of God'" (p.26).

Meanwhile, besides Beta, listed as including the phrase are eight uncials (including Aleph "corrected"), 37 minuscules, the Byzantine lectionaries, ten Old Latin manuscripts, the Vulgate, 8 copies of early versions and 5 Fathers.

Green lists the evidence as follows: "Evidence for omitting Son of God: Codex Sinaiticus (Aleph), cursives 28, 255, Origen." Meanwhile, "Evidence for the authenticity of Son of God: All other uncials, all other cursives (over 2,000 mss. have these words), Irenaeus (170 A.D.)" (Green, *Gnostics*, p.39).

Mark 16:9-20:
THE LONGER ENDING TO "THE GOSPEL ACCORDING TO MARK."

The issues surrounding this passage are too complex to be pursued in this book, but one point will be made. In the previous chapter the textual note in EARLIER editions of the NIV was quoted as saying, "The two most reliable early manuscripts do not have Mark 16:9-20."

The reason for emphasizing "earlier" is more recent editions of the NIV leave out the word "two" in the textual note. This is probably because they don't want to give away that Aleph and Beta are the ONLY early manuscripts which omit this passage. The only other Greek manuscript which omits it is a twelfth century minuscule (#304). Several manuscripts, however, have notes indicating the passage is doubtful.

John 3:13:

"No one has ascended to heaven but He who came down from heaven, the Son of Man WHO IS IN HEAVEN."

Was Jesus in heaven at the same time He was on earth talking to Nicodemus? If He was, then Jesus was omnipresent even during the time of His incarnation, and this verse would then be a strong proof-text for His Deity. It would also raise some interesting theological questions about the nature of the incarnation.

But the key words, "who is in heaven" are omitted in the CT. Metzger explains, "...the majority of the committee, impressed by the quality of the external attestation supporting the shorter reading, regarded the words (who is in heaven) as an interpretive gloss, reflecting later Christological development" (p.204).

First, Metzger assumes the variant originated with people who believed in the Deity of Christ. But is it not possible that Gnostic or other heretics who did not believe in the Deity of Jesus removed the words? This is a distinct possibility since most of the manuscripts which omit the key words have an Egyptian origin.

Second, what is the "impressive external support" Metzger is referring to for omitting the phrase? The UBS apparatus lists two early papyri (p66,75), Aleph, Beta, and five other uncials, three minuscules, four copies of the Coptic version, an Ethiopic version and five Church Fathers.

Meanwhile, listed manuscripts which include the key words are: nine uncials, 37 minuscules, the Byzantine lectionaries and 11 other lectionaries, 11 copies of the Old Latin version, the Vulgate and nine copies of other early versions, including one Coptic version, and 17 Church Fathers.

J.P. Green summarizes the situation as follows: "Evidence for the Omissions: MANUSCRIPTS: p66, p75, Aleph, B, L, T, and 33 = 2 papyri, 4 uncials, 1 cursive (the first 4 executed in Egypt at a time when the Gnostics dominated that nation; the latter 3 are late manuscripts executed by those who, like our modern critics, venerated Aleph and B)."

Meanwhile, "Evidence the words are divine: MANUSCRIPTS: More than 1800, and that many more lectionaries = at least 99.5% of all manuscripts" (*Gnostics*, p.23). So on which side is there really "impressive external support?"

John 7:53-8:11:
THE STORY OF THE WOMAN TAKEN IN ADULTERY.

This is again a very complex variant and only one general comment will be made. There is no doubt in this writer's mind this passage records a genuine incident in the life of Christ. It fits well with other confrontations Jesus had with the Jewish leaders where they tried trapping Him with a "no win" question. But, of course, Jesus was never able to be caught with such futile attempts (see Matt 12:9-14; 22:15-33).

1Corinthians 2:4:
And my speech and my preaching were not with persuasive words of HUMAN wisdom, but in demonstration of the Spirit and of power.

Should Christians utilize logical reasoning (apologetics) in spreading the Gospel? Or should they just proclaim Christ and depend on miracles to uphold the message? Those who believe the latter often point to this verse. But is Paul saying he didn't use "wisdom" in evangelism of the Corinthians, or just not "human wisdom?"

Metzger explains why the word "human" is omitted in the CT, "If the word was original, there is NO GOOD REASON why it would have been deleted; on the contrary, it has the appearance of AN EXPLANATORY GLOSS inserted by copyists (at different places) in order to identify more exactly the nuance attaching to *sophias* (wisdom)" (p.546).

Again, Metzger is trying to guess why Christian scribes deliberately altered the text. But could not a "good reason" for its omission and slightly different placement in some manuscripts be simply scribal mistakes?

Moreover, there is a "good reason" a Gnostic might have omitted the word. The Gnostics, with their mystical attitudes, were opposed to any kind of "wisdom" other than their esoteric wisdom.

Further, as always, Metzger assumes the autographs were written in a difficult language style, but the scribes tried to smooth out God's language. Here, they added "an explanatory gloss" because God wasn't clear in what He was trying to say.

As for the manuscript evidence, listed in the UBS apparatus as omitting "human" are: the uncials Aleph, Beta, and D, along with in one papyri (p46), five minuscules, nine copies of various early versions, and several Church Fathers.

Listed as including "human" are: five uncials (one is Aleph "corrected"), 23 minuscules, nine copies of early versions, seven Church Fathers (three of which are also listed as omitting it), and many other Byzantine texts which are not listed individually.

Now for the question of Paul's evangelistic methods, in Acts 18, Luke records Paul's mission in Corinth. He says that Paul "REASONED in the synagogue every Sabbath and PERSUADED both Jews and Greeks" (v.4, see also v.13).

Moreover, preaching "in Spirit and in power" is NOT a reference to miracles. No miracles are mentioned by Luke in Acts 18. Further, John the Baptist's ministry is described in the same way, but he performed no miracles (Luke 1:17; John 10:41).

In his evangelism, Paul did not use "human" or "fleshly" wisdom (see 1Cor 2:13; 2Cor 1:12). These terms probably refer to Socratic, rhetorical dialog. This approach used a series of questions to "corner" someone into agreeing to something before they are ready. Christians are not to use such pressure tactics.

But Paul did, "speak the wisdom of God" (1Cor 2:7). And this includes answering people's questions and objections to the Gospel (1Cor 15:1-58; Col 4:5,6; 1Pet 3:15).

1Timothy 3:16:
And without controversy great is the mystery of godliness: GOD was manifested in the flesh.

The variant here is "God" (used in the TR/ MT) vs. "who" (followed by the CT). The former would make this a proof-text for the full Deity and full humanity of Christ.

The problem is difficult since in Greek "God" (*theos*) rhymes with "who" (*os*). Also, scribes often used shorthand for "God" by rendering it with the symbol *OS*. So a scribe could have easily made an accidental mistake.

But the distinct possibility of an accidental mistake doesn't prevent Metzger from speculating about a reason for a deliberate alteration. Assuming "who" was original, Metzger says a scribe might have changed it to "God" – "either to supply a substantive for the following six verbs, or, with less probability, to provide greater dogmatic precision" (p.641).

As for his less probable conjecture, why could not a heretic have changed "God" to "who?" This is especially possible for the Gnostics since the idea of God becoming flesh completely contradicted their entire belief system.

As for the former conjecture, Metzger admits that with the word "who" there is no substantive for the verse. This is evident when modern versions which follow the CT try to translate this verse. Virtually every one renders *os* as "He." But this is an impossible translation of the word. Then again, for the CT people, the fact that "who" doesn't make sense is proof it is original.

As for the manuscript evidence, the UBS apparatus list with "who" eight uncials (including Aleph), one lectionary, four copies of early versions, and eight Church Fathers.

Listed as containing "God" are also eight uncials (including Aleph "corrected"), twenty minuscules, the Byzantine lectionaries, and five later Church Fathers.

Green lists the evidence as, "For *who*, of the uncials, ONLY Aleph, 33, 442, 2147, three lectionaries, one version (Gothic), and not one single [early] patristic father!"

Meanwhile, "For *God*, A, Cvid, F/Gvid, K, L, P, over three hundred cursives and lectionaries ... 3 versions, and 20 Greek fathers, going back to Ignatius in the first century" (pp. 53,54).

Additional Important MT vs. CT Variants

Matt 6:15; 9:13; 17:21; 18:11; 20:23; 23:13; 26:28; 28:9.
Mark 2:17; 3:15; 6:11; 7:8,16; 9:38,44,45,46; 10:24; 11:8,26; 13:14; 14:24,27,70; 15:28.
Luke 1:28; 2:14,33; 4:4,8,18; 6:16, 8:45,54; 9:55; 11:2,4,11; 12:39; 17:9; 20:23,30; 22:43-44; 23:17,38; 24:46,53.
John 1:18,27; 3:15; 5:16; 6:47,55; 7:46; 8:59; 11:41; 16:16; 21:15.
Acts 1:14; 2:30,47; 10:11,32; 15:24; 18:21,26; 28:29.
Rom 1:16; 8:1,26; 9:28; 10:15; 11:6; 14:6,21, 24-26; 16:24,25-7.
1Cor 6:20; 10:28; 11:24,29; 15:55.
Gal 3:1.
Eph 3:9; 5:30.
Phil 1:16,17; 3:16.
Col 1:2,14, 2:11.
1Thes 3:2.
2Thes 2:4,13.
1Tim 1:4; 3:3; 6:5.
Heb 1:3; 10:1
James 4:4,5.
1Peter 1:22,23; 2:2; 3:,13,15; 4:14; 5:2.
2Peter 3:10.
1John 3:1; 4:3; 5:13.
Jude 1:1,22,23,25.
Rev 2:5; 9:16; 21:6,24; 22:21.

A complete listing of significant variants between the MT and the CT is contained in an appendix to this writer's *Analytical-Literal Translation.*

Conclusion

This discussion of the debate between the TR/ MT and the CT will close with a couple of pointed questions by John W. Burgon.

This MT advocate asks:
Does the truth of the Text of Scripture dwell with the vast multitude of copies, uncial and cursive, concerning which nothing is more remarkable than the MARVELOUS AGREEMENT which subsists between them? Or is it rather to be supposed that the truth abides exclusively with a very little handful of manuscripts, which at once differ from the great bulk of the manuscripts, and also differ widely among themselves? (quoted in Green, *Unholy*, Vol. I, p.9).

Final Note:
Before ending this discussion it needs to be emphasized, this whole debate does NOT impinge on the overall integrity of the New Testament text. As the preface to the NKJV states, "Readers may be assured that textual debate does not affect one in a thousand words of the Greek New Testament."

Further, "Differences among the Greek manuscripts such as omission or inclusion of a word or a clause, and two paragraphs in the Gospels, should not overshadow the overwhelming degree of AGREEMENT which exist among the ancient records" (pp.iv,v; emphasis in original). See Chapter Six: "Introduction to Textual Criticism" for more on the textual integrity of the New Testament text.

Bibliography:

The New King James Version. Nashville: Thomas Nelson, 1982.

Barker, Kenneth. ed. *The NIV: The Making of a Contemporary Translation*. Colorado Springs, CO: International Bible Society, 1991.

Clark, Gordon. *Logical Criticisms of Textual Criticism*. Jefferson, MD: The Trinity Foundation, 1986.

Green, J.P. *The Interlinear Greek - English New Testament*. Peabody, MA: Hendrickson, 1989.

The Gnostics, the New Versions, and the Deity of Christ. Lafayette, IN: Sovereign Grace Publishers, 1994.

Unholy Hands on the Bible. 2 Volumes. Lafayette, IN: Sovereign Grace Trust Fund, 1990, 1992.

Lightfoot, J.B. & J.R. Harmer. *The Apostolic Fathers*. Grand Rapids: Baker Book House, 1988.

Metzger, Bruce. *A Textual Commentary on the Greek New Testament*. New York: United Bible Societies, 1975.

United Bible Societies. *The Greek New Testament*. ed. by Kurt Aland et.al. Germany, 1983.

Chapter Ten
Significant Textual Variants
TR vs. MT

The *Textus Receptus* (TR) and the Majority Text (MT) are very similar. Most of the significant variants in the New Testament occur between the TR/ MT and the Critical Text (see the previous chapter).

However the TR and the MT are not identical. There are some differences between them, although, the places where there are significant differences are few and far between. Only in the Revelation are there many such variants.

However, there are occasionally places where there are important differences between the TR and the MT. Below is a discussion of two of the most significant ones. The verses will be quoted from the *New King James Version* with disputed parts in capitals.

Acts 9:5,6:

And he said, "Who are You, Lord?" And the Lord said, "I am Jesus, whom you are persecuting. IT IS HARD FOR YOU TO KICK AGAINST THE GOADS." SO HE, TREMBLING AND ASTONISHED, SAID, "LORD, WHAT DO YOU WANT ME TO DO?" AND THE LORD SAID TO HIM, [BUT] "Arise and go into the city, and you will be told what you must do."

Bruce Metzger says about this passage:

After *diokeis* [persecuting] (and omitting *alla* [but] of ver[se] 6) the *Textus Receptus* adds..."it is hard for thee to kick against the pricks. (6) And he trembling and astonished said, Lord, what wilt thou have me to do? And the Lord said unto him." So far as is known, no Greek witness reads these words at this place; they have been taken from 26.14 and 22.10, and are found here in codices of the Vulgate....

Metzger explains that the spurious passage came to be in the *Textus Receptus* when Erasmus translated this passage from the Latin Vulgate into Greek and inserted it in the first edition of his Greek New Testament of 1516 (Metzger, p. 362).

And so the reader knows that this is not just the ramblings of a CT advocate, even such a strong MT proponent as J.P. Green has a similar comment in the preface to his interlinear.

Green writes:
Although it is admitted that Erasmus has added to his Received Text two or three readings from the Latin Vulgate, without Greek manuscript authority (e.g. Acts 9:5,6), and also one from the Complutension Bible has no Greek manuscript authority (1 John 5:7). We have not deleted these from the Greek text as supplied by the Trinitarian Bible Society, though we do not accept them as part of the true deposit of the Holy Scriptures (*The Interlinear Bible*, Vol. IV, p. xi).

So the evidence for this passage is rather weak, to say the least, hence why it is not included in the MT. But, it must be noted that the words themselves are genuine. As Metzger indicates, part of the words can be found in Acts 22:10 and the rest in 26:14.

1John 5:7,8:
For there are three that bear witness IN HEAVEN: THE FATHER, THE WORD, AND THE HOLY SPIRIT: AND THESE THREE ARE ONE. AND THERE ARE THREE THAT BEAR WITNESS ON EARTH: the Spirit, the water, and the blood; and these three agree as one."

Metzger writes about the disputed part in these verses, "That these words are spurious and have not right to be in the New Testament is certain in light of the following considerations."

Metzger then lists three points under "External Evidence:

(1) The passage is absent from every known Greek manuscript except four, and these contain the passage in what appears to be a translation from a late recension of the Latin Vulgate....

(2) The passage is quoted by none of the Greek Fathers, who, had they known it, would most certainly have employed it in the Trinitarian controversies....

(3) The passage is absent from the manuscripts of all ancient versions...(Metzger, pp.715,716).

So how did this passage originate? Metzger says this passage could be, "an interpretation which was first written as a marginal note that afterwards found its way into the text" (p.716).

In other words, a scribe may have written this passage as a note to himself in the margin of his Bible (as many Christians write notes in their Bibles today). But a later scribe copying from this manuscript thought the passage was supposed to be in the text itself and inserted the words.

Erasmus then included the passage in his Greek NT, but not without dispute. The words were then included in the TR (Barker, p.56). However, both the CT and the MT omit the passage. The MT omits the words since they are not found in the vast majority of the manuscripts.

Basically, the only people who believe this passage is genuine are KJV only advocates. For instance, KJV onlyist Robert J. Sargent writes, "A footnote in the NKJB rendering of 1John 5:7 casts some doubt on the authority of this verse. This is a standard trinitarian verse which is naturally missing from all corrupt Greek texts and modern perversions passed off as Bibles" (p.4).

The footnote in the NKJV Sargent is upset about reads, "Only four or five very late manuscripts contain these words in Greek." And this sounds similar to the first point Metzger mentions.

Moreover, even J.P. Green acknowledges these words are not genuine. As quoted above in the discussion on Acts 9:5-6, Green writes, "We have not deleted these from the Greek text as supplied by the Trinitarian Bible Society, though we do not accept them as part of Holy Scripture" (p.xi). The words are then placed in italics in his *Literal Translation of the Bible*, the marginal reading in the interlinear.

However, it must be mentioned, by omitting this verse, the doctrine of the Trinity is NOT called into question. As Metzger indicated above, even without quoting this verse during the early Trinitarian controversies, the Trinity was established as being an essential and Biblical doctrine in the early Church.

The reason for this is there are hundreds of other verses in the Bible which demonstrate the three-in-one nature of the one, true God. This writer's *Scripture Workbook* has a chapter listing and arranging these hundreds of verses by topic.

The Revelation

Percentage wise, there are more variants between the TR and the MT in the Revelation than in any other NT book. And in many of these cases, the CT agrees with the MT. But why is the pattern different in the Revelation from what is seen in the rest of the NT?

The answer to this lies in the history of the TR. First, it should be mentioned, there is some disagreement as to exactly what Greek text *"Textus Receptus"* refers to. Basically, it is the text first developed by Erasmus, and later edit by Stephens and others.

Arthur L. Farstad provides further details:

When the Dutch scholar Desiderius Erasmus (1469-1536) published the first Greek New Testament in 1516, he had just a few late manuscripts with which to work. Later editions of the Greek Testament were also based on similar manuscripts. So, apart from minor variations, all the early printed editions are essentially the same.

The Greek New Testaments used by the King James translators other than Erasmus' texts included the Complutensian Polyglot printed in 1514 (but not published till 1520), Stephanus' texts, and Beza's texts. "The editions of Beza, particularly that of 1598, and the two last editions of Stevens were the chief sources used for the English Authorized Version of 1611."

The Elzivir brothers of the Netherlands published several editions of the Greek New Testament with essentially the same text as that of Erasmus, Beza, and Stephanus. In the Latin introduction to the 1633 edition, Elzivir stated that this text was the *"textum ab omnibus receptum"* ("text received by all"). This was shortened to "Textus Receptus," and was later applied to Stephanus' text of 1550. This name was also applied in a general way to all texts of the Byzantine type. The traditional Greek text has been called the *Textus Receptus* ever since that time (pp. 106-7).

But whichever specific text is being referred to, the TR was developed from a small handful of manuscripts. And of these, many lacked the Revelation. In fact, Erasmus had only one manuscript with the Revelation, and it was missing the last few verses. So to complete his Greek NT he translated the passage from the Latin Vulgate back into Greek.

Stephens and the others may have had additional manuscripts with the Revelation, but far less than for the rest of the NT. So with only a few manuscripts, the probability of the resultant text having errors was greatly increased.

By the time the CT and the MT were developed, many more and earlier manuscripts of the NT were discovered, including many more copies of the Revelation. And these additional manuscripts showed the manuscripts the Revelation of the TR was developed from had some errors in them, whether one goes with the general principle of the earliest manuscripts being the most accurate (CT) or the majority of the manuscripts reflecting the most accurate text (MT). For this reason, the MT and CT often agree together against the TR in the Revelation.

The reasons for there being far less manuscripts containing the Revelation than the rest of the NT has to do with the history of the transmission of the Revelation.

First, there is the practical issue of a scribe, for whatever reason, not finishing when copying the NT. Obviously, with the Revelation being last in the canon, it would be the most likely not to be copied if the scribe didn't finish. In fact, one of the earliest "complete" manuscripts of the NT actually lacks the Revelation.

Secondly, the Revelation was one of the "antilegomena" (Greek for "spoken against"). It was one of the seven books of the NT that were in dispute in the early Church as to its authenticity. More specifically, 20 of the 27 books were accepted throughout the Church without question as being written by an apostle or an apostolic delegate and as being inspired. These included the Gospels, Acts, the 13 epistles of Paul (Hebrews not included), 1John, and 1Peter. So these 20 books were copied more frequently in the early centuries than the other seven. By about the fourth century the canon was finalized, but the Revelation was probably one of the last books to be universally accepted.

In addition, sections of the NT, namely the four Gospels (sometimes with Acts) and the *Pauline Corpus*, were collected together and being copied as "sets" very early. There are several manuscripts containing these two sections of Scripture dating from the third century, but only one manuscript from this time of the Revelation (UBS text, pp.xii-xv).

Additional Important TR vs. MT Variants

For each of the following passages, the discussion would be about the same as for the verses above. The manuscript evidence supporting the TR reading is sparse, while the majority of the manuscripts support the MT reading. It is for this reason this writer prefers the MT to the TR.

As indicated above, the TR was based on the handful of manuscripts available at the time it was developed while the MT is based on the now over 5,000 known manuscripts. And in such cases as in the following verses, the TR reading simply was not supported in the many more manuscripts that were discovered later.

Matt 15:5; 23:13,25; 26:39,61; 27:35.
Mark 6:28; 15:3.
Luke 9:55-56; 17:35.
Acts 3:20; 8:36; 10:6; 13:23; 15:33; 24:6-8.
Rom 12:2; 14:24-26; 16:25-27.
Eph 1:18.
1Thes 2:11-12
Heb 2:7.
1John 2:23.
James 5:12.
Rev 1:8,11; 3:2; 7:5-8; 8:7; 9:16; 15:3; 19:12; 20:2,14; 21:6.

A complete listing of significant variants between the TR and the MT is contained in an appendix to this writer's *Analytical-Literal Translation*.

Bibliography:

Farstad, Arthur L. *The New King James Version in the Great Tradition* (Nashville: Thomas Nelson, 1993), and quoting from the preface to The New Testament: The Greek Text Underlying the English Authorized Version of 1611. London: The Trinitarian Bible Society, n.d.

Green, J.P. *The Interlinear Greek-English New Testament.* Peabody, MA: Hendrickson, 1989.

Metzger, Bruce. *A Textual Commentary on the Greek New Testament.* New York: United Bible Societies, 1975.

New King James Version. Nashville: Thomas Nelson, 1982.

Sargent, Robert. J. "Is the 'New King James Bible' the Word of God?" Halifax: The People's Gospel Hour, n.a.

United Bible Societies. *The Greek New Testament.* ed. by Kurt Aland et.al. Germany, 1983.

Chapter Eleven
Meaning of "Majority Text"

Throughout this book, I recommend the "Majority Text" (MT) for use in translating the Greek New Testament. But exactly what does this term refer to? This short chapter will answer this question and look at a few related items.

Published Majority Greek Texts

In the most simplified terms, the MT refers to the Greek text established on the basis of the reading found in the vast majority of the Greek manuscripts. There are two published Greek texts which would be considered to represent a MT type of text. They are:

Zane C. Hodges and Arthur L. Farstad. *The Greek New Testament According to the Majority Text*. Nashville: Thomas Nelson, 1985.

The Greek New Testament According to the Byzantine Textform. As edited by Maurice A. Robinson and William G. Pierpont. Revised edition, 2001.

Differences in Methodology

For both of the above Greek texts, "number" is an important point considered in determining the correct text, but it is not the only point that is considered. Each will appeal to other criteria, especially when the manuscript evidence is divided. And each has different criteria they will appeal to.

Hodges and Farstad explain their premises and methodology:

The premises which underlie the present edition and determine its methodology are two. Both of these premises need to be clearly understood by the users of this text.

(1) Any reading overwhelmingly attested by the manuscript tradition is more likely to be the original than its rival(s). This observation arises from the very nature of manuscript transmission. In any tradition where there are not major disruptions in the transmissional history, the individual reading which has the earliest beginning is the one most likely to survive in a majority of documents. And the earliest reading of all is the original one....

(2) Final decisions about readings ought to be made on the basis of a reconstruction of their history in the manuscript tradition. This means that for each New Testament book a genealogy of the manuscripts ought to be constructed (pp.xi-xii).

Robinson and Pierpont, however, discount the genealogy method. They write, "No procedures are utilized which rely upon mere numerical 'nose-counting,' nor are hypothetical stemmatic or genealogical principles employed. The leading criteria for textual selection have been [John] Burgon's seven canons of textual criticism, carefully applied ..." (p.liii).

Burgons' seven canons for textual restoration are: Antiquity, Number, Variety, Continuity, Respectability of Witnesses, Context, and Internal Reasonableness (p.ix). Though not with these exact terms, the concepts underlying some of these "canons" are discussed in the two chapters on "The Majority Text vs. the Critical Text."

Similarity in Published Texts

So for each of the two published MTs, "Number" is an important criterion, but they differ as to what other criteria should be appealed to. But in actual practice, how much of a difference do these two different philosophies make? Answer: Not very much. These two published Greek text are virtually identical.

Wilbur N. Pickering (Master's degree in theology, Ph.D. in linguistics and author of the book *The Identity of the New Testament Text*) writes in an article distributed by the Majority Text Society, "... I take it that the Hodges and Farstad Majority Text represents at least 99.8% of the original wording, and that the Robinson's and Pierpont Byzantine/ Majority Text represents at least 99.9%."

So there is only a 0.1% difference between the two texts. The reason for this is that the vast majority of the time a vast majority of the manuscripts has the same reading. As a result, "number" becomes the overriding criterion. The other criteria simply confirm what "number" indicates.

In the rare cases where there is not a vast majority of manuscripts agreeing, the other criteria take on more importance. Pickering discusses some such examples in his article. But whichever of the above methods that are used, again, they do tend to produce similar results. And using either method gives a very high degree of confidence. As Pickering indicates, only about 0.1-0.2% of the text is still in doubt.

In these rare cases where a decision cannot be definitely made between variant readings, each Greek text handles the situation differently. Hodges and Farstad's text has an extensive textual apparatus. In such cases, the apparatus would indicate that the textual evidence is divided.

Robinson and Pierpont's text has no textual apparatus. Instead, questionable words are placed in brackets. But it needs to be emphasized that such questionable words are few and far between. Altogether, there are 150 bracketed words or phrases, with seven of them being in the adultery story (John 7:53-8:11) and 64 in the Revelation.

Additional Points and Summary

Two additional points from Pickering's article are worth mentioning here. First, Pickering writes, "Is there a ceiling above which a reading may be considered 'safe' or secure; that is, beyond reasonable challenge? Personally, I have tended to regard 80% as such a ceiling."

Pickering writes further, "a 90% attestation will be considered unassailable, and 80% virtually so." Also, "Burgon's 'notes of truth' will come into play, especially where the attestations falls below 80%."

In other words, when at least 80% of the manuscripts agree on a reading, and especially when 90% or more agree, it is considered to be a consensus sufficient to establish the reading. Below 80% level of agreement, then the other criteria take on greater importance.

It should also be noted that for the vast majority of the words in the NT, at least an 80% and most often a 90% or greater level of agreement is seen in the textual evidence.

Second, what would it take to produce a Greek text that is 100% representative of the autographs? Pickering writes, "To reach 100% we must have full collations [comparisons] of most, if not all, extant MSS [manuscripts]. Surely modern technology is to the point where the MSS can be scanned into a computer, which can do the basic collating (verified by the human eye)."

In other words, the difficulty is not for the lack of manuscript evidence. With over 5000 manuscripts available, there is more than enough evidence to fully establish the text. It is simply a matter of more work being done with the manuscripts.

Overall, Pickering basically advocates utilizing all of the above-mentioned criteria: Number, genealogy, and the rest of Burgon's "canons." I would tend to agree with Pickering here, though I would probably lean more toward Robinson and Pierpont's method.

With all of that said, by "Majority Text" in this book is meant either of the above published Greek texts. Despite the somewhat different methodologies, the resultant texts are virtually identical. And most importantly, either text very accurately represents the originals. In fact, the difference between either published text and the autographs would be very insignificant indeed.

Bible Versions

So if the MT very accurately represents the original writings of the apostles, what Bible versions are translated from it? The first completed English translation available of the MT was the interlinear reading in Farstad and Hodges' *The NKJV Greek-English Interlinear New Testament* (Nashville, TN: Thomas Nelson, 1994). It, of course, used Hodges and Farstad's version of the MT.

The first regular translation to be based on the MT was the *World English Bible* (WEB). This version was produced by Rainbow Missions, Inc. as a copyright-free, Web based Bible (hence the acronym). It is based on Robinson's and Pierpont's MT.

Another translation based on Robinson's and Pierpont's MT is this writer's own *Analytical-Literal Translation* (ALT).

A final MT-based version in process is Robinson's own *Modern American Standard Version* (MASV). As with the *New American Standard Bible* (NASB), it is an updating of the *American Standard Version* of 1901. But the difference is, the NASB is based on the Critical Text while the MASV is being based on the MT, Robinson and Pierpont's version, of course.

So that's four translations that are currently available or are in the process of being produced which are based on the MT. It should also be noted that the *Textus Receptus* (TR) is very similar, but not identical, to the MT. The TR was based on a handful of manuscripts available in the sixteenth century. But these were reflective of the readings found in the vast majority of the now over 5,000 available manuscripts. So the TR basically reflects today's MT scholarship.

The TR is the basis for several Bible versions including: *The King James Version, The New King James Version, The Modern King James Version,* and *The Literal Translation of the Bible.* All of these versions are discussed elsewhere in this book.

Variants

While working on my translation, I was utilizing the 2001 edition of Robinson and Peirpont's MT, but I was also consulting the *NKJV Interlinear* (which is based on Hodges and Farstad's text) for help in translating passages. Following is a list of verses I noticed with differences between these texts. But note that many of these are so minor they would not even show up in translation. In addition, all 150 bracketed passages in Robinson and Peirpont's text would differ simply because Hodge's and Farstad's text uses footnotes rather than notations within the text to indicate words and phrases with split textual evidence.

The most significant difference is probably in Romans 12:2. In this verse Robinson and Peirpont's text has two infinitives while Hodge's and Farstad's has imperatives. The TR and CT also have imperatives. See Chapter Twenty-two for translations of this verse. But it should be noted, the WEB, even though it is based on Robinson and Pierpont's text, translates these infinites as imperatives.

Note also how many differences there are in the adultery story of John 7:53-8:11. These would be in addition to the seven bracketed passages in Robinson and Pierpont's text. This probably reflects the textual difficulty of this passage, along with the fact that Robinson has spent extensive time collating the manuscripts for this passage.

Luke 3:33; 9:22; 12:36; 20:31; John 8:2,6,7,9,10; Acts 2:37; 7:38; 22:12; 28:11; Rom 12:1,2; 13:9; 2Cor 3:14; 7:11; 13:5;

Eph 1:11; 5:21; Phil 3:8; 2Tim 1:1; Heb 5:4; Rev 3:12; 16:15; 18:23.

Bibliography:

Zane C. Hodges and Arthur L. Farstad. *The Greek New Testament According to the Majority Text*. Nashville: Thomas Nelson, 1985.

Maurice A. Robinson and William G. Pierpont. *The New Testament in the Original Greek According to the Byzantine/ Majority Textform*. Atlanta: Original Word Publishers, 1991.

Pickering, Wilbur N. "Majority Text Theory in Acts." Distributed by The Majority Text Society ~ PO Box 141289 ~ Dallas, TX 75214-1289 (www.thelordjesus/majtext.html).

KJV Only-ism

Chapter Twelve
Critique of KJV-Only Arguments:

This chapter will critique the arguments of KJV-only advocates. The sources for these arguments will be the many KJV-only tracts that have been sent to this writer, along with several KJV-only Web sites and the book *New Age Bible Versions* (which an Internet friend sent this writer after he got disgusted with it due to its very harsh language).

Note: The KJV is often referred to as the *Authorized Version* (AV) in KJV-only literature, and this name or abbreviation will be seen in some of the following quotes.

Infallible, Perfect, Inspired KJV?

Jack Chick writes, "Your old *King James Version* (the *Textus Receptus* in English) is the infallible Word of God ... Don't allow it to be thrown out of your church" (p.20; ellipse in original). And David Cloud claims about his KJV, "I believe I have a perfect Bible in my hands."

Similarly, Robert J. Sargent writes that the KJV is, "...the infallible, inspired, inerrant [without error] Word of God" (p.1). And Jack Moorman writes, "God has preserved in the *King James Version* His original work of inspiration" (Moreland, *Part 2*). And D. B. Loughran refers to "the real Bible—the *King James Version*."

But are these claims true? And what arguments do KJV-only advocates put forth to support their claims? A summary of some of these arguments will follow, with a critique of each. But first, another question needs to be answered.

Which KJV?

When KJV-only advocates claim the KJV is infallible or inspired, which KJV are they referring to? The KJV has undergone four revisions, in 1629, 1638, 1762 and 1769. The KJV in general use today is the 1769 version (Lockyer, pp. 172,176).

So this raises the important question, if the KJV translation is itself inspired, which one of these five versions of the KJV is the inspired one?" The original 1611 version? The one in use today? Or maybe one of the in-between three?

If the original 1611 version is the inspired one, then the KJV in use today is not inspired. If the one in use today is the inspired one, it must be asked, why did it take God five tries to get it right?

If, however, the 1611 KJV was simply a translation of the inspired texts, then each of these revisions would simply be attempts to improve the translation. Moreover, if changes needed to be made to the KJV text several times, at what point did it become infallible? If the 1611 were infallible, why were changes made to it? If the KJV-only advocates claim that today's edition is, how can they be sure? Why stop at four revisions? Why not a fifth?

KJV only advocates try to dismiss the changes made to the text over the years as being minor corrections of spelling errors and the like. But even if this were true, it would still argue against inspiration and infallibility. An inspired, infallible text should not have any errors in it.

However, some of these changes were more than minor spelling corrections. For instance, 1Corinthians 12:28 in the 1611 KJV had "helps in government" while the 1769 edition has "helps, governments."

Examples of other significant changes are: "covenant, even the Lord" vs. "covenant of the Lord" (Josh 3:11); "in the temple" vs. "in the temple of the LORD" (2Kings 11:10); "God" vs. "the LORD" (Isaiah 49:13); "be satisfied with goodness" vs. "be satisfied with my goodness" (Jer 31:14); "their" vs. "her" (Jer 51:30); "that he may" vs. "that ye may" (Ezek 6:8); "him" vs. "them" (Ezek 24:5); "poured it upon the ground" vs. "poured it not upon the ground" (Ezek 24:7); "they" vs. "ye" (Ezek 48:8);

"fiery furnace" vs. "burning fiery furnace" (Dan 3:15); "oathes" vs. "oath's" (Matt 14:9); "And" vs. "After" (1Cor 15:6); "Son" vs. "Son of God" (1John 5:12) (Hudson, pp.3,4).

Moreover, even today, there are actually two different editions of the KJV available: the Oxford edition and the Cambridge edition. The Oxford edition has "whom he had set" in Jeremiah 34:16 while the Cambridge edition has "whom ye had set." Another verse with a difference is 2Timothy 2:2 ("heard of me" vs. "heard from me"). So which one of today's two KJVs is the infallible and inspired one?

Less anyone thinks this is a minor point, while I was teaching a home-group, Bible study, someone mentioned that at a church he used to attend, the difference between KJVs in 2Timothy 2:2 made quit a stir. The difference changes the meaning of the verse significantly, and major debates broke out in the church over which was correct. In fact, "from" would be the most correct rendering of the Greek word *para* (Friberg's lexicon). But, unfortunately, the edition of the KJV most people have today has "of" in it, including the KJVs of everyone at the Bible study.

"Uniquely Blessed"

The first main argument by KJV only advocates for the KJV's "perfection" is put forth by Jack Moorman, "That the *Authorized Version* is such a Standard and the only Standard in the English language for nearly 400 years argues convincingly that it is God's preserved word in that language" (Moreland, *Part 2*).

Sargent expresses this idea by saying, the KJV has been "uniquely blessed of God for well over 300 years" (p.1). Moreover, the KJV is the version which God has "providentially preserved in the English language" (p.2).

And Edward Hills writes, "For more than 350 years, therefore, the reverent diction of the *King James Version* has been used by the Holy Spirit to bring the Word of life to millions upon millions of perishing souls. Surely this is a God-guided translation on which God, working providentially, has placed the stamp of His approval" (Hills, p. 65).

To respond to these claims, first it should be noted that the KJV was not the first English version of the Bible. Working from the Latin *Vulgate*, John Wycliffe first translated the Bible into English in 1384. A second edition was issued in 1395.

And then, the 216 years from 1395 to 1611, "...were fruitful years for new versions of the Bible. The stage was set for the monumental *King James Bible* by five different English translations that were issued in these years."

The first of these five versions was William Tyndale's version in 1525 with a revision in 1535. One important difference between Tyndale's version and Wycliffe's was Tyndale worked from Hebrew and Greek texts, not a Latin translation.

Next came *Coverdale and Matthew's Bible* in 1535-37, then *The Great Bible* in 1539, *The Geneva Bible* in 1560, and lastly, *The Bishops' Bible* in 1568.

Then came the KJV. The 54 scholars who worked on it, "...used the 1602 edition of the Bishop's Bible as the basis of their revision, but they had access to many other versions and helps, as well as the texts in the original biblical languages."

One of the "other versions" was Tyndale's, and, "His wording in those portions of the Bible which he translated was retained in the *King James Version* to a great degree." So the KJV was not a totally new version. It was mainly a revision of earlier English versions. So, as before, it must be asked, "Why did it take God several tries to get it right?"

In other words, if God is in the business of inspiring translations, why didn't He just "inspire" Tyndale and be done with it? Why the above long string of tries?

If, however, the KJV was simply the product of human scholarship, then the above makes sense. Each new version improved upon, and in some cases replaced the previous one.

Furthermore, all of the above versions were "blessed" by God to one degree or another. The translations of Wycliffe and Tyndale were powerful forces in bringing about the Reformation in England, "What Luther did for the Germans, William Tyndale did for the people of England."

Moreover, "To this day the Psalter in the *Book of Common Prayer* that is sung in the services of the Church of England is the Psalms contained in the *Great Bible*." And all of the above versions were read by many people to their spiritual benefit.

For instance, "*The Geneva Bible* was printed until 1644 and was still found in use 30 years later." This would mean the *Geneva Bible* was used by God's people for over a century. Furthermore, "This was the Bible the Pilgrims took with them to the new world in 1620." So the *Geneva Bible* was influential in the founding of the United States (the above information and quotes from Lockyer, pp.169-172).

But one could still argue that the blessing of God upon the KJV has been "unique." But this would be a difference of degree, not of kind.

As for the KJV being the "providentially preserved" English version of the Bible, it is true it had been the best-selling English version for over 350 years. And this could be interpreted as being duo to the providence of God. But does this mean the KJV is inspired, or simply that the KJV is a quality translation?

Interpreting providence can be a rather tricky business. This is especially the case here since there is no promise in Scripture that any translation of the inspired Hebrew and Greek texts will itself be inspired.

Moreover, the sales of the NIV and other versions that KJV only advocates claim are "corrupted" are now exceeding sales of the KJV. In addition, countless numbers of people are now reading these versions to their spiritual benefit, and yes even coming to a saving knowledge of Christ through them. Could not these facts be interpreted as God's "blessing" on these versions as well?

Furthermore, KJV onlyists claim the KJV is the "inspired" ENGLISH Bible. But what about the thousands of other languages out there? Has God inspired a version for each one of these? That's a lot of inspired Bibles.

Overall, an appeal to "blessing" and "providence" cannot demonstrate the KJV, or any other version for that matter, is inspired. It is a *non-sequitur* (it does not follow logically) that God's blessing on a book means that the book is infallible.

The KJV vs. the Original Texts

Sargent asks a very interesting question, "Did God preserve His word in the original languages, or, for all English speaking peoples, in the A.V.?" He claims it must be the KJV since it is still around while the original Hebrew and Greek manuscripts are not.

But, as was detailed previously, the original manuscripts are not around today because they wore out. Materials durable enough to last millennia simply were not used at the time the original autographs were written. But we do have thousand of original language manuscripts to work with.

But the main point here is, Sargent appears to trust the KJV more than the Hebrew or Greek text. David Cloud makes this claim explicitly, "We are convinced that the KJV is accurate in all textual matters, and if there is a difference between a KJV reading and any certain edition of the Received Text, we follow the KJV" (Cloud, *Which*).

Needless to say, such dogmatism is difficult to argue against. Demonstrating that there are readings in the TR, and thus in the KJV, that have very little manuscript support, as was done in Chapter Ten, would have little effect, and neither would showing that the KJV does not have the best possible translation of select verses, as will be done later.

However, facts are fact. There ARE readings in the TR which have very little manuscript support. And there ARE translations in the KJV that are less than perfect.

And, as KJV onlyists Donald Waite writes:

Some people say they like a particular version because they say it's more readable. Now, readability is one thing, but does the readability conform to what's in the original Greek and Hebrew language? You can have a lot of readability, but if it doesn't match up with what God has said, it's of no profit (Waite, "Superiority").

This writer has said just about the same in previous chapters. But what Waite says about other versions applies to the KJV as well. If a translation of the KJV "doesn't match up with what God has said, it's of no profit," and it will be shown later that there are cases when it does not.

Confusion of Greek Texts

Throughout this book, a clear distinction has been made between the *Textus Receptus* (TR) and the Majority Text (MT). It has also been said that the KJV is based on the TR. However, some KJV onlyists confuse these two texts and try to claim the KJV is based on the MT.

For instance, Riplinger writes:

The overwhelming majority of these manuscripts, lectionaries, and writers agree generally with each other as to the readings of the New Testament. Manuscripts from the second Century (P66) down through the Middle Ages (A.D. 1500) attest to the readings of this 'Majority Text,' as Kurt Aland terms it. Dean Burgon, who found this 'Majority Text' in most of the early writers collated, calls it 'The Traditional Text.' It is also called the Syrian Text, the Byzantine Text and the K (Kappa) or Common Text.

> This text type is available today in English in the *Authorized Version*, or as it is called in the United States, the *King James Version* (p.471).

This passage is a mixture of truth and misinformation. The first two sentences are true. However, Dean Burgon lived in the 1800's. The text he was referring to by "Traditional Text" was the TR. The term "Majority Text", as Chapter Eleven makes clear, refers to either the text by Robinson and Pierpont or the text by Hodges and Farstad. None of these men were even alive in the 1800s. The other names given refer to the MT, not the TR. But most importantly, the KJV is NOT based on the MT. It is based on the TR.

Loughran writes similarly:

> Before we consider the *King James Version* (KJV) and a few of the modern translations in use today, let us first consider certain Greek texts from which all New Testament translations are derived. Foremost amongst these is the Traditional Received Text (*Textus Receptus*), also called the Byzantine Text or the Majority Text because it is based on the vast majority of manuscripts still in existence....
>
> Textus Receptus is based on the vast majority (90%) of the 5000+ Greek manuscripts in existence. That is why it is also called the Majority Text.

All of this is true, for the MT. It would also be true for the 99% of the time that the TR and the MT agree. But for the other 1% it is not true. As already demonstrated, there are readings in the TR, and thus the KJV, which have very little manuscript support. So for these readings the numbers would be reversed. It would more like less than 10% of the manuscripts have the reading of the TR, while greater than 90% do not. As a result, these readings are not included in the MT.

The point of all of this is that the KJV onlyists are trying to ride on the back of the evidence for the MT in defending the KJV. But to do so requires them to confuse the issues.

They also confuse the issues when referring to the textual base of the NKJV. They often claim the NKJV is not based on the TR and lump it in with versions based on the CT.

For instance, when talking about the CT, Hills writes, "This false Greek text, with its approximate 10,000 alterations, was the basis for virtually all of the modern English versions and perversions, including the ERV, ASV, NIV, NASV, **NKJV**, RSV, NRSV, TEV, JB, NEV, LV and the rest" (bolding added). Notice how the NKJV is lumped together with a list of versions which are based on the CT.

Loughran writes similarly:

> Most, if not all, modern translations are based on the *Revised Version* (1881-5) which, as we have already learned, was influenced throughout by the Alexandrian manuscripts Sinaiticus and Vaticanus. In effect there really are only Two English language Bibles to choose from. The *King James Version*: which is based on the Masoretic Hebrew Text and the Majority Greek Text. The Revised Version: which is based on the Minority Text. This version has spawned a whole generation of inaccurate translations: which, like their unholy mother the RV, all rely heavily on the Minority Text.

So Loughran lumps in not only the NKJV with CT versions, but also all the other versions that have been mentioned in this book as being based on the TR or MT. And he explicitly says it's either the KJV or a CT based version, which is far from the truth.

And finally for KJV confusion on Greek texts, Jack Chick even confuses the MT with the CT when he writes, "Check this verse; over 95% of all corrupted versions tamper with it. [quoting 1John 5:7]. If that verse is messed up in the Book you call 'The Bible,' then you know you're looking at a translation that came from Satan's mutilated Alexandrian manuscripts" (p.21).

The MT does not have the "extra" section of 1John 5:7, but it is not based on "Alexandrian manuscripts." It is primarily based on Byzantine manuscripts. Now to be fair, Chick's tract was probably written before there were any translations available based on the MT. But still, Chick should be aware that along with the Alexandrian manuscripts, the vast majority of the Byzantine manuscripts also omit the extra words in this verse.

KJV Translators Superior?

Hill claims:

> The second reason for defending the KJV is because it has superior translators. This correctly implies that the various versions and perversions of the Bible have inferior translators. Let's take a brief look at the superior translators of the KJV. Why do I say that the KJV translators are superior? I say they are superior because they ARE superior! I think that there is no question about the expertise and ability of the translators who gave us our KJV.

As indicated in Chapter Five, it is true there were quality translators who worked on the KJV, but it is also true quality translators worked on the KJV, the NIV, and most other Bible versions. All of them were God-fearing men with the necessary qualifications for translating the Bible. There is really no basis for claiming that the KJV translators were "superior"—other than dogmatism.

Differences between the KJV and other versions are not due to the KJV translators being "better." Rather, they are due to the different groups of translators having different opinions as to what constitutes the best method of translating, the best way to translate a particular word, and what is the best Greek text- type.

Now I agree that the translators of many newer versions have made the wrong decisions on some of these matters, but that doesn't mean they are "inferior", just that we disagree. And it definitely doesn't mean that these translators should be disparaged the way KJV onlyists do.

For instance, in the writings of KJV onlyists, the translators of the NKJV are said to be: ignorant, deluded, corrupters of the pure bread of life, horrendous liars, money-mad apostates, lovers of filthy lucre, and phony Greek scholars. The NKJV itself is called: crummy, corrupted, perverted, polluted, apostate, a deadly version, communist, Satan's ultimate deception, Satanic nonsense, and New King Rat's nest. And to make matters worse, readers of the NKJV are called: foolish, gullible, suckers, and madmen (gleaned from various KJV onlyist sources).

Is such language really necessary?

Translation Method Confusion

Hill writes:

The third reason for defending the KING JAMES BIBLE is because it has superior technique of translation. This correctly implies that the various versions and perversions of the Bible have inferior technique of translation. The KJV translators used the superior technique of verbal equivalence and formal equivalence—not dynamic equivalence.

The modern versions and perversions have used, to a greater or lesser degree, the inferior technique of dynamic equivalence and have disdained both verbal and formal equivalence.

It is true that most modern versions use the dynamic equivalence method, and this writer agrees that it is an inferior method. However, not all modern versions use this method. As previously chapters have shown, quite a few more recent versions use the same method as the KJV, formal equivalence, and a few even use the more accurate literal method. So the KJV onlyists are just creating confusion when they lump all versions together without discrimination.

Archaic Pronouns

Moreland writes, "It seems strange that with the great increase of knowledge, people should have trouble with the "Thee's" and "Thou's" of the *Authorized Version*" (Moorman, Part 1).

And Reynolds writes further:
We do consider it a tragic mistake to eliminate the use of "Thee," "Thous" and "Thine where these refer to Deity. There is a disturbing trend toward stripping God of His Majesty both in word and deed. The substitution of the common pronouns "You" and "Yours" for "Thee," "Thou" and "Thine" which have historically been used to refer to Deity both in the Scriptures and the Hymns of the Church, only helps pave the way for further attempts of sinful men to bring God down to their level rather than exalting Him in every way possible.

As for Moorman's comments, it is true that many today would probably be able to figure out what the "Thee's" and "Thou's" in the KJV mean. But that's not the point. Simply put, for many people today they are very awkward to read, and even more awkward to read out loud since people don't talk that way today.

Reynold's comments are interesting for a couple of reasons First, it should be noted that the KJV does not only use these words for Deity but also for humans (e.g., Exod 20:12, "Thou shalt no kill"). So how these pronouns particularly "exalt" God is not quite clear.

Second, if these words were only used in reference to God, then such a practice would be less accurate. Hebrew and Greek do not have separate pronouns for God and humans.

Third, again, these words are awkward for many today. This writer finds them awkward to sing when my church sings some of the older hymns with them. And frankly, I really wish someone would come out with "updated" versions of these hymns well.

However, Waite does make an interesting point in this regard:

The Greek and Hebrew language contain a different word for the second person *singular* and the second person *plural* pronouns. Today we use the one-word "you" for both the singular and plural. But because the translators of the 1611 King James Bible desired an *accurate, word-for-word* translation of the Hebrew and Greek text - *they could NOT use the one-word "you" throughout! If it begins with "t" (thou, thy, thine) it's SINGULAR, but if it begins with "y" (ye) it's PLURAL.* Ads for the NKJV call it "the Accurate One", and yet the 1611 King James, by using "thee", "thou", "ye", is far more accurate! (italics and bolding in original).

Waite is correct here that Hebrew and Greek have different words for "you." The problem is, modern-day English does not. So Waite is correct that the KJV is more accurate by using different words for "you" to show this distinction. However, most readers of the KJV do not know about this feature, and more importantly, to show the distinction, the KJV uses archaic words. So which is "better" would be a toss-up.

For my own *Analytical-Literal Translation*, I decided to use an asterisk to indicate the plural "you" (i.e. you*), and "you" with no asterisk to indicate the singular. And this feature is clearly indicated in the introductory pages to the translation. This is not a perfect solution, but there really is none in this case given the deficiency of the English language in this regard.

And this discussion on archaic pronouns leads to the next point.

Readability of the KJV

Another claim made in defense of the KJV is that it is not really that difficult to read. Gail Riplinger, for instance, claims the reading grade level rating of the KJV is actually lower than modern versions. For Matthew chapter one, she puts the KJV at a 6.7 grade reading level, the NIV at 16.4, the NASB at 6.8, the GNB at 11.8, and the NKJV at 7.7.

She then states, "Why is the KJV easier to read? The KJV uses one or two syllable words while new versions substitute complex multi-syllable words and phrases. Their 'heady, high minded' vocabulary hides the hope of salvation from simple saints and sinners" (p.196).

Waite claims similarly, "Many people say, "The KJV is too hard for people to read, they can't understand it." Well, if you consult the readability index called "Right Writer" (a computer program) that is absolutely neutral on this subject, you will find readabilities for the portions of the KJV examined as follows."

Waite then gives the following figures: Passage Readability Grade Level: Genesis 1: 8th Grade; Exodus 1: 8th Grade; Romans 1: 10th Grade; Romans 3:1-23: 6th Grade; Romans 8: 8th Grade; Jude 1: 10th Grade. He then comments, "From the chart you can see that the KJV is NOT too difficult to understand— provided that you can read at a 6th to 10th grade level."

This claim is interesting as it conflicts with "reading grade level" charts this writer has seen previously. In these the KJV is consistently listed as the most difficult to read version.

For instance, a chart I picked up at a Bible distribution center gives the following reading levels: KJV: 12th grade; NAS77: 11th grade; NAB: 11th grade; NKJV: 8th grade; LB: 8th grade; NIV: 7th grade; GNB: 7th grade; NCV: 3rd grade ("How," pp. 6-7).

A flyer from Family Bookstores gives the following reading grade levels: KJV: 14.0; NAB: 14.0; NAS77: 11.3; Amplified: 11.1; NJB: 10.1; NKJV: 9.1; NRSV: 8.5; NIV: 7.8; GNB: 7.3; LB: 6.9; NCV: 3.9; ("Bible," front page).

So the KJV is rated at 12th grade in the first and at 14th grade in the second. This is a far cry from Riplinger's 6.7 and Waite's 6th to 10th grade. And note how close these two are for other versions, yet how far they are from Riplinger's claims. The NIV, for instance, is at 7th grade in the first and 7.8 in the second while Riplinger has it at 16.4.

Now Waite says to use a computer program, so I tried using the reading level checker in Microsoft Word 2000[tm] on Romans 12. I ended up with a level of five to six for several versions, including the KJV. The problem is, such programs only look at formatting issues such as the number of sentences in a paragraph, the number of words per sentence, and the number of letters in a word. It does not consider archaic words in its evaluation. And I would suspect, neither do the computer programs Waite and Riplinger are using. But the charts I quoted were probably developed by humans, most likely English teachers.

So a word like "ere" (Exod 1:19) would be considered to be an easy word by a computer program since it only has three letters and one syllable, but most readers today wouldn't even know what it means. The modern-day equivalent is "before," which a computer would consider to be a more difficult word since it has six letters and two syllables. However, an English teacher would evaluate them in the opposite manner.

Now in some cases the KJV has a word that is not archaic which has less letters or syllables than some modern versions. But in these cases it is because the KJV translation is less accurate than the modern versions. For instance, Riplinger lists the NASB's "reclining" as a more difficult word than the KJV's "sat" for Mark 4:3 (p.198). And it is true that "sat" has less syllables and letters than "reclining." However, in those days people reclined on the floor when they ate, they did not sit on

Gary Zeolla

chairs as we do today. So the NASB's "reclining" is more accurate.

But getting back to archaic words, how many of them are there in the KJV? KJV onlyists claim that there are not that many archaic words. Moorman writes, "Relatively few words in the *King James Version* would fall into the category of "Old English." This is not nearly so great a problem as is claimed. It is doubtful that more than twenty words would cause a problem, and here the dictionary will quickly give the meaning" (Moorman, Part 1).

So Moorman claims there are only 20 archaic words in the KJV. However, in order to update all of the archaic language in the KJV for the *King James Easy Reading Bible*, the KJER Web site states that the KJER "has *changed* about 700 old English words to modern English" ("Bibles" page; italics in original). And note, that is 700 DIFFERENT words. Each one of these words probably occurs dozens, hundreds, or even thousands of times (e.g. the above-mentioned archaic pronouns), so collectively there are probably tens of thousand archaic words in the KJV.

In any case, all of this talk about reading grade levels and archaic words is really irrelevant to any individual reader. What matters is what any particular person thinks when he or she begins to read a Bible version. If the person finds it too difficult, then he or she will probably give up on it. And that is probably what happens a lot of the time when people try reading the KJV; they give up on it, no matter how much the KJV onlyists scream that it is not difficult to read.

In fact, this writer has read the KJV, but has found it difficult to do so. See the next chapter for a list of passages I found difficult when reading just the Book of Exodus.

However, there is one point in this regard where I agree with KJV onlyists:

Many maintain that the KJV uses archaic language. Is this objection justified? Pause awhile and consider this

162

well known fact: every department of human learning uses language peculiar to that particular discipline: language which novices could easily refer to as being archaic. Biology, botany, geology, physics, chemistry, mathematics, music, medicine, law etc., all use strange sounding words, phrases and expressions which a novice will find difficult to understand.

The study of the Word of God is similar in this respect. It also uses words and expressions which a new believer will find hard to comprehend. Words like sin, repentance, baptism, atonement, sanctification, justification, resurrection etc. These words often baffle a new believer: but he/she must learn them in order to progress spiritually; because they are explicit Biblical terms which uniquely express vital spiritual concepts and processes. They are not archaic words and we dare not get rid of them or simplify them to such a degree that the Word of God becomes a paraphrase, a commentary. Can you imagine a novice biology, science or law student objecting to the strange sounding words or old-fashioned expressions in his text books? (Loughran, "Which").

The problem of "simplifying" theological terms has been discussed previously. When technical words are simplified, very often the full intended meaning is not expressed nearly as well in the "simpler" term than it is in the technical term.

Confusion Caused by Proliferation of Versions

A claim often made by KJV onlyists is that the proliferation of Bible versions since the late 1800's is causing confusion among Christians. In fact, while I was working on this chapter I received an e-mail from a KJV onlyists reiterating just this claim. But for a change, on this point the KJV onlyists are probably correct. Christians are confused about Bible versions. That is one reason I decided to write this book.

However, it doesn't help matters when KJV onlyists spread misinformation. KJV onlyists add to the confusion when they lump together TR-based versions like the NKJV with CT-based versions, confuse the differences between Greek texts, claim only the KJV follows a formal equivalence translation method, claim the KJV is the easiest to read Bible version, and simply declare the KJV to be the only "real" versions while calling all others "corruptions" (or worse).

In addition, the extreme caustic language seen in KJV only literature is simply un-called for. This writer does agree that many modern-day versions are less than reliable, but I see no reason to refer to them in such derogatory ways as KJV onlyists do. And more importantly, as this book has shown, there are many new versions that are just as if not more accurate than the KJV.

Now I can understand the KJV onlyists' complaint. Things were easier when the KJV was basically the only Bible version available, or at least by far the most popular version. But those days are long gone, and it is very doubtful there will ever again be a time when just about everyone is using the same Bible version. However, I for one am very thankful for this.

I shudder to think what would have become of my Christian walk if the KJV were the only Bible version I had to choose from. As I've said previously, I simply find the KJV too awkward to read. Now if it were my only choice, I am sure I would have struggled through it. But it would have been just that—a struggle. But more importantly, I am sure there are many today who would not have struggled. They would have just set the KJV aside and not bothered with reading the Bible at all.

I am also thankful there is more than one Bible version available, no matter what version that would be. As should be clear from previous sections of this book, this writer has spent much time comparing different Bible versions, and I have benefited spiritually by doing so.

Conclusion

These chapters will conclude by looking at one last KJV only claim:

> Now, frankly, after seventy attempts to replace the *Authorized Version*, one cannot help wonder whether God wants it replaced! This conviction is strengthened when we note that believers do not seem to study the modern versions as they once did the AV. They are not marked up and study worn. Passages are seldom memorized. Preachers do not quote verses from the NIV in the pulpit as they once did the AV. Nor is expository preaching and doctrinal study emphasized as it once was (Moorman, Part 1).

In the 17 years I have been reading the Bible I have gone through several Bibles. And I am sure there are many others who have gone through more than one Bible through the years. Now granted, the Bibles people put aside today when they buy new ones might not be as "study worn" as Bibles used to be, but that is probably because people buy new Bibles more often today than they used to.

As for memorizing, expository preaching, and doctrinal study, I don't know what churches Moorman has been attending, but there many churches which use versions other than the KJV and which emphasize such activities.

So, however much KJV onlyists may deny and even despise it, Christians today ARE reading, studying, and deriving spiritual profit from what they call "corrupted" versions.

To conclude, the KJV is a very good translation, done by godly scholars, based on an accurate Greek text, using an excellent translation method. However, the KJV is not perfect, infallible, or inspired, and it most definitely is not the only "real" Bible. There are many other trustworthy Bible versions besides the KJV.

Bibliography:

The KJV – NKJV Parallel Reference Bible. Nashville: Thomas Nelson, 1991.

Brown, Driver, Briggs, Gesenius. *Hebrew and English Lexicon*. Peabody, MA: Hendrickson, 1979.

Baur, Walter. *A Greek-English Lexicon of the New Testament*. Chicago: University of Chicago Press, 1979.

"Bible Translation Comparison." Family Bookstores, n.a.

Chick, Jack. "The Attack." Chino, CA, n.a.

Cloud, David, "Which Edition of the Received Text is the Preserved Word of God?" (http://wayoflife.org/~dcloud/fbns/whichtr.htm).

Friberg, Timothy and Barbara. *Analytical Lexicon to the Greek New Testament*. Copyright © 1994. As found on BibleWorks™ for Windows™. Copyright © 1992-1999 BibleWorks, L.C.C. Big Fork, MT: Hermeneutika. Programmed by Michael S. Bushell and Michael D. Tan.

Hills, Edward. *Believing Bible Study*, quoted in "The Superiority of the King James Version" (www.biblebelievers.net/BibleVersions/kjckjv1s.htm).

"How to Choose the Right Bible." Spring Arbor Distributors, 1990.

Hudson, Gary. "Revision is no 'Myth!'" Whitehouse, FL, n.a.

King James Easy Reading Sword Study Bible/ Word of God (KJER) Bible pages (www.abible.orgabible/BIBLES.html).

Lockyer, Herbert, ed. *Nelson's Illustrated Bible Dictionary*. Nashville: Thomas Nelson, 1986.

Loughran, D B. "Which is the real Word of God?" (http://rhema-av-1611.lima.net.pe/kjvbook.html).

Moorman, Jack. "Modern Bibles—The Dark Secret, Part 1." © Fundamental Evangelistic Association (www.fundamentalbiblechurch.net/fbcdark.htm.

"Modern Bibles—The Dark Secret, Part 2." © Fundamental Evangelistic Association (www.fundamentalbiblechurch.net/fbcdark2.htm.

Reynolds, M.H. "New King James Bible Examined." Los Cos, CA: Fundamental Evangelistic Association, n.a.

Riplinger, Gail. *New Age Bible Versions*. Ararat, VA: A.V. Publications Corp., 1993.

Sargent, Robert. "Is the New King James Bible the Word of God?" Halifax: The People's Gospel Hour, n.a.

Waite, Donald A., in "The Superiority of the King James Version," summarizing from Defending the King James Bible (www.biblebelievers.net/BibleVersions/kjckjv1s.htm).

Gary Zeolla

Chapter Thirteen
Difficult Terms in the KJV

I recently read the Book of Exodus in the *King James Version* (KJV) via Matthew Henry's commentary. As I was reading through it, I underlined terms and phrases in the KJV which I found difficult, awkward, or simply did not know the meaning of. But each time, when I compared the verse in the *New King James Version* (NKJV) the meaning of the verse was immediately clear.

Also, as I was studying, I was comparing the verses with the Hebrew text using J.P. Green's *Interlinear Bible*. The Interlinear also contains the *Literal Translation of the Bible* (LITV). So I compared that version as well.

Below are the verses in question. The words and phrases in the KJV I am referring, along with the corresponding terms in the NKJV and LITV, are capitalized.

Preliminary Notes: For definitions of Hebrew words, I consulted the *New Brown–Driver–Briggs–Gesenius Hebrew Lexicon* (abbreviated as BDBG) and *Whitaker's Revised BDB Lexicon*, copyright © 1995, Dr. Richard Whitaker (RBDB), as found on *BibleWorks™ for Windows™*. I also consulted the *Theological Wordbook of the Old Testament*. All English definitions are from copied from *Webster's Talking Dictionary/ Thesaurus*.

Words in italics in the KJV and NKJV and in brackets in the LITV are words added for clarity that are not in the original text.

Also, I have not been consistent in transliterating the Hebrew words. Sometimes I just followed the transliteration seen in the interlinear in the *PC Study Bible*. In these cases, the transliteration reflects the form of the word as it is seen in the verse. Other times I used my own transliteration. In these cases, the transliteration is the lexical form.

Verses

Exod 1:18:
KJV: And the king of Egypt called for the midwives, and said unto them, Why have ye done this thing, and have saved the MEN CHILDREN alive?

NKJV: So the king of Egypt called for the midwives and said to them, "Why have you done this thing, and saved the MALE CHILDREN alive?"

LITV: And the king of Egypt called to the midwives and said to them, Why do you do this thing and keep alive the MALE CHILDREN?

The phrase "men children" sounds like a contradiction in terms. In English today "men" refers to ADULT males. The NKJV rendering makes much more sense. Also, the LITV follows the Hebrew word order in putting "alive" before "male children" rather than after.

Exod 1:19:
KJV: And the midwives said unto Pharaoh, Because the Hebrew women *are* not as the Egyptian women; for they *are* lively, and ARE DELIVERED ERE the midwives come in unto them.

NKJV: And the midwives said to Pharaoh, "Because the Hebrew women *are* not like the Egyptian women; for they *are* lively and GIVE BIRTH BEFORE the midwives come to them."

LITV: And the midwives said to Pharaoh, Because the Hebrew women [are] not like the Egyptian women, for they [are] vigorous. BEFORE the midwives come to them they BEAR.

The LITV word order is closer to the Hebrew, but the wording is rather awkward.

Exod 3:5:

KJV: And he said, DRAW NOT NIGH HITHER: put off thy SHOES from off thy feet, for the place whereon thou standest *is* holy ground.

NKJV: Then He said, "DO NOT DRAW NEAR THIS PLACE. Take your SANDALS off your feet, for the place where you stand *is* holy ground."

LITV: And He said, DO NOT COME NEAR HERE pull off your SANDALS from your feet, for the place on which you [are] standing [is] holy ground.

Needless to say, "nigh" and "hither" are archaic words. No one today uses such terms. Also, the LITV's "here" is the most accurate rendering of the last word in the phrase in question (Hebrew, *halom*), although it is a bit awkward. In addition, though "shoes" is not a difficult term, "sandals" would be more historically accurate.

Exod 9:9:

KJV: And it shall become small dust in all the land of Egypt, and shall be a boil breaking forth *with* BLAINS upon man, and upon beast, throughout all the land of Egypt.

NKJV: "And it will become fine dust in all the land of Egypt, and it will cause boils that break out in SORES on man and beast throughout all the land of Egypt."

LITV: And let it become dust on all the land of Egypt, and let it become an inflammation breaking out into a BOIL on man and on livestock in all the land of Egypt.

The KJV and NKJV are slightly more accurate than the LITV since the Hebrew word in question is plural. However, I had to look "blain" up in *Webster's* dictionary to found that it meant "an inflammatory swelling or sore." So the NKJV "sores" is the most accurate and readable rendering.

Exod 9:31:
KJV: And the flax and the barley WAS smitten: for the barley *was* in the ear, and the flax *was* BOLLED.
NKJV: Now the flax and the barley WERE struck, for the barley *was* in the head and the flax *was* IN BUD.
LITV: And the flax and the barley WERE stricken. For the barley [was in] the ear, and the flax [IN] BLOSSOM.

In the first sentence, the verb is singular, so the KJV's "was" is more accurate than "were," but it is not correct English grammar and very awkward.

I had to look up "bolled." The word "boll" means, "a rounded seed vessel or pod of a plant, as of flax or cotton." But "boll" is a noun, as is the Hebrew word, but with the "ed" ending, it sounds like a verb. The Hebrew word means simply "bud" (RBDB), and since "bud" and "blossom" mean just about the same, both the NKJV and LITV are more understandable and accurate.

Exod 12:39:
KJV: And they baked unleavened cakes of the dough which they brought forth out of Egypt, for it was not leavened; because they were thrust out of Egypt, and could not tarry, neither had they prepared for themselves any VICTUAL.
NKJV: And they baked unleavened cakes of the dough which they had brought out of Egypt; for it was not leavened, because they were driven out of Egypt and could not wait, nor had they prepared PROVISIONS for themselves.
LITV: And they baked the dough which they brought out from Egypt [into] unleavened cakes. For it was

not leavened, because they were driven out from Egypt, and they were not able to delay. And also they had not prepared FOOD FOR A JOURNEY for themselves.

The Hebrew word in question (*tsedah*) can refer to food or provisions in general (BDBG, p.845).(6) The LITV captures both meanings rather well. Also, note, the NKJV and LITV follow the Hebrew word order in putting "for themselves" after the word rather than before it.

Exod 13:12:

KJV: That thou shalt set apart unto the LORD all that openeth the MATRIX, and every FIRSTLING that cometh of a beast which thou hast; the males *shall be* the LORD's.

NKJV: "that you shall set apart to the LORD all that open the WOMB, that is, every FIRSTBORN that comes from an animal which you have; the males *shall be* the LORD's.

LITV: you shall set apart to Jehovah every one opening the WOMB, and every FIRSTLING, the offspring of animals which are yours; the males [are] Jehovah's.

"Matrix" means, "something that constitutes the place or point from which something else originates." So it could be a reference to the womb. But "womb" is much more accurate and understandable. And "firstling" does make sense, but again, "firstborn" is more accurate and understandable

Exod 19:18:

KJV: And mount Sinai was ALTOGETHER ON A SMOKE, because the LORD descended upon it in fire: and the smoke thereof ascended as the smoke of a furnace, and the whole mount quaked greatly.

NKJV: Now Mount Sinai was COMPLETELY IN SMOKE, because the LORD descended upon it in fire. Its smoke ascended like the smoke of a furnace, and the whole mountain quaked greatly.

LITV: And the mountain of Sinai was SMOKING, ALL OF IT, because Jehovah came down on it in fire. And its smoke went up like the smoke of a furnace; and the mountain quaked exceedingly.

The KJV is very awkward. The LITV is the most literal in that the Hebrew word (*aashan*) is a verb, not a noun. And the LITV also follows the Hebrew word order.

Exod 20:13:
KJV: Thou shalt not KILL.
NKJV: "You shall not MURDER."
LITV: You shall not MURDER.

The KJV word is not a difficult term, but the NKJV and LITV is a more precise and accurate rendering of the Hebrew word (Harris, p.860). The words "kill" and "murder" are not entirely synonymous. You can kill someone without it being murder, such as in self-defense.

Exod 23:1:
KJV: Thou shalt not RAISE a false report: put not thine hand with the wicked to be an unrighteous witness.
NKJV: "You shall not CIRCULATE a false report. Do not put your hand with the wicked to be an unrighteous witness.
LITV: You shall not UTTER a false report; You shall not put your hand with the wicked, to become a violent witness.

This is one case where the KJV is more literal than either the NKJV or LITV. The Hebrew word *tisaa* most literally means, "lift up" as Green's interlinear renders it. However, the word is variously translated otherwise even in the KJV. Moreover, in this verse, "raise" does not make sense given the context, while both "circulate" and "utter" do. But both of these are less literal, especially the latter. So there is a trade-off however the word is rendered. If it were up to me, I would probably choose the NKJV's "circulate." It fits the context and is not too far from a literal rendering.

Exod 23:3:

KJV: Neither shalt thou COUNTENANCE a poor man in his cause.

NKJV: "You shall not SHOW PARTIALITY to a poor man in his dispute.

LITV: And you shall not FAVOR the lowly in his lawsuit."

When used as a verb, "countenance" means, "to permit or tolerate, to approve or encourage." Meanwhile, the Hebrew verb in this form means, "honour, pay honour to … in a bad sense, of partiality, favoritism" (BDBG, pp.213,214). So the KJV rendering is not accurate while the renderings of either the NKJV or LITV would be.

Exod 23:6:

KJV: Thou shalt not WREST the judgment of thy poor in his cause.

NKJV: "You shall not PERVERT the judgment of your poor in his dispute.

LITV: You shall not PERVERT the judgment of your needy one in his lawsuit.

I had to look up "wrest" to find out it means "twist," and twist is the most literal meaning of the Hebrew word. However, "pervert" is a possible figurative meaning and is more understandable in the context.

Exod 23:19:

KJV: The first of the firstfruits of thy land thou shalt bring into the house of the LORD thy God. Thou shalt not SEETHE A KID in his mother's milk.

NKJV: "The first of the firstfruits of your land you shall bring into the house of the LORD your God. You shall not BOIL A YOUNG GOAT in its mother's milk.

LITV: The first, the firstfruits of your ground you shall bring to the house of Jehovah your God. You shall not BOIL A KID in its mother's milk.

I know that "kid" can refer to a young goat. But I wonder how many city "kids" today would know this?

Exod 24:18:

KJV: And Moses went into the midst of the cloud, and GAT HIM UP into the mount: and Moses was in the mount forty days and forty nights.

NKJV: So Moses went into the midst of the cloud and WENT UP into the mountain. And Moses was on the mountain forty days and forty nights.

LITV: And Moses came into the midst of the cloud, and HE WENT UP into the mountain. And Moses was in the mountain forty days and forty nights.

Webster's refers to "gat" as, "*archaic*, pt. [past participle] of get." But I really didn't need *Webster's* to tell me "gat" is an archaic word. Moreover, the way the phrase is worded in the KJV, it makes it sound like the verb is a passive and that Moses was "taken up" into the mountain, but this is not the case.

175

Exod 27:1:

KJV: And thou shalt make an altar of shittim wood, five cubits long, and five cubits broad; the altar shall be FOURSQUARE: and the height thereof *shall be* three cubits.

NKJV: "You shall make an altar of acacia wood, five cubits long and five cubits wide—the altar shall be SQUARE—and its height *shall be* three cubits.

LITV: And you shall make the altar of acacia timbers; five cubits long and five cubits wide. The altar shall be SQUARE, and its height three cubits.

The Hebrew word means simply "square." The awkward "foursquare" is simply unnecessary.

Exod 28:11:

KJV: With the work of an engraver in stone, *like* the engravings of a signet, shalt thou engrave the two stones with the names of the children of Israel: thou shalt make them to be set in OUCHES of gold.

NKJV: "With the work of an engraver in stone, *like* the engravings of a signet, you shall engrave the two stones with the names of the sons of Israel. You shall set them in SETTINGS of gold.

LITV: You shall engrave the two stones, the work of an stone engraver, the engravings of a signet, according to the names of the sons of Israel; you shall make them set *in* PLAITED WORK of gold.

Webster's defines "ouches" as, "Archaic.... the setting of a precious stone." So it means about the same as "settings," but again, I didn't need *Webster's* to tell me the word is archaic. The LITV is slightly more accurate in that the term in question is actually two words in Hebrew. However, the words are plural, not singular.

Exod 28:14:

KJV: And two chains *of* pure gold at the ends; of WREATHEN WORK shalt thou make them, and fasten the WREATHEN CHAINS to the OUCHES.

NKJV: "and you shall make two chains of pure gold like BRAIDED CORDS, and fasten the BRAIDED CHAINS to the SETTINGS.

LITV: and two chains of pure gold, you shall make them WOVEN WORK, a work of cord; and you shall put CHAINS OF THE CORDS on the PLAITED WORK.

I couldn't even find "wreathen" in *Webster's*, so I'm not sure of its meaning. I would assume it's an archaic word for "braided" or "woven."

Exod 28:42:

KJV: And thou shalt make them linen BREECHES to cover their nakedness; from the loins even unto the thighs they shall reach:

NKJV: "And you shall make for them linen TROUSERS to cover their nakedness; they shall reach from the waist to the thighs.

LITV: And make linen BREECHES for them, to cover the naked flesh, from the loins as far as the thighs they shall be.

"Breeches" are "knee-length trousers, often with buckles or decoration at the bottoms, worn by men in the 17th to early 19th centuries." So "breeches" were not worn in Biblical times. And this is the 21st century. So it makes no sense to translate the Hebrew word *miknaseey* by the name of a garment that is over 100 years out-of-date.

Meanwhile, "trousers" are, "a usu[ally] loose-fitting outer garment for the lower part of the body, having individual leg portions, usu[ally] of full length." It is not certain exactly what

177

the clothing being referred to looked like, so it can't be said with certainty if this is an accurate description or not. However, at least most people today know what "trousers" are.

Exod 29:13:
KJV: And thou shalt take all the fat that covereth the INWARDS, and the CAUL *that is* above the liver, and the two kidneys, and the fat that *is* upon them, and burn *them* upon the altar.

NKJV: "And you shall take all the fat that covers the ENTRAILS, the FATTY LOBE *attached* to the liver, and the two kidneys and the fat that *is* on them, and burn *them* on the altar.

LITV: And you shall take all the fat that covers the INWARD PARTS, and the LOBE on the liver, and the two kidneys, and the fat on them, and you shall burn on the altar.

The KJV's "inwards" is not even in *Webster's* dictionary. But the NKJV's "entrails" means the "inner organs of the body" which is what the Hebrew word *qereb* means (BDBG, p. 899). The LITV's "inward parts" would also be a good translation and possibly even a little clearer to some.

The KJV's "caul" makes no sense. The word means, "a part of the amnion sometimes covering the head of a child at birth." Either "lobe" or "fatty lobe" are understandable and accurately render the Hebrew word *yeteret*, although "appendage" is also possible (BDBG, p.452).

Exod 29:34:
KJV: And IF OUGHT of the flesh of the consecrations, or of the bread, remain unto the morning, then thou shalt burn the remainder with fire: it shall not be eaten, because it *is* holy.

NKJV: "And IF ANY of the flesh of the consecration offerings, or of the bread, remains until the morning, then you shall burn the remainder with fire. It shall not be eaten, because it *is* holy.

LITV: And IF [ANY] is left of the flesh of consecration, and of the bread, until the morning, you shall burn what is left with fire; it shall not be eaten, for it [is] holy.

I have no idea what "ought" is supposed to mean in this context. The only definition in Webster's is as a verb, which makes no sense in the context. Also, the word should be italicized as added, and so should "any" in the NKJV. Only the LITV accurately offsets the word.

Exod 30:18:

KJV: Thou shalt also make a laver of brass, and HIS FOOT *also* of brass, to wash *WITHAL*: and thou shalt put it between the tabernacle of the congregation and the altar, and thou shalt put water therein.

NKJV: "You shall also make a laver of bronze, with ITS BASE also of bronze, for washing. You shall put it between the tabernacle of meeting and the altar. And you shall put water in it,

LITV: And you shall make a bronze laver for washing, and ITS BASE bronze. And you shall put it between the tabernacle of the congregation and the altar; and you shall put water there.

The word "base" is a more accurate rendering of the Hebrew word *wakanow* (BDBG, p.487). Also, though it is true the Hebrew word is masculine, this is only because all words in Hebrew are masculine or feminine. In other words, Hebrew has no neuter, but English does. And we generally do not use masculine (or feminine) pronouns when referring to inanimate objects. So using "his" in the KJV for the laver is very awkward.

The "withal" in the KJV is in italics in the text indicating it is not in the original, and it is rather unnecessary, not to mention a rather archaic English word. As such, the other two versions have no equivalent for it.

The LITV uses "And" instead of "also." The LITV's translation is the more common way of rendering the Hebrew *waw*, but "also" is possible as well. The second "also" in the KJV and NKJV is not in the Hebrew. Hence why the LITV has no equivalent to it.

Exod 30:25:

KJV: And thou shalt make it an oil of holy ointment, an ointment compound after the art of the APOTHECARY: it shall be an holy anointing oil.

NKJV: And you shall make from these a holy anointing oil, an ointment compounded according to the art of the PERFUMER. It shall be a holy anointing oil.

LITV: And you shall make it an oil of holy anointing, ointment compound, the work of a PERFUMER, an oil of holy anointing it shall be.

"Apothecary' means, "a druggist; pharmacist." But the Hebrew word has no sense of mixing medicine. It refers to one who makes ointments or mixes spices or perfumes (BDBG, p.955). Hence, "perfumer" is both more accurate and more understandable.

Exod 32:1:

KJV: And when the people saw that Moses delayed to come down out of the mount, the people gathered themselves together unto Aaron, and said unto him, Up, make us gods, which shall go before us; for *as for* this Moses, the man that brought us up out of the land of Egypt, WE WOT NOT what is become of him.

NKJV: Now when the people saw that Moses delayed coming down from the mountain, the people gathered together to Aaron, and said to him, "Come, make us gods that shall go before us; for *as for* this Moses, the man who brought us up out of the land of Egypt, WE DO NOT KNOW what has become of him."

LITV: And the people saw that Moses delayed to come down from the mountain. And the people gathered to Aaron. And they said to him, Rise up, make for us gods who may go before our face. As for this Moses, the man who brought us up from the land of Egypt, WE DO NOT KNOW what has become of him.

Webster's defines "wot" as, "*Archaic.* first and third pers[on]. Sing[ular]. Pres[ent]. of WIT²." So again, Webster's says it's an archaic word, a form of "wit." But when I looked up "wit" I couldn't find any definition that made sense in this context.

Exod 32:18:
KJV: And he said, *It is* not the voice of *them that* shout for MASTERY, neither *is it* the voice of *them that* cry for being overcome: *but* the noise of *them that* sing do I hear.

NKJV: But he said: "*It is* not the noise of the shout of VICTORY, nor the noise of the cry of defeat, *but* the sound of singing I hear."

LITV: And he said, It is not a sound of a cry of MIGHT, nor a sound of a cry of defeat; I [am] hearing the sound of singing.

The Hebrew word *gabuwrah* means most literally "strength" or "might" (BDBG, p. 150). So the LITV is the most literal. Both the KJV and NKJV are extending the meaning somewhat, but at least the NKJV uses a word that is more understandable in this context.

Exod 32:25:
KJV: And when Moses saw that the people *were* NAKED; (for Aaron had made them NAKED unto *their* shame among their enemies:)

NKJV: Now when Moses saw that the people *were* UNRESTRAINED (for Aaron had NOT RESTRAINED them, to *their* shame among their enemies),

LITV: And Moses saw the people, that it was UNLOOSED, for Aaron had LET [IT] LOOSE for a derision among their enemies.

The Hebrew verb *parua* can mean, "uncover." Hence the KJV rendering "naked." However, in the "qal" verb form (used in both places in this verse though in different tenses) it more specifically means to, "let go, let loose, people, i.e. remove restraint from them." BDBG even cites this verse as an example of this usage (p.828). So the NKJV and LITV more precisely render the verb than the KJV. However, the NKJV rendering is more readable.

Exod 34:21:
KJV: Six days thou shalt work, but on the seventh day thou shalt rest: in EARING TIME and in harvest thou shalt rest.

NKJV: "Six days you shall work, but on the seventh day you shall rest; in PLOWING TIME and in harvest you shall rest.

LITV: You may work six days, and on the seventh day you shall rest. In PLOWING TIME and in harvest you shall rest.

Webster's has no definition of "earing" that makes sense in this context. The Hebrew word means, "plowing, plowing time" (RBDB). So the NKJV and LITV are accurate and readable.

Exod 35:11:
KJV: The tabernacle, his tent, and his covering, HIS TACHES, and his boards, his bars, his pillars, and his sockets,
NKJV: 'the tabernacle, its tent, its covering, ITS CLASPS, its boards, its bars, its pillars, and its sockets;
LITV: the tabernacle, its tent, and its cover, ITS HOOKS, its boards, its bars, its pillars, and its sockets;

Webster's again has no definition of "tach" that makes sense in this context. The Hebrew word in this context would mean, "hook" (RBDB). So the LITV version is most accurate, but the NKJV's "clasp" means about the same. And again, the pronoun is masculine, but a neuter translation is less awkward.

Exod 35:35:
KJV: Them hath he filled with wisdom of heart, to work all manner of work, of the engraver, and of the CUNNING WORKMAN, and of the embroiderer, in blue, and in purple, in scarlet, and in fine linen, and of the weaver, *even* of them that do any work, and of those that devise CUNNING WORK.
NKJV: "He has filled them with skill to do all manner of work of the engraver and THE DESIGNER and the tapestry maker, in blue purple, and scarlet *thread*, and fine linen, and of the weaver—those who do every work and those who design ARTISTIC WORKS.

LITV: He has filled them *with* wisdom of heart, to do every work of a smith, and AN ARTISAN, and an embroiderer in blue, and in purple, and in crimson, and in bleached *linen*, and a weaver; doers of every work and devisers of DESIGNS.

"Cunning" means, "1. skill employed in a shrewd or sly manner, as in deceiving; craftiness; guile. 2. adeptness in performance; dexterity." So if one is thinking of definition number two, the KJV's rendering would fit the context. However, in most common usage today, the word has the first, rather negative connotation. So the NKJV's and LITV's renderings are more understandable.

Exod 36:4:
KJV: And all the wise men, that WROUGHT all the work of the sanctuary, came every man from his work which they MADE;
NKJV: Then all the craftsmen who WERE DOING all the work of the sanctuary came, each from the work he was DOING,
LITV: And all the wise men came, those DOING every kind of work [for] the holy place, each one from his work they [were] DOING.

The first word in question is an active participle. This verb form in Hebrew indicates "continuous occurrence or state of activity" (from my seminary, Hebrew class notes). So the NKJV and LITV are not only more understandable but also more accurate. The last word in the verse is the same Hebrew word in the same form. So both the NKJV and LITV are more consistent in their translation, and again more accurate. However, the verb is plural, so the NKJV is less accurate in making it singular (note: the pronoun is implied in the verb).

Exod 38:8:

KJV: And he made the laver of brass, and THE FOOT
      OF IT of brass, of the LOOKINGGLASSES of *the*
      women assembling, which assembled *at* the door of
      the tabernacle of the congregation.

NKJV: He made the laver of bronze and ITS BASE of
      bronze, from the bronze MIRRORS of the serving
      women who assembled at the door of the tabernacle
      of meeting.

LITV: And he made the laver bronze, and ITS BASE
      bronze, from the MIRRORS of the serving women,
      those assembling, who served [at] the door of the
      tabernacle of the congregation.

The awkwardness of "foot" has already been discussed. But
note that this time the KJV uses a neuter pronoun in reference to
it. So the KJV is not consistent in its handling of the "gender" of
pronouns.

As for "looking-glass," I know that it is a mirror. But I
wonder how many young people today would? The KJV is
somewhat more accurate in rendering the words "assembling"
and "assembled" with the same root word, as the root words in
Hebrew are the same. However, the more basic meaning of the
word that would fit this context is "serve" (BDBG, p.838). So, if
it were up to me, I would render the phrase as "the serving
women who served."

Conclusion

In this comparison I have not capitalized all the "thee's" and
"thou's" and archaic verb forms found in the KJV. These
permeate the entire version. Also, many additional difficult terms
in the KJV could be produced from the other 65 books in the
Bible.

But this comparison list from just one book should suffice to
demonstrate why I prefer the NKJV and LITV to the KJV. The

NKJV is much more readable than the KJV, yet, in almost every case, the NKJV was every bit as faithful to the Hebrew text as the KJV. In some cases the KJV was actually inaccurate while the NKJV had an accurate translation.

Meanwhile, the LITV, in almost every case, was even more accurate than the KJV and the NKJV, but it is still also more readable than the KJV, though less so than the NKJV.

As such, the claims of the KJV onlyists cited in the previous chapter are not true. The KJV is not a "perfect" translation. There are times when its rendering are less than accurate. And these examples show that it definitely is not the most readable translation as some KJV onlyists try to claim.

The NKJV, however, is a very reliable and very readable translation, hence why it is my primary Bible. The LITV is not quite as readable as the NKJV, but it is even more accurate. So it is my secondary Bible for Old Testament studies. It is the first version I check when I want to compare a verse in another version. (I will, of course, first consult my own *Analytical-Literal Translation of the New Testament* for NT studies.)

As for the KJV, since it is no more accurate than any of these versions, yet more difficult to read, I only refer to it occasionally. And, of course, I cannot avoid reading it given its inclusion in so many reference works, especially older ones like Matthew Henry's excellent commentary.

Bibliography:

Green, J.P. ed. *The Interlinear Bible: Hebrew-English.* (Peabody, MA: Hendrickson Publishers, 1985).

Harris, R. Laird, et.al. *Theological Wordbook of the Old Testament*, Vol. II (Chicago: Moody Press, 1980). Also as found on *BibleWorks™ for Windows™* Copyright © 1992-1999 *BibleWorks*, L.C.C. Big Fork, MT: Hermeneutika. Programmed by Michael S. Bushell and Michael D. Tan.

Henry, Matthew and Thomas Scott. *Commentary of the Holy Bible*, Vol. I (Nashville: Thomas Nelson, 1979).

New Brown-Driver-Briggs-Gesenius Hebrew and English Lexicon (BDBG). Peabody, MS: Hendrickson Publishers, 1979.

Whitaker's Revised BDB Lexicon, copyright © 1995, Dr. Richard Whitaker (RBDB). As found on *BibleWorks™ for Windows™*.

Online Bible. Ontario: Online Bible Foundation and the Woodside Bible Fellowship, 1997.

PC Study Bible. Seattle: Biblesoft, 1996.

Webster's Talking Dictionary/ Thesaurus. Licensed property of Parson's Technology, Inc. v. 1.0b. Software Copyright 1996 by Exceller Software Corp. Based on Random House *Webster's College Dictionary*. Copyright 1995 by Random House, Inc. Note: All English word definitions are copied from this source.

Chapter Fourteen
KJV Only Arguments Against the NKJV

The *New King James Version* (NKJV) comes under particular fire from *King James Version* (KJV) only advocates. This fact first surprised this writer. I simply never believed the differences between the two versions were great enough to warrant such an attack. But it is because the versions are rather similar that KJV onlyists attack it so vigorously.

For instance, D. B. Loughran writes:
> The truth of the matter is that the *New King James Version* represents Satan's ultimate deception to oppose God's remnant in the closing days of the New Testament age. Having enlisted the lukewarm materialist with his NIV, the devil sets a trap for the diligent soul winner with the NKJV. Although his worldly counterparts embraced the oldest is best theory of manuscript evidences, the true Bible believer refused to abandon the Majority Text, retaining the Divine commendation of, 'thou has kept my word.' Thus we find Satan attempting to wean him away from his *Authorised Version* with the deceitful half-step of a generic look-alike, TRANSLATED FROM THE TRUSTWORTHY TEXTUS RECEPTUS! ...(capitals in original).

And Terry Watkins writes similarly:
> And among his [Satan's] greatest counterfeit's is the *New King James Bible* (NKJV). Christians that would never touch a *New International Version* (NIV), *New American Standard* (NASV), *Revised Standard* (RSV), the *New Revised Standard* (NRSV) or other *per*-versions are being "seduced" by the subtle NKJV.
> And though the *New King James* does indeed bear a "likeness" to the 1611 King James Bible, as you'll soon

see, there's something else coiled (see Genesis 3:1) *"underneath the cover"* of the NKJV (emphasis in original).

Terry Watkins, along with James L. Melton, writes further:

> We will now give some special attention to one of the deadliest translations on the market—the *New King James Version*, first published in 1979. It is a deadly version because it's editors have succeeded in deceiving the body of Christ on two main points: (1) That it's a King James Bible (which is a lie), and (2) that it's based on the Textus Receptus (which is only a partial truth). The following information should be helpful when dealing with Christians who have been swindled by the Laodicean lovers of filthy lucre.

Watkins and Melton then give 16 reasons to support their claims. The first four are general comments about the NKJV and will be dealt with in this chapter. The rest of them deal with verses the writers claim are mistranslated in the NKJV. Such verses will be discussed in the next two chapters.

NKJV Copyright

Watkins and Melton give their first reason:
> 1. The text of the NKJV is copyrighted by Thomas Nelson Publishers, while there is no copyright today on the text of the KJV. If your KJV has maps or notes, then it may have a copyright, but the text itself does not.

This statement is true. The NKJV, as with most modern versions, is copyrighted. But be sure to note the word "today" in this quote. The KJV was copyrighted when it was first produced, but its copyright has long since run out. The same would be true for any other version which was published more than 70 years ago.

A version previously mentioned that would fit this category is *Young's Literal Translation*. Other such versions would be the *Revised Version*, the *American Standard Version*, *The Darby Bible*, and probably many others this writer is not aware of.

In addition, the *Revised Webster's Bible*, even though it was done in 1995, is also in the public domain. And the *World English Bible*, from its inception, was designed to be a public domain version.

Moreover, given that "the labourer is worthy of his hire" (Luke 10:7; KJV, see also 1 Tim 5:18), this writer sees no reason why the translators and publishers of Bible versions should not profit from their efforts. Much work goes into producing a Bible version.

NKJV Logo

Watkins and Melton's second reason is:
2.   There's nothing "new" about the NKJV logo. It is a "666" symbol of the *pagan* trinity which was used in the ancient Egyptian mysteries. It was also used by satanist Aleister Crowley around the turn of this century. The symbol can be seen on the *New King James Bible*, on certain rock albums (like Led Zepplin's), or you can see it on the cover of such New Age books as *The Aquarian Conspiracy* (emphasis in original).

This is a claim often made by KJV onlyists. And it is true that the triquetra symbol seen on the cover of the NKJV is used as a pagan symbol.

Watkins correctly notes:
One of the most occultic television shows ever aired is "Charmed". "Charmed" details the spells and occultic practices of three witches. The "NKJV symbol" is the

show's primary symbol of witchcraft and is splattered throughout the series. Notice the "NKJV symbol" displayed on "The Book of Shadows". The Book of Shadows is commonly used in witchcraft and satanism.

But Watkins is incorrect when he states, "And why does *The Aquarian Conspiracy*, a key New Age "handbook", bear a similar symbol? New Agers freely admit it represents three inter-woven "6"s or "666".

When I took a class on "Christianity and the New Age" at seminary, we used *The Aquarian Conspiracy* as one of our sources for New Age teachings, and we specifically talked about the symbol on the cover. The professor mentioned about this "666" claim, but refuted it as being untrue. The symbolism behind it in New Age circles is to show the unity of all things, i.e. pantheism.

All that said, it must be asked, why did the editors of the NKJV choose this symbol? Can it seriously be believed that Thomas Nelson used this symbol so that they would have a pagan symbol on the Bible's cover? Or could there be another reason?

Inside most editions of the NKJV is the following explanation, "The triquetra (from a Latin word meaning "three-cornered") is an ancient symbol for the Trinity. It comprises three interwoven arcs, distinct yet equal and inseparable, symbolizing that the Father, Son, and Holy Spirit are three distinct yet equal Persons and indivisibly one God" (NKJV, p. ii).

So, it would seem, there is a completely different meaning for the triquetra than the pagan interpretation that KJV onlyists refer to. Now which came first, the pagan interpretation or the Christian one, this writer cannot say. But it really doesn't' matter. There is nothing inherently "sinister" about a symbol. It is the meaning that is attached to it that matters.

For instance, a decorated evergreen tree was used in some pagan ceremonies in times past. And for this reason, some fundamentalist Christians will refuse to have a Christmas tree in their homes. But most Christians don't give this a second thought. No Christian today puts up a Christmas tree to use as part of pagan ceremony.

The same would be true for the triquetra. Any possible pagan connotations are only there if one reads them into it. But if someone is using it to illustrate the doctrine of the Trinity, then there are no pagan connotations to it.

But along these lines, Watkins writes:

Thomas Nelson Publishers (publishers of the NKJV) claim, on the inside-cover, the symbol, "...is an ancient symbol for the Trinity." But Acts 17:29, clearly FORBIDS such symbology: "...we ought NOT to think that the Godhead is like unto gold, or silver, or stone, GRAVEN BY ART and man's device."

The triquetra is not an "image" of God that people create to worship, which is what Paul is referring to in this verse. It is a symbol used to illustrate a very difficult theological concept. This writer has used this very symbol for this purpose in articles I have written defending the doctrine of the Trinity. And, by the way, the doctrine of the Trinity is not "pagan" as Watkins and Melton assert. It is a Biblical doctrine. Three chapters in my *Scripture Workbook* are devoting to demonstrating the Biblical basis for the doctrine.

NKJV Changes

Watkins and Melton's third reason is actually three reasons combined into one:

3. It is estimated that the NKJV makes over 100,000 translation changes, which comes to *over eighty changes per page and about three changes per verse*! A great number of these changes bring the NKJV in line with the readings of such Alexandrian perversions as the NIV and

the RSV. Where changes are not made in the text, subtle footnotes often give credence to the Westcott and Hort Greek Text (emphasis in original).

Each of the three arguments in this paragraph will be addressed separately. First is the statement about the number of changes in the NKJV as compared to the KJV.

Lougran writes similarly in this regard, "Conservative estimates of the total translation changes in the NKJV are generally put at over 100,000! This is an average of 82 changes for each of the 1219 pages in the NKJV."

This writer doesn't doubt this number. It was mentioned in Chapter Twelve that there are probably tens of thousands of archaic words in the KJV that would need changed to update the KJV into modern-day English.

Moreover, the NKJV does have the word "New" in its title. There are many other versions today that also have this word in their titles. And generally speaking, if one compares the "New" version with the old one, they will find there are very different. For instance, the *New American Standard Bible* differs considerably from the *American Standard Version* it is based on.

So it is not surprising that the NKJV differs considerably from the KJV. The important question is, are these changes for the better or for the worse? In the case of the updating of archaic words, they are definitely for the better, as the previous chapter showed. And in the cases of changes in translation, they are also generally for the better. This will be demonstrated in the next two chapters.

As for the second point about the NKJV being in line with Alexandrian readings, this issue will be addressed later.

NKJV Textual Notes

Watkins and Melton's third point above is about the textual notes in the NKJV. These show textual variants between the *Textus Receptus* (TR, which the NKJV is based on), the Critical Text (which this book uses the abbreviation CT for, but for which the NKJV uses "NU," referring to Nestle-Aland/ United Bible Societies, the two groups publishing a CT type of text), and the Majority Text (which this book uses the abbreviation MT for, but for which the NKJV uses "M").

These textual notes are a source of major complaint in KJV only writings. David Cloud, for instance, wrote an entire article on, "The Doubt Producing Margin of the New King James Version." In it, he states, "The editors of the NKJV claim they are honoring the Received Text with their *New King James Bible*, but they have given credibility to the corrupted UBS text by placing its doubt-producing readings in the margin of their Bible."

I can understand the KJV onlyists' complaints in this regard. I struggled considerably over whether I should include textual variants in my own translation, the *Analytical-Literal Translation* (ALT). As indicated previously in this book, I personally have found the variant notes in the NKJV to be helpful. And I do believe they help to dispel confusion that can be caused at Bible studies by different readings in different versions.

However, the KJV only people have a point. The variant notes do seem to give credence to the CT. They can make it sound like the CT is just as good as the TR or MT.

So for the ALT, I came up with a compromise. I decided to include the textual variants, but in a separate appendix in the back of the Bible rather than as notes on the same page as the text. I also did not use any kind of superscript footnote markers like the NKJV does to indicate where there are variants within the text. So someone can easily ignore the variants by simply not turning to the back of the Bible.

Moreover, the first two sentences in the appendix read, "*The Analytical-Literal Translation* is based on the 2001 edition of the *Byzantine Majority Text.* The translator believes this Greek text most accurately reflects the original manuscripts." So I made it clear in the introduction to the notes that I believe the MT is superior to the CT and even the TR. I also referred readers to this book for a discussion one why this is so.

But it should be noted, so does the NKJV. The "Preface" to the NKJV mentions briefly some of the arguments discussed in detail in this book. It mentions the fact that the CT is based on a relatively few number of manuscripts and that these manuscripts disagree with each other substantially.

The Preface then states:
On the other hand, the great majority of existing manuscripts are in substantial agreement...

A new group of New Testament scholars are persuaded that the best guide to a precise Greek text is the close consensus of the majority of the manuscripts. The Greek text obtained by using this rule is called the Majority Text" (p.v).

But Cloud mentions another reason he dislikes the NKJV notes:
The marginal notes in the NKJV New Testament largely show the omissions and changes from the Nestle-Aland Greek text, a revision of the Westcott-Hort text of 1881. The note at 1 Timothy 3:16 says, "NU Who," telling the reader that "God" is removed from this important verse and is replaced with the almost meaningless "Who." The reader is left wondering why. If he were to pick up the popular *New International Version* to check further, he would be led even farther astray, as already noted, by being told that only "some manuscripts" have the word "God."

This variant was discussed in detail in Chapter Seven. There it was noted that only a few manuscripts have "who" while literally hundreds have "God." So yes, the NIV note is misleading, to say the least. And also, yes, someone only reading the NKJV would wonder why one text has "who" and another has "God." And it would have been possible for the NKJV, and for my ALT, to have said something like, "A few manuscripts have 'who'." But even this wouldn't tell the whole story. It requires an extensive discussion to fully explain it.

However, such an explanation would have been needed not just for 1Timothy 3:16, but also for every one of the hundreds of significant variants between the three Greek texts. But with the limited space available in the margin (or appendix) of a Bible version, this simply is not possible.

So this writer did basically the same thing as the NKJV did: list the variants without comment. If people are left wondering why there are such variants, then maybe they'll be motivated to research the issue and end up reading a book like this.

The bottom line is, there is no perfect solution. The KJV onlyists want the CT to simply be ignored. But, unfortunately, this is not going to happen. There are millions of Bible versions based on the CT floating around. So even if someone is using a TR or MT based version, he or she is eventually going to come across a CT based version, and the question of why they differ will be raised anyway. At some point, the serious student of the Bible will have to study and make a decision on this difficult issue, whether there are textual notes in Bible versions or not.

NKJV Textual Base

Watkins and Melton give their final reason to be discussed in this chapter:

4. While passing off as being true to the Textus Receptus, the NKJV IGNORES the Receptus over 1,200 times (capitals in original).

Lougran again writes similarly:

Along this line of abuse, the most shocking revelation about the *'New' King James Version* is that it is literally laced with **'old'** readings from the *Revised Standard* and *New American Standard Versions*. This revival of Alexandrian readings is one of the best-kept secrets of the decade (bolding in original).

This type of claim was mentioned in Chapter Twelve. There, KJV onlyists were quoted as saying the NKJV is based on the CT, not the TR. Here the claim is that the NKJV is based on the TR, but that it deviates from it and follows the CT at times.

However, neither of these articles nor any others I have been able to find actually list verses where the NKJV is supposedly following the CT. So it is hard to comment.

Watkins and Melton do state, "there are 22 omissions of "hell," along similar supposed omissions in the NKJV. However, the NKJV does not omit "hell"—it simply translates the word differently than the KJV. For instance, the KJV has "hell" in Matthew 11:23 while the NKJV has "Hades." The same is true for the other supposed omissions. It is a translation difference, not a textual one.

And such translation differences are probably what Watkins and Melton, along with Lougran, are thinking of when they claim that the NKJV has Alexandrian readings in it. The NKJV is not following the CT; instead, in places where the TR and CT agree, the NKJV has the same translation of a passage that some CT versions have. The question then is, is this a correct translation? Again, such a question will be addressed in the next two chapters.

In addition, while I was translating the textual notes for the ALT, I had all three Greek texts open in my *BibleWorks*™ *for Windows*™ program. I also had several versions of the Bible open, including the NKJV. And at no time did I notice an instance of where the NKJV followed the CT rather than the TR.

However, I do notice a couple of times where the KJV deviated from the TR.

But in theses rare cases, I think the problem was that the KJV was based on a different edition of the TR than I was using. There is actually not one TR, but several Greek texts which go by the name *Textus Receptus*. These editions are virtually identical, but they do have some minor differences between them (see Chapter Ten for further details).

I was using F.H.A Scrivener's 1894 edition. This is the most recent edition of the TR, and the one I suspect the NKJV translators used. But the KJV was probably based on Beza's and Stevens' texts from the late 1500's. So in the rare places where the NKJV differs from the KJV due to a textual not translation difference, it is probably because the NKJV is based on a slightly different TR than the editions the KJV translators used.

Conclusion

The KJV onlyists do a lot of screaming about the NKJV. But when their arguments are looked at logically, not emotionally or with dogmatism, they simply do not hold up. The next two chapters will look at verses where the KJV onlyists claim the NKJV is mistranslated, while the KJV has the "correct" translation.

Bibliography:

BibleWorks™ *for Windows*™ Copyright © 1992-1999 *BibleWorks*, L.C.C. Big Fork, MT: Hermeneutika. Programmed by Michael S. Bushell and Michael D. Tan.

Cloud, David. "The Doubt Producing Margin of the New King James Version" (http://wayoflife.org/~dcloud/fbns/nkjvdoubt.htm).

Loughran, D B. "Which is the real Word of God?" (http://rhema-av-1611.lima.net.pe/kjvbook.html).

New King James Version. Nashville, TN: Thomas Nelson Publishers, 1982.

Watkins, Terry. "The New King James Bible: Counterfeit" (http://www.av1611.org/).

Watkins, Terry and James L. Melton. "The Attack on the Bible!" (http://rhema-av-1611.lima.net.pe/kjv.html).

Chapter Fifteen
Verse Evaluations: KJV vs. NKJV

Part One

In their diatribes against the *New King James Version* (NKJV), *King James Version* (KJV) onlyists will often list passages where they claim the KJV has the correct translation while the NKJV has mistranslated the passage. In this and the next chapter, these claims will be answered by evaluating many of these passages.

But first, an important point needs to be noted about how KJV onlyists come up with these supposed mistakes in the NKJV. In none of their examples do they ever refer to the Hebrew or Greek texts. They simply assume the KJV rendering is better simply because it is the KJV. But without demonstrating the KJV is the better rendering of the original Hebrew or Greek, their charts are meaningless. They are nothing but circular reasoning.

What they do appeal to, however, is what they believe is correct theology to "prove" the KJV has the correct translation of a passage. But translators should not allow their own theological biases to influence how they translate a passage. The lexical and grammatical details of the original text should be the primary consideration.

It is for this reason that in the following evaluations a wide variety of Hebrew and Greek reference works will be utilized. A possible interpretation will be mentioned at times, but only after the correct translation has been established on lexical and grammatical grounds. See the Bibliography at the end of the next chapter for a complete list of all resources consulted.

The verses to be evaluated are taken from a variety of KJV only sources, including Web pages, KJV only tracts, and personal correspondences this writer has had with KJV onlyists. In most cases, below the verses is first a quote or two by KJV onlyists, then my response. But in some cases, the KJV onlyists' claims from these sources will be summarized, not specifically quoted. In the Bibliography at the end of the next chapter are listed all the KJV only sources that were consulted.

The "changes" the KJV onlyists are complaining about are in capitals in the verses. All emphases in the KJV onlyists quotes are in the originals. And they do "emphasize" a lot of things, as will be seen!

Matthew 11:23

KJV: And thou, Capernaum, which art exalted unto heaven, shalt be brought down to HELL: for if the mighty works, which have been done in thee, had been done in Sodom, it would have remained until this day.

NKJV: "And you, Capernaum, who are exalted to heaven, will be brought down to HADES; for if the mighty works which were done in you had been done in Sodom, it would have remained until this day.

In his "Bible Version Comparison Chart," Watkins indicates that the NKJV omits "hell" in this and in many other verses. However, the NKJV does not omit this word. It simply translates it differently than the KJV.

But at least Watkins gets this part correct in an article elsewhere:

How about that *"obsolete word"* - **"hell"**. The NKJV removes the word "hell" 23 times! And how do they make it "much clearer"? *By replacing "hell" with "Hades" and "Sheol"! Webster's New Collegiate Dictionary* defines Hades: *"the underground abode of the dead in Greek **MYTHOLOGY"**. By making it "much clearer" - they turn your Bible into **MYTHOLOGY**!* Not only that, Hades is not always a place of torment or terror! The Assyrian Hades is an abode of blessedness with silver skies called "Happy Fields". *In the satanic New Age Movement, Hades is an intermediate state of purification!*

Who in their right mind would think "Hades" or "Sheol" is "up-to-date" and "much clearer" than "hell"? (Watkins, "Counterfeit").

All this shouting is rather interesting given that *hades* is the Greek word. The NKJV has simply transliterated the Greek letters into English letters. So *hades* is what Mathew originally wrote, which would make the Gospel writer the "myth writer" given Watkins' reasoning. Moreover, Watkins is allowing his theological viewpoint of there necessarily being torment in *Hades* to determine which rendering he declares to be correct.

It is difficult to say whether it is best to translate or transliterate controversial and theological charged words. But it should be noted that along with *hades*, the KJV also translates *gehenna* as "hell" (e.g. Matt 5:22), while the NKJV only translates the latter as "hell." So the distinction between these two words is lost in the KJV but retained in the NKJV.

As for the meaning of *hades*, Friberg defines it as, *Hades* (lit[erally]. *an unseen place);* (1) the place of the dead *underworld* (AC 2.27); (2) usu[ally] in the NT as the temporary underworld prison where the souls of the ungodly await the judgment (LU 16.23); (3) personif[ied] as following along after Death (RV 6.8). But Newman has, " Hades, the world of the dead; death; perhaps hell, the place of final punishment."

So the lexicons disagree as to whether *hades* is synonymous with "hell" or not. Friberg says it is where souls go before the final judgment, but Newman indicates it is the same place as "hell," the place of eternal torment after judgment. There is also disagreement over whether *hades* is a place of torment or the place where all souls go before the final judgment.

Given these disagreements, it would at least be best to render *hades* and *gehenna* differently and not to render *hades* in a way which must include torment. The NKJV has done neither while the KJV has done both. And by doing so, the KJV has intruded interpretation into the text.

Matthew 12:32

KJV: And whosoever speaketh a word against the Son of man, it shall be forgiven him: but whosoever speaketh against the Holy Ghost, it shall not be forgiven him, neither in this WORLD, neither in the *WORLD* to come.

NKJV: "Anyone who speaks a word against the Son of Man, it will be forgiven him; but whoever speaks against the Holy Spirit, it will not be forgiven him, either in this AGE or in the *AGE* to come.

In order to "harmonize" with the satanic New Age Movement (and of course the NIV, NASV, RSV, NRSV!), the NKJV changes *"end of the WORLD"* to *"end of the AGE"*! And in it's no longer the *"WORLD to come"* but *"AGE to come"*. The New Age Movement teaches a series of ages (hence the name: New **AGE**). See Matthew 12:32, 13:39, 13:40, 13:49, 24:3, 28:20, Mark 10:30, Luke 13:30, 20:34,35, 1 Cor 1:21 (Watkins, "Counterfeit").

The Greek word means:
era, time, age; (1) as a segment of contemporary time, *lifetime, era, the present age* (LU 16.8); (2) of time gone by *the past, earliest times* (LU 1.70); (3) of prolonged and unlimited time *eternity* (1T 1.17); (4) of time to come *eternity, the age to come* (LU 20.35); idiomatically *eis ton aiona* lit[erally] *into the age,* i.e. *forever, eternally* (JN 6.51); *eis ton aiona ton aionon,*

lit[erally] *into the ages of the ages,* i.e. *forever and ever, forevermore* (HE 1.8); (5) pl[ural] as a spatial concept, of the creation as having a beginning and moving forward through long but limited time *universe, world* (HE 1.2, 9.26, 11.3) (Friberg).

Note that "age" or something similar to it is the most basic meaning of the word. "World" is not even mentioned until the last possible definition. So "age" is definitely the most literal rendering.

Furthermore, note that the phrase "forever and ever" (as it is rendered in both the KJV and NKJV) is literally "into the ages of the ages." If Watkins were correct that the word must be translated as "world," then this phrase would have to be, "into the worlds of the worlds." Not only would this not make any sense, but it would also be impossible to get the figurative rendering of "forever and ever" from it.

As for Watkins' rants about the New Age, the fact that "age" is in the name of their movement does not make the NKJV "New Age" for using this translation. "Age" in this context simply means, "a particular period of history" (*Webster's*). With this definition, there *is* "a series of ages," but this simply indicates the progression of time. There's nothing "New Age" about it.

Matthew 12:40

KJV: For as Jonas was three days and three nights in the WHALE'S belly; so shall the Son of man be three days and three nights in the heart of the earth.

NKJV: "For as Jonah was three days and three nights in the belly OF THE GREAT FISH, so will the Son of Man be three days and three nights in the heart of the earth.

change *"whale"* to *"fish"* (ditto NIV) I don't guess it matters (what's the truth got to do with it?), the Greek word used in Matthew 12:40 is *ketos*. The scientific study of whales just happens to be - ***CETOLOGY*** - from the Greek *ketos* for whale and *logos* for study! The scientific name for whales just happens to be - ***CETACEANS*** - from the Greek *ketos* for whale! (Watkins, "Counterfeit").

Watkins has committed a very common fallacy here. He is reading the current use of a word back into the Bible. What a word means today may or may not have a relationship to what it meant in Biblical times.

That said, Friberg defines the word as, "*sea monster, large fish* (MG 12.40)." Lidell and Scott have, "*any sea-monster* or *huge fish*." Newman has, "large sea creature." Louw and Nida have, "any large sea monster - 'big fish, huge fish.'" And A.T. Robertson has, "Sea-monster, huge fish."

So no lexicon, older or newer, has "whale" here. So the NKJV is more accurate than the KJV. It simply is not known what kind of creature Jonah was in. It is possible that it was no known creature at all, but one God specially "prepared" for Jonah (Jonah 1:7).

Matthew 18:26 – Matthew 20:20

KJV: The servant therefore fell down, and WORSHIPPED him, saying, Lord, have patience with me, and I will pay thee all.

NKJV: "The servant therefore fell down before him, saying, 'Master, have patience with me, and I will pay you all.'

KJV: Then came to him the mother of Zebedee's children with her sons, WORSHIPPING *him*, and desiring a certain thing of him.

NKJV: Then the mother of Zebedee's sons came to Him with her sons, KNEELING DOWN and asking something from Him.

Matthew 18:26; 20:20: The NKJV removes *"worshipped him"* (robbing worship from Jesus) (NIV, NASV, RSV, NRSV) (Watkins, "Counterfeit").

Matthew 20:20: Worshipping and kneeling are two very different words. Worshipping is directed toward God and is an attitude of the heart. Kneeling is an attitude of the body, and can be directed toward anyone. (You don't have to kneel to worship!). Even the Greek says "worship" is the correct word. (Sargent, p.5).

First off, I cannot help but comment on Sargent's last sentence, "Even the Greek says "worship" is the correct word." He makes it sound like this is something "special." But a translation should always report what "the Greek says."

That said, Watkins is half correct in his comment on these two passages. In the first verse the NKJV does appear to have omitted a word. The phrase "fell down" and the word "worshipped" are translations of two different Greek words, but the NKJV only has "fell down", unless "before" is supposed to be a translation of the second word. However, in the second verse, the NKJV uses "kneeling down" where the KJV has "worshipping." In any case, it is the same Greek word in question in both verses.

Friberg defines the word as:

(1) fr[om] a basic sense *bow down to kiss* someone's feet, garment hem, or the ground in front of him; (2) in the NT of worship or veneration of a divine or supposedly divine object, expressed concr[etely] w[ith] falling face down in front of someone *worship, venerate, do obeisance to;* (a) toward God (MT 4.10); (b) toward

Jesus (MT 2.2); (c) toward the devil and demons (MT 4.9; RV 9.20); (d) toward idols (AC 7.43); (e) toward human beings as given or claiming to have divine power or authority (RV 3.9; 13.4b).

Liddell and Scott have, "Plut.:-*to make obeisance* to the gods, *fall down and worship, to worship, adore,* **2.** of the Oriental fashion of *making the* salam or *prostrating oneself before* kings and superiors, ... *to make obeisance* to him as king."

So the word can mean, "to fall down before someone and worship" or it can mean, "to prostrate oneself before someone in reverence" as was in done in those times before kings. So neither the KJV nor the NKJV capture both parts of the meaning of the word. Both the physical action and the reason for the action are included in the verb. But which reason is correct for the falling down, reverence or worship, needs to be determined by the context.

In the first passage, Jesus is telling a parable. The "Lord" or "Master" is not Jesus, but an earthly king. So "worship" is definitely incorrect while "fell down" is closer. Since there is a separate word for "fall down" in the verse, the most correct rendering would be something like, "fell down and prostrated himself in reverence."

In the second passage, Jesus is the subject. So either "fell down in worship" or "fell down in reverence" could be correct. The difference would be what was the woman's state of heart. Was she showing Jesus worship or just reverence? It is impossible to determine from the context. But it is doubtful that the deity of Jesus was well known at this early point in salvation history, and given she was a Jew, she would not have been quick to accept Jesus' deity. So "fall down in reverence" would probably be most correct.

Matthew 21:32

KJV: For John came unto you in the way of righteousness, and ye believed him not: but the publicans and the harlots believed him: and ye, when ye had seen *it*, REPENTED NOT afterward, that ye might believe him.

NKJV: "For John came to you in the way of righteousness, and you did not believe him; but tax collectors and harlots believed him; and when you saw *it*, you DID NOT afterward RELENT and believe him.

Another one of those "obsolete words" is "repent". They take it out 44 times! And how does the NKJV make it "much clearer"? In Matthew 21:32 they use "relent". Matthew 27:3 it's "remorseful" Or Romans 11:29 they change "repentance" to "irrevocable" (Watkins, "Counterfeit).

The Greek word here is *metamalomi*. It means, "(1) *feel remorse, become concerned about afterwards, regret* (MT 27.3); (2) *change one's mind, think differently afterwards* (HE 7.21)" (Friberg).

This word differs from *metanoeo*, "strictly, *perceive afterwards,* w[ith] the implication of being too late to avoid consequences; (1) predom[innately] of a relig[ious] and ethical change in the way one thinks about acts *repent, change one's mind, be converted* (MT 3.2); (2) as feeling remorse *regret, feel sorry* (LU 17.3, 4)" (Friberg).

So there is overlap between these two words, but only the second properly means, "repent." The KJV translates both words as "repent." So it blurs the distinction between these two words, while using a translation for the first that is not strictly accurate.

The NKJV, however, renders the two differently, showing the distinction. It also more correctly uses "repent" only for the second. But its "relent" is a bit too weak for the first word. Something like "regret" would be better.

Mark 13:6

> KJV: For many shall come in my name, saying, I AM *CHRIST*; and shall deceive many.
> NKJV: "For many will come in My name, saying, 'I AM *HE,'* and will deceive many.

> removes *"Christ"* (NIV, NASV, RSV, NRSV) (Watkins, "Counterfeit").

It's interesting that Watkins would say the NKJV and other versions "removes Christ" given that the word Christ is in italics in the KJV. This means the word was added by the translation. A version cannot "remove" a word that is not in the original text.

The question only is, what word should be added? This writer thinks that none should be! It is very possible that the ones coming in Jesus' name are saying, "I am!"—making a claim to deity (compare John 8:58). So I would say both versions are wrong for adding anything here and hiding this possibility.

Luke 7:19

> KJV: And John calling *unto him* two of his disciples sent *them* to Jesus, saying, Art thou HE THAT SHOULD COME? or look we for another?
> NKJV: And John, calling two of his disciples to *him,* sent *them* to Jesus, saying, "Are You THE COMING ONE, or do we look for another?"

The New Age Movement and the occult are longing for one called the Maitreya. The Bible calls him the Anti-Christ. New Ager's refer to him as the *"the Coming One"* - *AND SO DOES THE NKJV!* In Luke 7:19, 20 (see also Matt 11:3) John told his disciples to ask Jesus: *"Are You THE COMING ONE..."* In the "The Great Invocation", a "prayer" highly reverenced among New Agers and chanted to "invoke" the Maitreya, says, *"Let Light and Love and Power and Death, Fulfil the purpose of the Coming One"* (Watkins, "Counterfeit").

The Greek text here is a definite article followed by a substantival participle (*ho erchomenos*). The most literal way to render this grammatical form is by "the Coming One." Most any interlinear would have this rendering. So the NKJV is not being "New Age" but is using a literal rendering of the Greek text while the KJV is deviating significantly from a literal rendering. It must be Luke, the Gospel writer, who is "New Age."

John 1:3

KJV: All things were made BY him; and without him was not any thing made that was made.
NKJV: All things were made THROUGH Him, and without Him nothing was made that was made.

change *"All things were made BY him;"* to *"All things were made THROUGH Him"* (NIV, NRSV, RSV) (Watkins, "Counterfeit").

The preposition in question is *dia*. Prepositions in Greek, as in English, can have a wide variety of meanings. Deciding which is correct in a particular context can be difficult, especially since there can be theological implications to different renderings.

In addition, prepositions in Greek have different possible meanings based on the case of the noun they modify. In this instance, the case of the noun is a genitive. And with a genitive, *dia* can mean, "through, by means of, with; during, throughout (*dia panto*, continually); through, among, throughout" (Newman).

So "through" is a legitimate rendering, but so is "by means of." This latter rendering is similar but not quite identical to "by." But other lexicons (e.g. Friberg's) do give "by" as a possible rendering. So which is correct in this context?

A.T. Robertson writes:

By him (*dia autou*). By means of him as the intermediate agent in the work of creation. The Logos is John's explanation of the creation of the universe. The author of Hebrews (Heb 1:2) names God's Son as the one "through whom he made the ages." Paul pointedly asserts that "the all things were created in him" (Christ) and "the all things stand created through him and unto him" (Col 1:16). Hence it is not a peculiar doctrine that John here enunciates. In 1Co 8:6, Paul distinguishes between the Father as the primary source (*ex ou*) of the all things and the Son as the intermediate agent as here (*dia ou*).

So other passages clearly show Jesus was the "intermediate agent" in creation. Hence, "by" would not be correct as it would make Jesus, not the Father, the "primary agent" in creation. So "through" or "by means of" would be the most correct translation.

John 4:24

KJV: God is A SPIRIT: and they that worship him must worship him in spirit and in truth.

NKJV: God is SPIRIT, and those who worship Him must worship in spirit and truth.

change *"God is a spirit"* to the impersonal, New Age pantheistic, *"God is spirit"* (NIV, NASV, NRSV, RSV) (Watkins, "Counterfeit").

First off, there is no indefinite article ("a") in the Greek language. So in no sense can it be said that the NKJV has "omitted" the word "a" as KJV onlyists have said to this writer in personal correspondences. But there is a definite article in the Greek language. When it appears with a noun it is generally translated as "the."

When a noun does not have the article it is called an "anarthrous" construction. The most important distinction between a noun with the article versus a noun without it is explained by Dana and Mantey, "An object of thought may be conceived of from two points of view: as to identity or quality. To convey the first point of view the Greek uses the article; for the second the anarthrous construction is used" (p.149).

In this instance, "Spirit" is used without the article. So it is referring to the "quality" of God. "Quality" means, "1. a. An inherent or distinguishing characteristic; a property. b. A personal trait, especially a character trait...2. Essential character; nature" (*American Heritage® Dictionary*). Words that have been used in theology to describe this concept are: essence, nature, or substance.

Putting all of the above together, an expressive way to render this passage would be something like, "God is as to His essence Spirit." But given the awkwardness and interpretative nature of this rendering, the NKJV's translation is probably best. It comes closest to the more expansive rendering in showing that God's "essence" is being discussed. And saying that God is in essence Spirit does not mean He is an "impersonal, pantheistic God." It means He does not have a physical body.

John 14:2

KJV: In my Father's house are many MANSIONS: if *it were* not *so*, I would have told you. I go to prepare a place for you.

NKJV: "In My Father's house are many MANSIONS; if *it were* not *so,* I would have told you. I go to prepare a place for you.

CHG [change] "mansions" TO "rooms", "dwelling places" - NI, NAS, **NKJ**, RS, NRS, LB, NC (Watkins, "Comparison")

Watkins lists the NKJV with other versions as rendering the word in question as "rooms" or "dwelling places". But as can be seen, the NKJV is the same as the KJV here. So Watkins is either being dishonest, or, giving him the benefit of the doubt, maybe he just made a mistake.

That said, the word in question means, "(1) *a staying, tarrying* ... (2) *dwelling place, abode, home* (JN 14.2)." So the idea of "mansion" is not really contained in the word. It simply means a "dwelling place." So the versions that do use "rooms" or "dwelling places" are actually more correct.

Acts 3:13/ Acts 4:27

KJV: The God of Abraham, and of Isaac, and of Jacob, the God of our fathers, hath glorified his SON Jesus; whom ye delivered up, and denied him in the presence of Pilate, when he was determined to let him go.

NKJV: "The God of Abraham, Isaac, and Jacob, the God of our fathers, glorified His SERVANT Jesus, whom you delivered up and denied in the presence of Pilate, when he was determined to let Him go."

KJV: For of a truth against thy holy CHILD Jesus, whom thou hast anointed, both Herod, and Pontius Pilate, with the Gentiles, and the people of Israel, were gathered together,

NKJV: "For truly against Your holy SERVANT Jesus, whom You anointed, both Herod and Pontius Pilate, with the Gentiles and the people of Israel, were gathered together

Acts 4:27,30: CHG [change] "holy child" TO "holy servant" (attacks deity) (Watkins, "Comparison Chart").

The Greek word is the same in Acts 3:13 and 4:27,30, along with in Acts 3:26. The NKJV uses "Servant" in all four verses; the KJV uses "Son" in the first two and "child" in the latter two. And, of course, KJV onlyists complain about the "change" in the NKJV. But what does the word actually mean?

Copying from the *Online Bible*:
3816 *pais* {*paheece*} perhaps from 3817; TDNT - 5:636,759; n m/f
AV - servant 10, child 7, son (Christ) 2, son 1, manservant 1, maid 1, maiden 1, young man 1; 24
1) a child, boy or girl
1a) infants, children
2) servant, slave
2a) an attendant, servant, spec. a king's attendant, minister

And Friberg defines the word as:
child; (1) in ref[erence] to age *child,* either *boy* (MT 2.16) or *girl* (LU 8.51); (2) in ref[erence] to descent *son, child* (JN 4.51); (3) in ref[erence] to social position *servant, slave "boy"* (LU 7.7, cf. *doulos* v2); as a servant in a ruler's household *attendant, courtier* (MT 14.2); (4) fig[uratively] in ref[erence] to relation to God *servant* (AC 4.25).

So in the KJV, the word is rendered "servant" as often as "son" or "child," and it can have any one of these meanings depending on the context. Moreover, the same word is used in Acts 4:25 in reference to David, and both the KJV and NKJV render it as "servant" in that verse. This use is especially significant as "son" would not fit the context. Also, it occurs right in between the four times the word is being applied to Jesus.

Now KJV onlyists will declare that "servant" cannot be correct in this context since God cannot be a servant of God. But Robertson explains, "**His servant** (*ton paida autou*). As in verse 13, the Messiah as God's Servant." So it is in His humanity as Messiah that Jesus is God's Servant. As such, there is no "attack" on Jesus' Deity here. Jesus' was full God and full man.

In addition, it should be noted that the NKJV is more consistent in its translation of the word in question in Acts chapters three and four. The word occurs five times in these chapters, and four times the NKJV renders it as "Servant" and once as, "servant." The KJV, however, translates it variously as: servant (once), Son (twice), and child (twice).

Acts 7:45 and Hebrews 4:8

KJV: Which also our fathers that came after brought in with JESUS into the possession of the Gentiles, whom God drave out before the face of our fathers, unto the days of David;

NKJV "which our fathers, having received it in turn, also brought with JOSHUA into the land possessed by the Gentiles, whom God drove out before the face of our fathers until the days of David,

KJV: For if JESUS had given them rest, then would he not afterward have spoken of another day.

NKJV: For if JOSHUA had given them rest, then He would not afterward have spoken of another day.

> *"Jesus"* is changed to *"Joshua"* (NIV, NASV, RSV)
> (Watkins, "Counterfeit").

It's interesting that Watkins would list these verses as mistakes in the NKJV as they are ones that are often pointed to as "obvious" mistakes in the KJV.

The Greek word in these verses is the same one that is translated elsewhere in the NT as "Jesus." It is for this reason that I had a KJV onlyist claim to me that the word "literally means Jesus." However, the word here is the same one that is used for "Joshua" in the Septuagint (a second century BC Greek translation of the OT).

So the word can be rendered as either "Jesus" or "Joshua." Context determines which is correct. It is rendered in these verses as "Joshua" in all modern versions since the context indicates that it is the OT figure that is being referred to, not the Lord Jesus Christ, especially in the second passage.

It was Joshua, not Jesus, who went in with the "fathers" of the Jews into "the possession of the Gentiles" (i.e. the Promised Land). This can be seen throughout the Book of Joshua.

However, in Exodus 33:2, God says He will send "an angel" before the Israelites to drive out the current inhabitants. In the NKJV the word reads, "*My* Angel." With the word capitalized, this could be a reference to Jesus. So in this sense, it could have been Jesus who went in with the Israelites, and the KJV reading could be correct. But note that one needs to turn to the NKJV to defend the KJV reading!

But the second passage is more difficult for the KJV onlyists. Joshua did not give the Israelites "rest" since there was still fighting to be done after his death (Judges 1:1). Jesus, however, gave us true rest (Heb 4:9,10). Note, the "He" in Hebrews 4:8 is God, not Joshua, hence why it is capitalized in the NKJV. The reference is to God speaking in the OT passages quoted in verses 3-7.

That said, I have read KJV onlyists' attempts to interpret this passage with the translation being "Jesus." It is very long and involved, not simple like what was just presented. And frankly, I personally could not understand the intricate explanation, so I really cannot say if it could be correct or not.

Acts 12:4

> KJV: And when he had apprehended him, he put *him* in prison, and delivered *him* to four quaternions of soldiers to keep him; intending after EASTER to bring him forth to the people.
>
> NKJV: So when he had arrested him, he put *him* in prison, and delivered *him* to four squads of soldiers to keep him, intending to bring him before the people after PASSOVER.

change *"Easter"* to *"Passover"* (NIV, NASV, RSV, NRSV) (Watkins, "Counterfeit").

This is again an interesting verse for Watkins to list as a mistake in the NKJV as it is another one that is often pointed to as an "obvious" mistake in the KJV.

The Greek word is *pascha* and is translated in the KJV and in other versions as "Passover" every place else it occurs (e.g. Matt 26:2,17; John 6:4; 1Cor 5:7, etc.). So why the KJV translators rendered it as "Easter" here is unclear.

The word means:

the Passover; (1) as the Jewish festival, which incl[udes] the Feast of Unleavened Bread (LU 2.41); (2) in a narrower sense, of the actual Passover meal, as ordained in the OT (MK 14.1); (3) by meton[omy], the lamb slain for the Passover meal *the Passover* or *Paschal lamb* (MK 14.12a); fig[uratively] of Christ Jesus in his sacrificial death (1C 5.7).

No lexicon that I could find even gives "Easter" as a possible meaning. So there is no idea of "Easter" in the word. It's a reference to the Jewish festival, not the Christian celebration of the resurrection of the Lord.

Acts 17:22

KJV: Then Paul stood in the midst of Mars' hill, and said, *Ye* men of Athens, I perceive that in all things ye are too SUPERSTITIOUS.

NKJV: Then Paul stood in the midst of the Areopagus and said, "Men of Athens, I perceive that in all things you are very RELIGIOUS;

The word "superstitious" (AV 1611) was too strong for their stomachs (*no one is more superstitious than Conservatives and Evangelical scholars!*), so they altered it to match the words of the Modernists and Liberals whom it scaled first. Here JFV reads with the RSV and ASV. *It is not an "edition" of the AV in any sense of the word* (Ruckman).

First note that for some reason which he really doesn't explain, Ruckman refers to the NKJV as the "Jerry Falwell Version" (JFV). Secondly, he gives no support for his claim that conservative and evangelical scholars are superstitious.

That said, the meaning of this word is hard to pin down as it is a *hapax legomena* (i.e. "spoken once") meaning this is the only verse in which it occurs in Scripture. In such cases it is always hard to get an exact meaning for a word.

However, Friberg defines it as, "(1) in a bad sense *superstitious;* (2) in the NT in a neutral sense of carefulness and precision in relig[ion]. *Religious.*" Lidell and Scott define it as, "*fearing the gods:* **I.** in good sense, like *eusebes, pious, religious,* Xen. **2.** in bad sense, *superstitious, bigoted.*"

So the word can mean either superstitious or religious. So either of these is possible and neither is inaccurate. However, note that the most basic meaning for the word that Lidell and Scott give, "fearing the gods." The problem is, what does "fearing" mean? It could mean a reverent awe ("religious") or it could mean an unjustified fear ("superstitious").

The question is, does Paul first complement the Athenians before he begins to point out the deficiencies in their religious beliefs, or he does start off with declaring a major problem with their belief system, namely that it leaves them in a state of fear?

Given the difficulty of pinning down the exact meaning, possibly the best translation would be something like, "fearful of the gods." This rendering is as ambiguous as the Greek text is.

Acts 17:29

KJV: Forasmuch then as we are the offspring of God, we ought not to think that the GODHEAD is like unto gold, or silver, or stone, graven by art and man's device.

NKJV: "Therefore, since we are the offspring of God, we ought not to think that the DIVINE NATURE is like gold or silver or stone, something shaped by art and man's devising."

*And to REALLY show their sympathy with the satanic New Age Movement - **BELIEVE IT OR NOT** - in Acts 17:29 the New Age NKJV changes "Godhead" to "Divine Nature"! (ditto NIV, NASV)* (Watkins, "Comparison").

I really don't see much of a difference here. "Nature" in this context would not be referring to nature in the sense of plants and animals but in the sense of "essence" or "being." Paul is saying that the "essence" of God cannot be displayed using precious metals or stone.

Or to put it another way, "How can God's nature be copied in gold, silver, or stone?" That is the point Paul is trying to make to the Athenians.

In any case, there is strong lexical support for "divine" and even "divine nature." Rienecker defines this word in this context as, "*theios* divine" (p.309). Robertson has, "*To theion* is strictly 'the divine' nature like *theiotes* (Rom 1:20)."

Friberg defines it as, "as related to God by nature *divine* (2P 1.3); subst[antive]. *To theion, the divine nature, the divine being* (AC 17.29). And definition "1b" in Baur is, "subst[antive]. '*to theion*' divine being, divinity" (p.353). And "being" in this context would be similar to the NKJV's "Nature."

As for the KJV's "Godhead," none of the lexicon's I checked has this word as a definition. However, the meaning of "Godhead" is, "the essential being or nature of God; the Almighty" (*Webster's*). So the KJV's translation means the same as the NKJV's rendering.

With such overwhelming lexical support and with the KJV's rendering meaning the same as the NKJV's, there is no way the NKJV is "New Age" or "satanic" in this verse. What is it, however, is probably more understandable to most people today.

This discussion will be continued in the next chapter.

Bibliography:
See end of Chapter Sixteen.

Chapter Sixteen
Verse Evaluations: KJV vs. NKJV

Part Two

This discussion is continued from the previous chapter.

Romans 1:25

KJV: Who CHANGED the truth of God INTO a lie, and worshipped and served the creature more than the Creator, who is blessed for ever. Amen.

NKJV: who EXCHANGED the truth of God FOR the lie, and worshiped and served the creature rather than the Creator, who is blessed forever. Amen.

Since the NKJV has "changed the truth of God into a lie", it has also changed Romans 1:25 to read "exchanged the truth of God for the lie". This reading matches the readings of the new perversions, so *how say ye it's a King James Bible?* (Watkins and Melton).

The first Greek word in question means, *"exchange, alter, change"* (Friberg). So either rendering is correct. But a greater difficulty comes with the preposition. The word is *ev*, and when used with the dative as it is here, it can mean, "in, on, at; near, by, before; among, within; by, with; into (= *eis*); to, for (rarely)" (Newman). And Friberg states, "The primary idea is *within, in, withinness*."

So neither translation renders the proposition with its most basic meaning of "in." The NKJV's rendering only uses "rarely," but it is used. So again, neither is ideal, but either is possible. And on a final note, there is a "the" before the word "lie." So the NKJV is more accurate in this regard.

Romans 4:25

KJV: Who was delivered FOR our offences, and was raised again FOR our justification.

NKJV: "who was delivered up BECAUSE OF our offenses, and was raised BECAUSE OF our justification.

KJV onlyists claim the NKJV rendering makes Jesus' resurrection dependent on our justification, but, in reality, our justification was dependant on His resurrection.

The preposition here is *dia*. Used with the accusative as here, it means, "because of, on account of, for the sake of; through, by (rarely)" (Newman). However, Dana and Mantey indicate the meaning "because of" is "very common", but they make not such remark for the meaning "For the sake of, for" (p.102). So "because of" is more likely correct.

As for the interpretation, Jesus shed His blood and died for our justification (Matt 26:28; Mark 10:45; Rom 3:25; 5:9; Eph 1:7; 2:13). All was "finished" that was necessary for our salvation "through the blood of the cross" (John 19:30; Col 1:14,20). His resurrection came afterwards. Nowhere in Scripture is Jesus' resurrection linked to our justification. So it could be said that the KJV rendering is not accurate.

I taught a Bible study through the Book of Romans a few years back. While preparing my lessons, I struggled over the meaning of this verse. I finally concluded that Paul's point is that God raised Jesus so that we could know He had accepted Jesus' propitiation for our sins (cp. Acts 17:31).

If Jesus had stayed dead then we would have had no way of knowing that His death was "unique." But the resurrection was "because of" God's acceptance of the sacrifice.

John Gill comments on this verse:

Christ's resurrection did not procure the justification of his people, that was done by his obedience and death;

but was for the testification of it, that it might fully appear that sin was atoned for, and an everlasting righteousness was brought in; and for the application of it, or that Christ might live and see his righteousness imputed, and applied to all those for whom he had wrought it out (from the *Online Bible*).

So this commentator agrees with me that our justification depends not on Christ's resurrection, but on His death, and that this verse could be saying that His resurrection is the "proof" that our sins have been forgiven. Gill also gives the possibility that the verse is referring to Jesus being raised so that He could see the fruits of His labors. Either way, "because of" makes perfect sense in this verse while "for" does not.

1 Corinthians 1:21

KJV: For after that in the wisdom of God the world by wisdom knew not God, it pleased God by the foolishness of PREACHING to save them that believe.

NKJV: For since, in the wisdom of God, the world through wisdom did not know God, it pleased God through the foolishness of THE MESSAGE PREACHED to save those who believe.

change *"foolishness of preaching"* to *"foolishness of the message preached"* (ditto NIV, NASV, NRSV, RSV) There's nothing foolish about the gospel of Jesus Christ. ***Unless you're not saved!*** 1 Cor. 1:18 says: *"For the preaching of the cross **is to them that perish FOOLISHNESS..."** I wonder where that leaves the translators of the NKJV, NIV, NASV, RSV, NRSV?* (Watkins, "Counterfeit").

223

The Greek word under question is *kyregma*. It means, "as the content of a sacred message *what is preached, preaching, proclamation* (1C 2.4)" (Friberg). So the basic meaning of the word refers to the content of what is preached, not to the act of preaching. So the NKJV rendering is most accurate.

As for Watkins comments, as he correctly points out, previously Paul had said that the Gospel is foolishness to the unsaved, and that is probably what Paul is referring to here.

And I must add, I would never take it upon myself to judge the salvation of another as Watkins apparently does. I leave that in the hands of the only One capable of making such a judgment (James 4:11,12).

1Corinthians 1:22

KJV: For the Jews REQUIRE a sign, and the Greeks seek after wisdom:

NKJV: For Jews REQUEST a sign, and Greeks seek after wisdom;

The Jews "require" a sign, according to I Corinthians 1:22 (and according to Jesus Christ - John 4:48), but the NKJV says they only "request" a sign. *They didn't "request" one when signs first appeared in Exodus 4*, and there are numerous places throughout the Bible where God gives Israel signs when they haven't requested anything (Exo. 4, Exo. 31:13, Num. 26:10, I Sam. 2:34, Isa. 7:10-14, Luke 2:12, etc). They "require" a sign, because signs are a part of their national heritage (Watkins and Melton).

Friberg defines the Greek word as, "*ask (for), request* (MT 7.10); *ask for, demand* (LU 23.23); as making a request in prayer *ask for* (MT 21.22)." Louw and Nida have "to ask for with urgency, even to the point of demanding - 'to ask for, to demand, to plead for."

Lidell and Scott have, "*to ask, beg,* Od., etc. **2.** c. acc. rei, *to ask for, crave, demand,* Hom., etc.; o`do.n aivt. *to beg* one's departure, i.e. *ask leave* to depart, Od.:-c. acc. pers. et rei, *to ask a person for* a thing, Hom., etc.; di,kaj aivtÅ tina. fo,nou *to demand* satisfaction from one for murder, Hdt. **3.** c. acc. pers. et inf. *to ask* one *to* do, Od., etc.

None of these three lexicons even mention "require" as a possible definition. I only found one that did, Newman's lexicon, "ask, request; require, demand." So it would seem the lexical evidence overwhelming favors "request." In addition, almost every place else this word occurs, the KJV translates it as "ask" or something similar. *BibleWorks* gives the following statistics for the KJV, "ask 48, desire 17, beg 2, require 2, crave 1, call for 1; 71."

As for the interpretation, it is because the Jews had signs given to them in the past that they are now "requesting" a sign. They want God to do for them now what he did in the past (compare John 6:30, 31). And as for the cross-reference Watkins and Melton mentions, in the previous verse, a Jew was seeking a sign from Jesus (John 4:48). So I don't see how this verse supports their argument.

1Corinthians 6:9

KJV: Know ye not that the unrighteous shall not inherit the kingdom of God? Be not deceived: neither fornicators, nor idolaters, nor adulterers, nor EFFEMINATE, nor ABUSERS OF THEMSELVES WITH MANKIND,

NKJV: Do you not know that the unrighteous will not inherit the kingdom of God? Do not be deceived. Neither fornicators, nor idolaters, nor adulterers, nor HOMOSEXUALS, nor SODOMITES,

KJV onlyists complain about "effeminate" being "removed" from this verse. Since this word and the next one are related, they will be dealt with together,

First, I was not quite sure what "effeminate" meant. So I looked it up, "ef·fem·i·nate (î-fêm¹e-nît) adjective 1. Having qualities or characteristics more often associated with women than men. 2. Characterized by weakness and excessive refinement" (*American Heritage Dictionary*). So the KJV rendering does not imply homosexuality as the NKJV does.

But what does the Greek word mean? The difficulty for the translator here is that there are two words being used, one right after the other, with very similar definitions. The first is *malakos*; the second is *arsenokoites*.

This second word is rendered "abusers of themselves with mankind" in the KJV and "sodomites" in the NKJV. Since I cannot look up a phrase in a dictionary, I am not really sure what the KJV means. The phrase could be taken in many ways. But the NKJV is clear that we are talking about sexual sins.

According to Baur, when used in reference to people as it is here, *malakos* means, "soft, effeminate, esp[ecially] of catamites, men and boys who allow themselves to be misused homosexually" (p.488).

Meanwhile, Baur defines *arsenokoites* as, "a male who practices homosexuality, pederast, sodomite" (p.109). So there is not doubt the words are referring to homosexual, sexual sins, just as the NKJV indicates, but as the KJV does not.

Rienecker's definitions of these two words are similar, "*malakos* soft, effeminate, a technical term for the passive partner in homosexual relations.... *arsenokoites* a male who has sexual relations with a male, homosexual" (p.402).

But what is the difference between these two words? Louw and Nida explain:

arsenokoites: a male partner in homosexual intercourse—'homosexual.' ... It is possible that *arsenokoites* in certain contexts refers to the active

partner in homosexual intercourse in contrast with
malakos, the passive partner.... As in Greek, a number
of other languages also have entirely distinct terms for
the active and passive roles in homosexual intercourse
(Vol. 2, pp.772,3).

So in no uncertain terms, Paul in this passage is declaring
that any person engaging in homosexual sex, be they the "active"
or the "passive" partner, "will not inherit the kingdom of God."
Note also that in none of the above definitions is this
homosexuality tied in with prostitution as some claim. It is
simply homosexuality of any form.

Moreover, the textual footnote in the NKJV for the first
word ("homosexual") reads, "catamites, those submitting
themselves to homosexuals." The footnote for the second word
("sodomites") is, "male homosexual."

So the NKJV in its text and especially with its footnotes
expresses the meaning of the Greek words very clearly and
accurately. But the KJV is neither clear nor accurate in its
translation.

2 Corinthians 2:10

KJV: To whom ye forgive any thing, I *forgive* also: for
if I forgave any thing, to whom I forgave *it*, for your
sakes *forgave I it* IN THE PERSON OF CHRIST;
NKJV: Now whom you forgive anything, I also *forgive.*
For if indeed I have forgiven anything, I have
forgiven that one for your sakes IN THE
PRESENCE OF CHRIST,

Since no modern apostate understands the Christian
being "IN CHRIST'S STEAD" and being "AS HE IS,"
the term "PERSON OF CHRIST" in 2Corinthians 2:10
had to be done away with. The purpose of this was to
erase the cross-reference to John 20:23, where the Holy

Spirit interpreted the passage in that fashion in ALL
EDITIONS OF THE KING JAMES BIBLE FROM
1611 TO 1892. The JFV is not an edition of the
Authorized Version. JFV's reading ... is the reading of
Modernists and Liberals in the NCCC and was first used
in the ASV of 1901 (Ruckman).

The word in question (*prosopon*) means:
(1) *face, countenance;* lit[erally]. as a part of the
body *face* (MT 6.16); fig[uratively]. (a) as denoting
personal presence *in person* (1TH 2.17); idiomatically,
w. the sense varied by controlling preps.; *prosopon pros
prosopon. face to face* (1C 13.12); apo prosopou *directly
from* (AC 3.20); *eis prosopon. before, in front of* (2C
8.24); *ev prosopo. in the presence of* (2C 2.10); *kata
prosopon. face to face, in person* (AC 3.13); *openly,
personally, to one's face* (GA 2.11); *meta prosopou with
the presence of, by being with* someone (AC 2.28); *pro
prosopou. in front of, ahead of* (MT 11.10); (b) as
denoting the front side of someth. *face;* of the earth
surface (LU 21.35); (c) as denoting the external form of
someth[ing] *appearance* (2C 5.12; JA 1.11); (2) by
synecdoche *person, individual* (2C 1.11 Friberg).

So the word literally means "face," so a literal rendering of
the phrase would be "in the face of Christ." But what would the
figurative meaning of this phrase be?" The word in question has
a wide variety of figurative meanings.
The KJV itself uses "presence" for the figurative meaning
seven times (e.g., 1Thes 2:17; Heb 9:24). Friberg specifically
gives 2Cor 2:10 as the example for the figurative meaning of "in
the presence of." And interestingly, Robertson comments, "**In
the person of Christ** (*ev prosopo christou*). More exactly, "in
the presence of Christ," before Christ, in the face of Christ. Cf.
evopion tou theou (4:2) in the eye of God, *evopion kuriou* (8:21).

So the reason the NKJV translators used "in the presence of Christ" is not because they are "modern apostates" as Ruckman says, but because it is a "more exact" rendering.

2Corinthians 2:17

KJV: For we are not as many, which CORRUPT the word of God: but as of sincerity, but as of God, in the sight of God speak we in Christ.

NKJV: For we are not, as so many, PEDDLING the word of God; but as of sincerity, but as from God, we speak in the sight of God in Christ.

With all the "corruptions" in the NKJV, you'd expect 2 Cor. 2:17 to change. ***IT DOES!*** They change, *"For we not as many which **CORRUPT** the word of God"* to *"For we are not, as so many, **PEDDLING** the word of God"* (ditto NIV, NASV, NRSV, RSV) (Watkins, "Counterfeit").

A striking word change involves changing "corrupt" to "peddling" in 2Corinthians 2:17. The KJV correctly says, "For we are not as many, which corrupt the word of God ...." But the NKJV, NASV, NIV and RSV, change "corrupt" to "peddling" (selling, for making a gain of) the Word of God and corrupting (adulterating) it.

Is there any great difference between peddling (selling, or making a gain of) the Word of God and corrupting (adulterating) it? Of course there is, and one does not have to be a Greek scholars to decide which is correct. When this warning was given in the 1st Century, was there any way for people to peddle (make a gain of) God's Word? Of course not—they were suffering for it. The warning clearly refers to corrupting God's Word, something that was common then as it is now (Reynolds).

First, it would help to define the words used in the two translations. "Corrupt" means:
1. Marked by immorality and perversion; depraved.
2. Venal; dishonest: *a corrupt mayor*.
3. Containing errors or alterations, as a text: *a corrupt translation*.

The definition of "peddle" is:
1. a. To travel about selling (wares): *peddling goods from door to door*.
   b. To engage in the illicit sale of (narcotics).
2. Informal. To seek to disseminate; give out: *peddling lies*.
verb, intransitive
   1. To travel about selling wares.
   2. To occupy oneself with trifles (*American Heritage Dictionary*).

"Corrupt" in this context refers to definition number three. So Paul would be talking about people who add "errors" or make "alterations" to the Word of God. "Peddle" on the other hand refers to people who travel about selling something, plus the word can be used in a "negative" sense ("peddling lies"). But which translation is closer to the meaning of the Greek word?

Rienecker states about this word:
kapeleuo to peddle, to pawn off a product for gain. The word is used in the LXX [Septuagint] in Isa 1:22 for those who mix wine with water in order to cheat the buyers (Plummer).... The word refers to those who peddle or merchandise the Word of God for profit (p.458).

So Rienecker uses the word "peddle" twice in his definition. And the idea of "selling" is definitely involved, but so is the idea of "altering" what is sold.

Bauer defines *kapeleuo* as, "trade in, peddle, huckster....Because of the tricks of small tradesman...the word comes to mean almost adulterate" (p. 403). So "peddle" appears to be primary meaning of the word, but an extended meaning could be "adulterate."

Interestingly, the NKJV footnote gives an alternate translation of, "adulterating for gain." The meaning of "adulterate" is, "To make impure by adding extraneous, improper, or inferior ingredients" (*American Heritage Dictionary*). This dishonest action is exactly what Rienecker was describing in regards to Isaiah 1:22.

So by combining the text reading and the footnote, the NKJV expresses the meaning of the Greek word very well, both its primary and secondary meanings. Paul is talking about people who travel about profiting from the Word while making it impure by adding improper elements to it. Meanwhile, the KJV's "corrupt" only expresses the secondary meaning of *kapeleuo*. The primary idea of "selling" is not in the KJV. So the NKJV is more accurate, especially when the footnote reading is included.

Now, Reynolds claims that people could not have been "peddling" the Word of God at the time this was written since "they were suffering for it." But in this statement he makes two errors. First, the "peddlers" would not have been true Christians, but false teachers.

Secondly, at the time 2Corinthians was written there was not widespread persecution of Christians. The Roman persecutions would not begin for a few years. There was some persecution from Jews, but it was not widespread, especially in Corinth, a Gentile city.

And yes there was a "way for people to peddle (make a gain of) God's Word." Paul did not make use of his "right" to live off of the Gospel in Corinth (1Cor 9:11-15). However, it was very possible for false teachers to insist on this right and take advantage of the ones supporting them. And while profiting from the Word by living off of believers, they would be presenting them with "adulterated" teachings.

Philippians 3:8

KJV: Yea doubtless, and I count all things but loss for the excellency of the knowledge of Christ Jesus my Lord: for whom I have suffered the loss of all things, and do count them but DUNG, that I may win Christ,

NKJV: Yet indeed I also count all things loss for the excellence of the knowledge of Christ Jesus my Lord, for whom I have suffered the loss of all things, and count them as RUBBISH, that I may gain Christ.

CHG [change] dung TO rubbish, trash (NI, NAS, NKJ, RS, NRS, LB, NC) (Watkins, "Comparison").

Friberg defines the word in question as, "anything that is to be treated as worthless and thrown out, transl[ated] acc[ording] to context *dung, rubbish, garbage, offscourings* (PH 3.8)." And Bauer defines it as, "refuse, rubbish, leavings, dirt, dung...." Phil 3:8 is then referred to with the rendering, "consider everything rubbish or dung" (p.758).

Friberg and Bauer give both the KJV and the NKJV translations. So the word could refer to human or animal excrement, but not necessarily. It can mean anything that is thrown out. So rubbish or garbage would work just as well.

However, there is a problem with the KJV translation. How many people today really use the word "dung?" I can think of several other much more common terms that are in use today for excrement, but most would not be appropriate for use in the Bible!

This type of problem is one that a translator will often face, how to render "sensitive" words (like those referring to sexual body parts, sexual acts, and human waste products). The translator could use the most "common" term, but it would often be considered "vulgar" in the receptor language. So a somewhat less common term might be used.

> Arthur L. Farstad, head of the NKJV New Testament translation committee, writes about why they used "rubbish" in this verse:
> Now if the Greek word definitely meant waste products, dung would have been left here in the NKJV. But it does not! The Greek word *skybala* is thought by some to be from an expression "throw to the dogs"— hence garbage or rubbish. Another view is that it comes from *skor*, an expression meaning dung. Since we are not sure, rubbish is a good choice (p. 86).

1Thessalonians 5:22

> KJV: Abstain from every APPEARANCE of evil.
> NKJV: Abstain from every FORM of evil.

> The NKJB is weaker on separation here, because the word "appearance" includes things which look wrong as well as are wrong—whereas the word "form" tends to mean things which are wrong (Sargent, p.5).

The KJV seems to be commanding a more stringent separation from evil than the NKJV. But is this the correct attitude Christians should have towards evil?

The Greek word here is *eidos*. Newman defines it as, "visible form, outward appearance; sight, seeing (2 Cor 5.7); kind, sort (1 Th 5.22)." Friberg has, "(1) w. pass. sense, as what is visible to the eye *form, (external) appearance* (LU 3.22); (2) w. act. sense *sight, what one sees* (2C 5.7); (3) *(particular) kind, sort* (1TH 5.22).

Liddell and Scott have, *that which is seen, form, shape, figure,* Lat. species, forma, Hom.; absol. in acc., ei=doj a;ristoj, etc. **II.** *a form, sort, particular kind* or *nature,* Hdt., etc. **2.** *a particular state* of things or *course* of action, Thuc. **III.** *a class, kind, sort,* whether *genus* or *species,* Plat., etc."

So each of these lexicons gives meanings like the KJV's "appearance" and the NKJV's "form." So either of these is possible. But note that the first two specifically give 1Thessalonians 5:22 as an example of "kind" or "sort," which mean the same as "form."

Moreover, Robertson has the following discussion:

> *Eidos* (from *eidon*) naturally means look or appearance as in Lu 3:23; 9:29; Joh 5:37; 2Co 5:7. But, if so taken, it is not semblance as opposed to reality (Milligan). The papyri give several examples of *eidos* in the sense of class or kind and that idea suits best here. Evil had a way of showing itself even in the spiritual gifts including prophecy.

Note that Robertson says, "it is not semblance as opposed to reality." Braumann writes similarly about the word, "It occurs from Homer onwards and denotes appearance, visible form, stressing the link between appearance and reality." And, "The *eidos* was the expression of the essence in visible form" (Braumann, pp.703,4).

So even though the Greek word can mean either "appearance" or "form," it does not allow for distinguishing between what something looks like and what it in reality is. So Sargent's comments cannot be correct, and the KJV's rendering is misleading. Paul cannot be saying to abstain from things that only look wrong but are not in fact wrong. They must be things that both look wrong and are wrong.

In addition, was Jesus concerned about abstaining from things which merely "look wrong?" Jesus ate with "tax-collectors and sinners" (Matt 9:9-11). To the Pharisees, this fellowship made it look like He was "a glutton and a winebibber, even though He was neither (Matt 11:19; NKJV). But rather than getting up and leaving this "appearance of evil," Jesus rebuked the Pharisees for their legalism (Matt 9:12,13; 11:19).

So which should be accepted? The more legalistic rendering of the KJV or the "weaker" translation of the NKJV indicated both by the full meaning of the Greek word itself and by the example of Jesus?

1 Timothy 6:5

KJV: Perverse disputings of men of corrupt minds, and destitute of the truth, supposing that GAIN IS GODLINESS: from such withdraw thyself.

NKJV: useless wranglings of men of corrupt minds and destitute of the truth, who suppose that GODLINESS IS A *MEANS OF* GAIN. From such withdraw yourself.

The NKJV changes *"gain is godliness"* to *"godliness is a MEANS OF gain"*. There are NO Greek texts with "means of" in them! Where, oh where, did they come from? Care to take a wild guess? **YOU GOT IT!** The NIV, NASV, RSV, NRSV! (Watkins, "Counterfeit")

First, it should be noted that "means of" is in italics in the NKJV. So even if it were true that "There are NO Greek texts with 'means of' in them" the NKJV has indicated the words are added.

However, the words "means of" are indicated by the Greek word. Friberg defines the word as, "as a process *a means of gain, a way to make money* (1T 6.5); fig[uratively] *advantage, profit* (1T 6.6)." Liddell and Scott have, "*a providing, procuring,*

Polyb.:-*a means of getting*, Plut.: *means of gain*, N.T." And Newman has simply, "gain, means of gain."

So the lexicons are unanimous that the word can mean "means of gain." As such, it is not incorrect for the NKJV to use these words. This would be true even if they were not in italics.

1Timothy 6:20

KJV: O Timothy, keep that which is committed to thy trust, avoiding profane *and* vain babblings, and oppositions of SCIENCE falsely so called:

NKJV: O Timothy! Guard what was committed to your trust, avoiding the profane *and* idle babblings and contradictions of what is falsely called KNOWLEDGE

Since all modern, apostate Fundamentalists think that science can sit in judgment on the AV of 1611, the word "science" has been removed from 1Timothy 6:20 … to match the Communist Bible of the NCC and the apostate NASV of Bob Jones University. The word "science" has occurred in every edition of the KJV from 1611 to 1982. (Ruckman).

Friberg defines the word in question (*gnosis*) as:

basically, as the possession of information *what is known, knowledge;* (1) as a characteristic of God and man *knowledge* (RO 11.33; 1C 8.1); (2) as the result of divine enlightenment *knowledge, understanding, insight* (LU 1.77); (3) of heretical claims to higher forms of knowledge available only to a select few *Gnosis, (esoteric) knowledge* (1T 6.20).

Newman has, "knowledge; esoteric knowledge; *kata gnosis* with understanding or consideration (1 Pet 3:7). Liddell and Scott have, "*a judicial inquiry* Dem. **II.** *a knowing, knowledge,*

Plat., N.T. **2.** *acquaintance with* a person, *pros tina a*p. Aeschin. **3.** *a knowing, recognising,* Thuc. **III.** *a being known, fame, credit,* Luc."

So the lexicons are unanimous that this is a general word for "knowledge" not a specific reference to the disciple of science. The Greek word is *gnosis*, which is where the name "Gnostics" comes from. As Friberg indicates, this heretical group claimed to have a "higher form of knowledge," or an "esoteric knowledge." The Gnostics were not scientists.

Moreover, this word occurs 29 times in the NT. Every other time it occurs, the KJV translates it as "knowledge" (e.g. Luke 1:77; 2Peter 1:5). Why the KJV uses "science" in this verse is not clear.

So the reason the NKJV translators used "knowledge" in this verse is not because they were "modern, apostate Fundamentalists" as Ruckman apparently calls them, but because of the overwhelming lexical data and in order for the translation of the word to be consistent throughout the NT.

2Timothy 2:15

> KJV: STUDY to shew thyself approved unto God, a workman that needeth not to be ashamed, rightly dividing the word of truth.
>
> NKJV: BE DILIGENT to present yourself approved to God, a worker who does not need to be ashamed, rightly dividing the word of truth.

In 2 Timothy 2:15, the NKJV (like the NIV, NASV, RSV, NRSV) remove that "obsolete" word - ***"study"***! The only time you're told to "study" your Bible. **AND THEY ZAP IT!** *Why don't they want you to "study" your Bible? Maybe they don't want you to look too close - **you might find out what they've ACTUALLY done to your Bible!*** The "real" KJV is the only English Bible in the world that instructs you to "study" your Bible! (Watkins, "Counterfeit").

The NKJB alters the familiar, 'Study to show thyself approved unto God,' to 'Be diligent to present yourself approved to God.' Since when has 'study' and 'diligence' meant the same? Imagine advising our College students to go home and be diligent! (Sargent, p.6).

Of course "study" and "diligence" don't mean the same. But the important question is, which word best translates the Greek word?

Friberg defines the word as, "(1) w[ith] inf[initive] foll[owing], to show the area of urgency *make haste to, hurry to, do your best to* (2T 4.9); (2) w[ith] inf[initive] foll[owing], to show the area of concern *be eager to, make every effort to, try hard to* (HE 4.11)." Baur has, "1. Hasten, hurry... 2. Be zealous or eager, take pains, make every effort.... (p.763).

So neither of these standard lexicons nor any others I checked gives the possible meaning of "study" for the Greek word. Instead, they give meanings similar to the term the NKJV uses. So why does the KJV has "study" in this verse? It's because of the context. Later in the verse, Paul writes that we need to be "rightly dividing the word of truth." And the only way to do this is to study the Scriptures.

For this reason the *Modern King James Version* (MKJV) renders this verse, "*Study* earnestly to present yourself approved to God, a workman that does not need to be ashamed, rightly dividing the Word of Truth."

The MKJV has the words "study" and a term similar to the NKJV's "diligent." But notice one important difference—the MKJV has "study" in italics. This indicates the word is added to help the reader understand the sense, but it is not in the original. And, as an aside, with the MKJV having this rendering, it is not true that the, "KJV is the only English Bible in the world that instructs you to "study" your Bible."

In any case, the KJV has used a word that is not in the Greek text without indicating it has done so, while not translating the word that is in the text. But by doing so it has helped to bring out the "meaning" of the passage. Meanwhile, the NKJV is more literal in regards to the actual wording of the Greek text.

So which is better? The KJV's rendering is more along the lines of a dynamic equivalence rendering than a formal equivalence translation. But this writer and KJV onlyists agree that dynamic equivalence is not the best method to use in translating. So the KJV onlyists are being inconsistent in trying to defend the KJV's "dynamic" rendering in this verse.

Titus 3:10

KJV: A man THAT IS AN HERETICK after the first and second admonition reject;

NKJV: Reject a DIVISIVE man after the first and second admonition,

The KJV tells us to reject a "heretick" after the second admonition in Titus 3:10. The NKJV tells us to reject a "divisive man". *How nice! Now the Alexandrians and Ecumenicals have justification for rejecting anyone they wish to label as "divisive men"* (Watkins and Melton).

The Greek word is a *hapax legomena*, so again, it is hard to get an exact meaning for the word. However, the word is *hairetikon* so "heretic" is basically a transliteration. Louw and Nida define it as: "pertaining to causing divisions—'divisive, one who causes divisions." Friberg has, "denoting loyalty to a separatist group *heretical, factious, causing divisions* (TI 3.10)."

So "heretical" is a transliteration while "causing divisions" is the meaning of the word. Which is best would depend on whether you want to just transliterate the word or to actually translate it. Moreover, the word is an adjective as the NKJV has it, not a noun as in the KJV. Also, the KJV rendering requires adding the words "that is" (which, by the way, are not italicized). So by grammar the NKJV's rendering would be preferred.

Watkins and Melton do not like the idea of the Bible saying that causing division is wrong as the KJV only movement has fractured more than one church. Now there is a time when separation is necessary (Rev 18:4), but separation should only occur over major doctrinal issues, not over which Bible version should be used, especially when the versions in question are all reliable.

Hebrews 10:14

KJV: For by one offering he hath perfected for ever them that ARE SANCTIFIED.
NKJV: For by one offering He has perfected forever those who ARE BEING SANCTIFIED.

The NKJV confuses people about salvation. In Hebrews 10:14 it replaces "are sanctified" with "are being sanctified" ... (Watkins and Melton).

The term "being sanctified" would be favorable to the Holiness movement, whereas in fact the believer IS sanctified (Sargent, p.7).

The Greek word is a present, passive, participle. These grammatical forms together mean the action of the verb is ongoing and is being done to the subject of the sentence by another. The NKJV's "are being" brings out each of these grammatical points much better than the KJV. God is continually sanctifying us, while justification is a one-time act.

As Millard J. Erickson writes, "Sanctification. The divine act of making the believer actually holy, that is, bringing the person's moral condition into conformity with the legal status established in justification" (p.147). So there is a clear distinction between sanctification and justification, but maybe the KJV onlyists are confusing the two.

1 John 5:13

KJV: These things have I written unto you that believe on the name of the Son of God; that ye may know that ye have eternal life, and that ye MAY BELIEVE on the name of the Son of God.

NKJV: These things I have written to you who believe in the name of the Son of God, that you may know that you have eternal life, and that you MAY *CONTINUE TO* BELIEVE in the name of the Son of God.

They add "CONTINUE TO" without any Greek text whatsoever! Not even the perverted NIV, NASV, NRSV and RSV go that far! A cruel, subtle (see Genesis 3:1) attack on the believer's eternal security! (Watkins, "Counterfeit")

First, it should be noted that the words "continue to" are in italics in the NKJV. So even if they are "without any Greek text whatsoever" the NKJV clearly indicates they are added. But, in fact, there is textual justification for these words.

The verb here is subjunctive mood, present tense. These grammatical forms together indicate the action is ongoing. So the translation could be something like, "may be believing" indicating one is always to believe. But this is somewhat awkward. However, the NKJV's, "continue to believe" brings out the ongoing sense in a more readable format.

Now this writer does believe in eternal security, but I never considered the NKJV's rendering to be an "attack on the believer's eternal security." True believers can loose their faith for a time in the sense of falling away from closely following Christ and turning to sinful ways. However, God will not let one of His children remain in sin. Eventually, He will convict and chasten wayward Christians and cause them to repent and return to Him. However, this chastisement and the following needed repentance can be painful. And John is trying to spare his "little children" this pain.

Moreover, what John says here is similar to what he wrote earlier in the epistle, "And now, little children, abide in him; that, when he shall appear, we may have confidence, and not be ashamed before him at his coming" (2:28; KJV). Telling us to "abide in him" is no more of an attack on eternal security than telling us to "continue to believe."

Conclusion

In rare cases, the KJV onlyists are correct: the KJV does have a better rendering than the NKJV. But in other cases either the rendering of the KJV or of the NKJV is legitimate. And in some cases, the NKJV has a somewhat better rendering than the KJV, while at times the KJV is simply inaccurate. And in some verses, neither version has the best possible translation.

These points produce two important conclusions. First off, the NKJV is not a "perversion" as the KJV onlyists claim. It is every bit as faithful to the original text as the KJV, even more so at times.

Secondly, the KJV is not "perfect" as KJV onlyists claim. There are times when its translations can be improved upon or actually need to be corrected. Overall it is a very good version, but it simply is not infallible.

What this means is this: Christians can choose to use either the KJV or the NKJV and be confident they are using a reliable Bible version. But since neither is perfect, it would also be helpful for Bible study to compare both of these versions, or one of these versions with another formal equivalence version, or even better, with a literal version.

Bibliography for Chapters Fifteen and Sixteen:

KJV Only Sources:
Reynolds, M.H. "New King James Bible Examined." Los Cos, CA: Fundamental Evangelistic Association, n.a.

Ruckman, Peter. "A Critique of the New King James Bible." Pensacola, FL: Bible Baptist Bookstore, 1979.

Sargent, Robert. "Is the New King James Bible the Word of God?" Halifax: The People's Gospel Hour, n.a.

Watkins, Terry. "The New King James Bible: Counterfeit" (www.av1611.org/).

"Bible Version Comparison Chart" (www.av1611.org/biblecom.html).

Watkins, Terry and James L. Melton. "The Attack on the Bible!" (http://rhema-av-1611.lima.net.pe/kjv.html).

Plus, personal correspondences the writer has had with KJV onlyists.

Greek References:
Baur, Walter. *A Greek-English Lexicon of the New Testament.* Chicago: University of Chicago Press, 1979.

Braumann, G. "eidos" in *New International Dictionary of New Testament Theology.* Vol.I. ed. by Colin Brown. Grand Rapids: Regency, 1986.

Dana, H.E. and Julius Mantey. *A Manual Grammar of the Greek New Testament.* New York: Macmillian, 1955.

Farstad, Arthur L. et.al. *The NKJV Greek-English Interlinear New Testament.* Nashville, TN: Thomas Nelson, 1994.

Friberg, Timothy and Barbara. *Analytical Greek New Testament.* Copyright © 1994 and *Analytical Lexicon to the Greek New Testament.* Copyright © 1994. Both as found on *BibleWorks™ for Windows™.*

Liddell-Scott Greek English Lexicon (Abridged). Public Domain. As found on *BibleWorks™ for Windows™.*

Green, Jay P. Sr. *Interlinear Bible.* LaFayette, IN: Sovereign Grace Publishers, 1988-1998.

Louw, Johannes and Eugene Nida, eds. *Greek-English Lexicon.* New York: United Bible Societies, 1988. And second edition, Copyright © 1998 as found on *BibleWorks™ for Windows™*.

Newman, Barclay M. Jr. *A Concise Greek-English Lexicon of the New Testament.* Copyright © 1971 by United Bible Societies and 1993 by Deutsche Biblelgesellschaft (German Bible Society), Sttugart. As found on *BibleWorks™ for Windows™*.

Robertson, A.T. *Word Pictures in the Greek New Testament.* Broadman Press, 1934. Also as found on *BibleWorks™ for Windows™* and the *Online Bible.*

Rienecker, Fritz. *A Linguistic Key to the Greek New Testament.* Trans. and ed. by Cleon Rogers. Grand Rapids, MI: Zondervan, 1980.

Software Programs:

American Heritage ® Dictionary of the English Language, Third Edition copyright © 1992 by Houghton Mifflin Company. Electronic version licensed from InfoSoft International, Inc. All rights reserved.

Hudson, Bob and Shelley Townsend, editors. *A Christian Writer's Manual of Style.* (Grand Rapids, MI: Zondervan), 1988.

BibleWorks™ for Windows™. Copyright © 1992-1999 *BibleWorks*, L.C.C. Big Fork, MT: Hermeneutika. Programmed by Michael S. Bushell and Michael D. Tan.

Online Bible. Ontario: Online Bible Foundation and the Woodside Bible Fellowship, 1997.

Webster's Talking Dictionary/ Thesaurus. Licensed property of Parson's Technology, Inc. v. 1.0b. Software Copyright 1996 by Exceller Software Corp. Based on Random House *Webster's College Dictionary.* Copyright 1995 by Random House, Inc. Note: unless otherwise indicated, all English word definitions are copied from this source.

Miscellaneous:

Erickson, Millard. J. *Concise Dictionary of Christian Theology*. Grand Rapids, Mich: Baker Book House, 1986.

Farstad, Arthur L. *The New King James Version in the Great Tradition*. Nashville: Thomas Nelson, 1993.

New King James Version. Nashville, TN: Thomas Nelson Publishers, 1982.

Gary Zeolla

Various Versions

Gary Zeolla

Chapter Seventeen
Review of the NAS95

As was discussed in the first chapter, my first Bible was a copy of the *New International Version* (NIV). But after using it for a couple of years I switched to the *New American Stand Bible* (NASB). I did so because the NIV is a dynamic equivalence ("thought for thought") type of translation while the NASB is a formal equivalence ("word for word") translation. It just made sense to me that since the Bible is the Word of God then a Bible version should translate God's actual words as closely as possible.

But after a few years of using the NASB as my primary Bible, I switched to the *New King James Version* (NKJV). I made this switch because I became convinced the Textus Receptus (TR) the New Testament of the NKJV is based on is more reliable than the Critical Text (CT) underlying the NASB (and the NIV). I also liked the NKJV's practice of footnoting the variants between the TR and the Majority Text (MT), which I think is slightly better than the TR. The NKJV also footnotes CT variants.

I also began to use the *Literal Translation of the Bible* (LITV) for my secondary version as it is, as the name implies, somewhat more literal than the NKJV. The LITV is also based on the TR.

But in 1995, the Lockman Foundation released an Updated NASB. It is also known as the NAS95, with the original NASB now sometimes being called the NAS77. This chapter will review the NAS95. It will first look at some background information on the NAS95 and then some verses from it.

Background Information

The following background information on the NAS95 is copied from: www.gospelcom.net/lockman/nasb/nasb.htm

The NASB Update continues the NASB commitment to accuracy, while increasing clarity and readability. Vocabulary, grammar, and sentence structure have been carefully updated for greater understanding and smoother reading. The NASB remains the most literally accurate Bible in the English language....

In order to be deemed acceptable by translators, updated material had to maintain the highest standards of literal translation. Thus the smoother reading NASB Update refines the differences in style between the ancient languages and current English. In the process, Old English "thees," "thys," and "thous," archaic vocabulary, and sentences beginning with "And" have been updated for better English, while verses with difficult word order were restructured....

Proper names or titles have been used in place of pronouns only when the context made it clear who the person was. Punctuation and paragraphing have been formatted to fit today's standards.

Also, the notes about ancient manuscripts, which have appeared in most editions of the NASB, have been reviewed and, in many cases, feature new and more specific interesting facts....

At NO point did the translators attempt to interpret Scripture through translation. Instead, the NASB translation team adhered to the principles of literal translation. This is the most exacting and demanding method of translation, requiring a word-for-word translation that is both accurate and readable....

To comment, one point I did not like about the NAS77 was the archaic language. So I am pleased it was updated in the NAS95. I am also glad to hear the textual footnotes were changed in the NAS95 as some of the ones in the NAS77 were somewhat misleading (e.g. saying "some manuscripts have..." when "some" is only two manuscripts).

But I disagree with the idea of "updating" the use of "And" at the beginning of sentences. By this is meant the Greek word *kai* at the beginning of sentences is not translated. If God inspired the *kai* then I believe it should be translated.

Also, I would disagree with changing pronouns to nouns for any reason. Again if God used a pronoun then I believe it should be rendered as such.

Otherwise, I wouldn't agree with saying the NAS95 is "the most literally accurate Bible in the English language." I would say the LITV is more literal. And the NKJV is about as literal as the NASB.

But the above are minor points compared with the major problems seen in the NIV and other dynamic equivalence types of versions. Such versions do "attempt to interpret Scripture through translation." What is most important is, "the NASB translation team adhered to the principles of literal translation." To produce "a word-for-word translation that is both accurate and readable" is, in my opinion, the most appropriate goal of a Bible translation.

Next, verse comparisons will be made of the NAS95 with each of the other four versions mentioned above.

Verse Comparisons

There are six verses I often turn to in order to "text" a Bible version. Below is a comparison of each of these verses from the NKJV, LITV, NAS77, NAS95, and NIV, followed by some comments.

Matthew 2:10
NKJV: When they saw the star, they rejoiced with exceedingly great joy.
LITV: And seeing the star, they rejoiced exceedingly [with] a great joy.

NAS77: And when they saw the star, they rejoiced exceedingly with great joy.

NAS95: When they saw the star, they rejoiced exceedingly with great joy.

NIV: When they saw the star, they were overjoyed.

This is one of the two "test" verses I used in the Chapter Four. I use it as it is very simple to translate and has an interesting feature in the Greek text. As can be seen, the first four versions are very similar. This is so as all four are following a formal equivalence translation principle and there are no textual variants in this verse. The NIV, however, being a dynamic equivalence version, is considerably different in the second clause.

One difference in the first clause is the LITV and NAS77 have "And" at the beginning of the verse while the NKJV, NAS95, and NIV do not. As indicated above, the "And" is a translation of the Greek word *kai*. So the NKJV and NIV do not translate the *kai* in this instance. And the omission of the *kai* in the NAS95 is what is referred to above about the NAS95 "updating" the use of 'And.'" Again, since God inspired Matthew to write the *kai* I think it should be translated.

Another difference between the first four versions is only the LITV offsets the word "with" indicating it is not in the Greek text but added for clarity. A minor point is the different placement of "exceedingly." This is due to a different decision as to whether it should be taken as an adjective modifying "joy" or as an adverb modifying "rejoiced." Either is grammatically possible, though as an adverb is most likely.

The interesting feature of the Greek text is the grammatical construction known as a "cognate accusative." What is interesting about this construction is it can easily be brought out in English. And in, fact, the first four versions do so. This construction refers to a verb and noun with the same root appearing together, and in this case, the English equivalents also have the same root (i.e. "rejoiced" and "joy"). So the first four versions are all closely following the word order and grammar of the Greek text.

However, the rendering of the NIV in the second clause is far from the Greek text. The NIV has combined "great" and "joy" into "overjoyed." Since it left out "rejoiced" it was forced to add "were" in order to have a verb. And the question of whether "exceedingly" is an adjective or an adverb has been "solved" by leaving the word untranslated. And the cognate accusative construction has been completely lost.

John 3:13
NKJV: No one has ascended to heaven but He who came down from heaven, that is, the Son of Man who is in heaven.

LITV: And no one has gone up into Heaven, except He having come down out of Heaven, the Son of Man who is in Heaven.

NAS77: And no one has ascended into heaven, but He who descended from heaven, even the Son of Man.

NAS95: No one has ascended into heaven, but He who descended from heaven: the Son of Man.

NIV: No one has ever gone into heaven except the one who came from heaven—the Son of Man.

I usually check this verse to see what Greek text a version is using. The final phrase ("who is in heaven") is in the TR and MT but not in the CT. The phrase is important as it shows Jesus was still in heaven during His incarnation. Thus He was in heaven and on earth at the same time. As such, the verse becomes a proof-text for His omnipresence and hence His Deity. But neither version of the NASB nor the NIV includes this important phrase since they are following the CT.

Otherwise, the verses in the first four versions are again virtually identical. Except, again, the NKJV and NAS95 (along with the NIV) omit the *kai* at the beginning of the verse while both the LITV and NAS77 translate it. This pattern shows why I said the LITV is somewhat more literal than the NKJV and demonstrates how the NAS95 is moving to be a little less literal than the NAS77.

As for the NIV, its renderings of "gone into" and "came from" ignore the fact that the Greek words indicate direction, going up and coming down respectively (Friberg's lexicon). These meanings are expressed in each of the first four versions.

Acts 13:48

NKJV: Now when the Gentiles heard this, they were glad and glorified the word of the Lord. And as many as had been appointed to eternal life believed.

LITV: And hearing, the nations rejoiced and glorified the Word of the Lord. And as many as had been appointed to eternal life believed.

NAS77: And when the Gentiles heard this, they *began* rejoicing and glorifying the word of the Lord; and as many as had been appointed to eternal life believed.

NAS95: When the Gentiles heard this, they *began* rejoicing and glorifying the word of the Lord; and as many as had been appointed to eternal life believed.

NIV: When the Gentiles heard this, they were glad and honored the word of the Lord; and all who were appointed for eternal life believed.

I check this verse to see if a version tries to eliminate "Calvinistic" verses. The second sentence was the passage of Scripture that began my "journey" into Calvinism. As I studied the verse I could see no way to avoid the implication that some (not everyone) at a time previous to Luke's writing "had been appointed" (Greek perfect tense indicating a prior action that has continuing results to the present) "to eternal life."

It was these who had been so "appointed" (or "ordained" as the word can also be rendered) who believed, and only these. The logical implication was that those who did not believe had not been so appointed. Some versions will try to evade this interpretation by mistranslating the phrase. *The Living Bible*, for instance, has "who wanted salvation"—which is not even close to the Greek text.

But there are no such problems with any of these versions. They all use "appointed" in the final phrase. However, the NIV misses the sense of the Greek perfect tense that the others express. The NIV renders the verb as if it was a simple past tense ("were") rather than a perfect tense ("had been").

The minor differences in the first sentence have to do with different decisions on how to best to render the vocabulary and grammar of the text. Each rendering is possible, except for the NIV's "honored." The basic meaning of the Greek word is "to glorify" (Friberg's lexicon). The rendering of "honored" is simply not strong enough.

The use of "rejoicing" and "glorifying" in both editions of the NASB does bring out the ongoing, past action sense of the Greek imperfect better than how the words are rendered in the other versions.

The use of the word "began" in both editions of the NASB is due to the translators taking it as an inceptive imperfect. This is also a legitimate rendering of the grammar. As such, in this writer's opinion, it is not really necessary to italicize the word.

1Corinthians 7:1

NKJV: Now concerning the things of which you wrote to me: *It is* good for a man not to touch a woman.

LITV: But concerning what you wrote to me, [it is] good for a man not to touch a woman;

NAS77: Now concerning the things about which you wrote, it is good for a man not to touch a woman.

NAS95: Now concerning the things about which you wrote, it is good for a man not to touch a woman.

NIV: Now for the matters you wrote about: It is good for a man not to marry.

This is the second "test" verse I used the Chapter Four, and again, it is very simple to translate—if one simply translates the actual Greek words. However, rather than translating the text, most of the versions evaluated in that chapter simply cannot resist trying to interpret what Paul meant when he wrote "it is good for a man not to touch a woman."

However, the first four of these versions simply render the Greek text literally and leave it up to the reader to decide what Paul meant by these words. So the above quote about the NAS95 was correct when it said, "At NO point did the translators attempt to interpret Scripture through translation." The same can be said for the NKJV and LITV.

But the NIV simply could not resist the temptation to try to interpret Paul's words. As a result, it's rendering of the last phrase is not even close to the Greek text.

Another difference in the second clause is that the NKJV and LITV offsets the words "It is" as not in the Greek text but added for clarity whereas neither version of the NASB nor the NIV does. Also, none of these latter three versions have the "to me" at the end of the first phrase since it is omitted in the CT.

Galatians 3:20
NKJV: Now a mediator does not *mediate* for one *only,* but God is one.

LITV: But the Mediator is not of one, but God is one.

NAS77: Now a mediator is not for one *party only*; whereas God is *only* one.

NAS95: Now a mediator is not for one *party only*; whereas God is *only* one.

NIV: A mediator, however, does not represent just one party; but God is one.

I check this verse since a strictly literal translation is very awkward and really makes little sense. Such a translation would read, "But the mediator is not of one, but the God is one." I want to see how many changes are made to the text to make it at least readable, and again if the translation simply cannot resist the urge to interpret the verse for its readers.

It can be seen that the LITV is the most literal of all of these versions. The only change it makes is to omit the "the" before "God." But this is standard practice even in literal versions as the definite article appears much more often in Greek than it is needed in English.

Otherwise, the only notable difference is the LITV capitalizes "Mediator" making it a reference to deity. This is somewhat interpretive as there are ways of taking the verse that do not make this verse a reference to one of the Persons of the Trinity.

The NKJV and both NASBs change "of one" to "for one." This is a minor point as using "for" is a legitimate way to render the Greek genitive.

Similarly, each of these versions changes the first "But" to "Now," and the two NASBs change the second "but" to "whereas." Again, these renderings are legitimate translations, but they do "hide" the fact that the same Greek word is used in both places.

Otherwise, each of these versions do add words to make the text readable and understandable. But each of these words is italicized, so readers know they are added. However, the NIV adds "represent just" without indicating it has does so. But at least this is the only significant change it makes to the text.

1Timothy 3:16

NKJV And without controversy great is the mystery of godliness: God was manifested in the flesh, Justified in the Spirit, Seen by angels, Preached among the Gentiles, Believed on in the world, Received up in glory.

LITV: And confessedly, great is the mystery of godliness: God was manifested in flesh, was justified in Spirit, was seen by angels, was

> proclaimed among nations, was believed on in [the] world, was taken up in glory.
>
> NAS77: And by common confession great is the mystery of godliness: He who was revealed in the flesh, Was vindicated in the Spirit, Beheld by angels, Proclaimed among the nations, Believed on in the world, Taken up in glory.
>
> NAS95: By common confession, great is the mystery of godliness: He who was revealed in the flesh, Was vindicated in the Spirit, Seen by angels, Proclaimed among the nations, Believed on in the world, Taken up in glory.
>
> NIV: Beyond all question, the mystery of godliness is great: He appeared in a body, was vindicated by the Spirit, was seen by angels, was preached among the nations, was believed on in the world, was taken up in glory.

I also check this verse to see what Greek text a version is following. The first word of the second sentence is "God" in the TR/ MT. This rendering makes this verse another proof-text for the Deity of Christ. The vast majority of the Greek manuscripts have this reading. The CT has "who" in it which causes this verse to cease to be a proof-text for Christ' Deity. A handful of Alexandrian manuscripts have this reading. A couple of manuscripts have "which," but all three published Greek texts consider this variant to be an obvious mistake.

However, NO manuscript has "He" as both versions of the NASB and the NIV have it. So none of these three versions is actually following any Greek text for this word. The reason why they changed the "who" in the CT they are supposed to translating to "He" is because "who" simply doesn't "fit" in the context. It makes it sound like it is a question when it is not.

That said, otherwise this is a difficult verse to translate. Although there are differences between these versions at various places, it would be hard to say for a certainty which is definitely correct. The one exception is the word order change in the NIV in the second phrase. The word "great" is first in the clause not last.

A couple of other minor points, notice how the NAS95 and NIV are the only versions to omit the "And" at the beginning of the verse. Also, the LITV is the only version to offset the "the" in the phrase "the world" as added for clarity.

Conclusion

Based on these six sample verses, I would say the LITV is the most literal of all. The NKJV and NAS77 are about equal, while the NAS95 has moved to being slightly less literal. The NIV would be dead last.

As compared to the NIV and other dynamic equivalence versions, the NAS95 looks very good. However, it is not as literal as its predecessor. It would have been preferable for it to have just updated the archaic language and misleading footnotes of the NAS77 and left the more literalness of the NAS77 intact.

But overall, the NAS95 is still basically an accurate version, translation wise. If the NAS95 had just followed the Majority Text rather than the Critical Text then I would have placed it on my list of recommended Bible versions. But as it is, the best I can do is to recommend it as a secondary version for comparison purposes.

Bibliography:

Friberg, Timothy and Barbara. *Analytical Lexicon to the Greek New Testament*. Copyright © 1994. As found on *BibleWorks™ for Windows™*. Copyright © 1992-1997 Michael S. Bushell. Big Fork, MT: Hermeneutika.

Green, Jay P. Sr. *Literal Translation of the Bible*. LaFayette, IN: Sovereign Grace Publishers, 1976 - 1998.

New American Standard Bible (NAS77 and NAS95). Copyright © 1960-1995. La Biblia de Las Americas. The Lockman Foundation.

Gary Zeolla

New King James Version. Nashville: Thomas Nelson Publisher, 1982.

New International Version. Grand Rapids: Zondervan, 1984.

Chapter Eighteen
Two NCC Bible Versions

The National Council of Churches (NCC) was founded in 1950. Many mainline (and often liberal) denominations are members of this organization. Conservative groups, however, are opposed to the liberal tendencies of the NCC. So many have formed opposing associations (Torbet, pp.428-430).

The NCC has commissioned two versions of the Bible. The first was the *Revised Standard Version* (RSV). The New Testament (NT) of the RSV was first released in 1946 and the Old Testament (OT) in 1952. A second edition of the NT was published in 1971.

The newer version is the *New Revised Standard Version* (NRSV). It was published in 1989. Its stated translation principle is, "As literal as possible, as free as necessary."

The NT of both of these versions is based on a Critical Text, Greek text-type. The latter follows the third edition, corrected by the United Bible Societies (NRSV preface, pp.ix-xi).

For the purposes of this chapter, liberalism will be defined as, "Any movement that is open to redefining or changing the traditional doctrines and practices of Christianity" (Erickson, p.96). A conservative, conversely, is one who adheres to the traditional doctrines and practices of historic Christianity.

The important question to be asked is, has liberalism influenced the translation of these two NCC Bible versions? Verses pertinent to one doctrinal and one practical issue will be examined in order to answer this question.

The Doctrine of the Trinity

The doctrinal issue to be covered is the essential doctrine of the Trinity. This doctrine teaches that within the one essence of God, there eternally exist three distinct yet equal Persons: God the Father, God the Son, and God the Holy Spirit. The first verse to be examined in this connection is the second verse of the Bible.

Genesis 1:2:

The second half of Genesis 1:2, in the *New King James Version* (NKJV), has a reference to the third Person of the Trinity, "And the Spirit of God was hovering over the face of the waters."

The RSV is similar, "and the Spirit of God was moving over the face of the waters." But a footnote in the RSV gives an alternate translation for "Spirit" as "wind." The NRSV takes this a step further by rendering this passage, "while a wind from God swept over the face of the waters." A footnote reads, "Or 'while the spirit of God' or 'while a mighty wind.'" But with "spirit" not being capitalized, neither of these are references to the Holy Spirit either. So the RSV footnote and the NRSV in its text and footnote eliminate any reference to the Holy Spirit in this verse.

But which of these translations is correct? There are three issues to be discussed. First, what is the meaning of the Hebrew word *ruach*? The word can be variously translated as: wind, breathe, mind, spirit, or Spirit (Harris, pp.836, 837). So the issue cannot be settled by the meaning of the word alone.

The second issue to address is the grammatical construction of the passage. The words *ruach* and *elohim* (God) are bound together by what is known as a Hebrew construct. This grammatical form is used to show genitival relationships between two nouns in Hebrew since the language does not have a separate word for "of." An example of this relationship can be seen in Joshua 4:9. In this verse mention is made of "the ark of the covenant."

Note, the words "ark" and "covenant" are connected by the word "of." This is the normal way of rendering the construct. Another method is to use a simple possessive, i.e. "Abraham's servant" (Gen 24:34; Seow, p.70).

Now back to Genesis 1:2. The NRSV tries to connect the words "wind" and "God" with the word "from." However, this is not the normal way of rendering the construct relationship as indicated above. To be true to the grammar, the NRSV would have to use, "a wind of God" or "God's wind." The same would be true if the RSV would put its alternate translation in the text. But neither of these makes much sense. However, "the Spirit of God" flows together nicely.

Third, and most importantly, is the meaning and tense of the verb (Hebrew, *rahap*). The verb in the grammatical form it is used here only occurs one other place in Scripture, in Deuteronomy 32:11. There, it is referring to an eagle that, "Hovers over its young" (NKJV). And the only meaning standard lexicons give for this word is "hovers" (see Harris, p.837; Brown, p.934).

The NRSV even has "hovers" in Deut 32:11. So why doesn't it use "hovers" in Genesis 1:2?—probably because it is pretty difficult for "wind" to "hover."

Moreover, in Genesis 1:2, the verb is a participle, which indicates ongoing motion (Seow, p.47). This is the reason for the NKJV's rendering, "was hovering" and even the RSV's "was moving." But the NRSV's "swept" misses the tense entirely.

Putting all of this together, the NRSV's rendering is simply impossible. It renders the Hebrew construct in an unnatural manner, and it gives the wrong meaning and tense for the verb. And if the RSV were to place its footnote rendering in the text, things wouldn't be much better.

However, the NKJV's translation fits well with all of these points. Moreover, with the NKJV, the picture is that of the Spirit hovering protectively over the newly formed earth. This then is not only a reference to the Holy Spirit, but a proof-text for His personality.

Isaiah 7:14:

Both the RSV and NRSV render the Hebrew word *almah* in this verse as "young woman" rather than the traditional "virgin" (KJV, NKJV). This difference is pertinent to this discussion since, if Jesus was not born of a virgin, He could not have been

God in the flesh. The copulation of two human beings could not have produced One who is full God and full man.

So which rendering is more appropriate? Three points will be mentioned. First, in the OT, "There is no instance where it can be proved that *almah* designates a young woman who is not a virgin" (Harris, p.672). The word appears in the following verses: Gen 24:43; Exod 2:8; Ps 68:25; Prov 30:19; Song 1:3; 6:8.

Second, the Septuagint (a second century B.C. Greek translation of the OT) translates *almah* in this verse by *parthenos*. This is the Greek word for virgin.

Third, and most importantly, Matthew follows the Septuagint when quoting this verse. He uses *parthenos* (Matt 1:23). So the rendering "virgin" is to be preferred.

Isaiah 48:16:

The second half of this verse in the NKJV reads, "And now the Lord GOD and His Spirit have sent Me." The footnote in the NKJV gives the alternate translation of, "Has sent Me and His Spirit. This rendering is probably to be preferred since the verb "sent" is singular.

The context indicates it is the LORD (Jehovah) who is speaking (48:3-5,12-15). So taking the alternate rendering, this verse is saying prophetically, God the Father has sent God the Son and God the Holy Spirit (cp. John 3:16; 14:16). So this OT passage is referring to all three Persons of the Godhead.

However, this very interesting proof-text for the Trinity is weakened in the NRSV. It reads, "And now the Lord GOD has sent me and his spirit." Notice that both the words, "me" and "spirit" are not capitalized. Thus, one could easily miss that these two words are referring to Deity.

Isaiah 61:1:

In addition to Genesis 1:2, there are many other references to "the Spirit of God" or "the Spirit of the Lord" in the OT (see for instance, Gen 41:38; Exod 31:3; Job 33:4; Judg 3:10; 2Sam 23:2; Isa 61:1).

But in every one of these instances, the NRSV does not capitalize the word "spirit." Thus, the reference to the third Person of the Trinity in all of these passages is weakened.

However, when one of these passages is quoted in the NT, "spirit" *is* capitalized in the NRSV (Luke 4:18, quoting Isaiah 61:1). So why is the word not capitalized in Isaiah 61:1 itself, and when "spirit" is used in these phrases elsewhere in the OT?

John 3:13/ 1Timothy 3:16:

In the KJV and NKJV, these two verses are proof-texts for the Deity of Jesus. But in the RSV and NRSV they are not. The reason for this difference is the two former versions are based on the *Textus Receptus*, whereas the two NCC versions are based on the Critical Text.

These textual variants are discussed in detail in Chapter Nine. Here, it will just be noted, two more proof-texts for the Trinity are lost in the RSV and NRSV vs. the KJV and NKJV.

Romans 9:5:

This verse reads in the KJV, "Whose *are* the fathers, and of whom as concerning the flesh Christ *came*, who is over all, God blessed for ever. Amen." This sounds like Paul is declaring Christ to be "God blessed for ever."

The NKJV is even clearer, "of whom *are* the fathers and from whom, according to the flesh, Christ *came*, who is over all, *the* eternally blessed God. Amen."

But the RSV renders this verse: "to them belong the patriarchs, and of their race, according to the flesh, is the Christ. God who is over all be blessed forever. Amen."

By putting a period after "Christ" instead of a comma the RSV makes the final clause a doxology to God the Father rather than a reference to Christ. The NRSV rendering is similar to the NKJV in its text, but an alternative translation given in a footnote reads like the RSV.

Gary Zeolla

So the RSV in its text and the NRSV in a footnote eliminate this verse as a proof-text for the Deity of Christ. The differences in the translations and resultant interpretations of this verse are discussed in-depth in a two-part article titled "Romans 9:5 Research" found on the Trinity section of Darkness to Light's Web site (www.dtl.org/trinity/).

Hebrews 1:3:
This verse presents a subtle loss of a proof-text for the Deity of Christ in the NCC versions. In this verse, in the KJV and NKJV, Jesus is said to be "the brightness" of God's glory. But the RSV says Jesus only "reflects" the glory of God. The NRSV says Christ is merely "the reflection" of God's glory.

But which is it? Does Jesus possess "the brightness" of God's glory within Himself, or does He merely "reflect" God's glory? The difference here is like that between the sun and the moon. The sun has its own brightness, but the moon, an inferior entity, only reflects the brightness of the sun.

The Greek word (*apaugasma*) can have either meaning. In the active sense it means "brightness" or "radiance." But in the passive it means "reflection." Since this is the only place in the NT where this word occurs, which meaning is meant can be difficult to determine.

However, the consensus of the early, Greek-speaking, Church Fathers favors the former sense (Baur, p.82). And *The New International Dictionary of New Testament Theology* concludes its discussion on this word by saying, "On balance, the active sense of 'radiance' is to be chosen in preference to 'reflection'" (Martin, p.290).

So the more liberal rendering of the NCC versions is unwarranted. As Greek scholar Gerhard Kittel declares, "Christ is the effulgence (radiance) of the glory of God as sunshine is of the sun or light of light" (p.87).

Conclusion:

Several proof-texts for the Deity of Christ, the personality of the Holy Spirit, and the Trinity in general are weakened or eliminated in the NCC versions. So it is apparent that doctrinal liberalism has influenced the translation of these versions.

However, it must be mentioned, even with these losses, the doctrine of the Trinity is not called into question. There are still hundreds of verses which show the three-in-oneness of the one true God. This writer's *Scripture Workbook* contains a chapter listing and arranging these hundreds of verses by topic.

The Role of Women in the Church

Moving to a controversial "practical" subject, the liberal tendency of these two NCC Bible versions can also be seen in how they handle verses relating to the role of women in the Church. This is especially true for the NRSV. A couple of places where its translators felt it was "necessary" to be "free" will also be noticed here.

Romans 16:1:

In the NKJV, this verse reads, "I commend to you Phoebe our sister, who is a servant of the church in Cenchrea." But in the RSV, Phoebe is called a "deaconess" and in the NRSV, a "deacon." But which is it? Was this woman simply a servant of her local church, or did she hold an official church office?

The Greek word in question is *diakonos*. It has both masculine and feminine forms, with the feminine form being used here. The word can be translated with any of the above three possibilities (Baur, p.184). But which one best fits here?

A little background on the use of the word in the NT is necessary to help answer this question. This word occurs 30 times in the NT. In 26 of these 30 uses of the word, the RSV and NRSV render it as "servant" or a similar term. Most importantly, the other three times Paul uses it in Romans it is translated as "servant" in both versions (13:4, twice; 15:8).

On the other hand, excluding Romans 16:1, both of these versions render *diakonos* as "deacon" only three times. And in each of these places, the term is clearly referring to an official church office (Phil 1:1; 1Tim 3:8,12).

So the question is, does Paul CLEARLY refer to Phoebe as the holder of an official office in the church at Cenchrea? If not, then the translations of "deaconess" or "deacon" are inaccurate. Since the evidence favors "servant" it should be the primary translation, but since "deaconess" or "deacon" are possible, placing one of these as an alternative translation in a footnote could be justified.

However, the NRSV doesn't even do the reverse. It has "deacon" in the text and "minister" in a footnote. But "minister" also has the connotation of an official church position. But elsewhere, the NRSV generally uses "servant" (e.g. Matt 23:11; Gal 2:17). So why not show both possibilities and at least use "servant" in a footnote here?

1Timothy 3:2:

In 1Timothy chapter three, Paul lists the qualifications for Church leaders. In verse two he writes, "A bishop then must be...the husband of one wife" (NKJV). In 3:12, Paul gives the same requirement for "deacons" and in Titus 1:6 for "elders."

Now it must be asked, how can a WOMAN be the HUSBAND of one WIFE? This question must be answered by anyone who believes women can be ordained.

The NRSV solves this dilemma by "translating" this requirement as, "married only once." Problem is, none of these words actually appear in the Greek text, but all of the words in the NKJV translation do.

James 3:1:

The last verse to be looked at on this subject is James 3:1. Here, the NKJV has, "My brethren, let not many of you become teachers, knowing that we shall receive a stricter judgment." However, the NRSV has, "Not many of you should desire to become teachers, my brothers and sisters, for you know we will be judged with greater strictness."

So the NRSV has "brothers and sisters" instead of "brethren." But a footnote in the NRSV reads, "Gk., brother." The question here is, in using the vocative "brothers," is James only addressing the men in the assembly he is writing to, or is he addressing both the men and women?

The word "brothers" is a masculine noun, so the former seems most likely. However, in the Greek language of the time, a plural masculine term was used when referring to a group of all men and when referring to a mixed group of men and women. The only time the feminine was used was if the group was only composed of women. To emphasize the point, one of my Greek professors at seminary would say that if you had a group consisting of one man and 99 women, a plural masculine would still be used. So a plural masculine term can include only men, or it can include men and women.

Looking at the meaning of the word, the most basic translation Baur gives for it is "brother." The same is true for Friberg and most any other lexicon. However, Baur adds later, "The plural can also mean *brothers and sisters*" (p.16).

What this means is, James could be addressing only the men in the assembly, or he could be addressing both the men and women. It is simply impossible to determine based on the gender or the meaning of the word.

So what is the best way to translate it? A rendering of just "brother" would eliminate the possibility of women being included, and a rendering of "brothers and sisters" would eliminate the possibility of only men being addressed. The NKJV has done the former while the NRSV has done the later. So the NRSV has "fixed" the meaning to include women for its readers. But at least it has given the literal rendering of "brothers" in its footnote.

Possibly the best solution is to use "brothers [and sisters]" within the text. This would indicate that the vocative definitely includes men but might also include women. However, since the

Gary Zeolla

NRSV does not offset added words, one has to wait for the footnote to see the alternative possibility.

Qualifier and Conclusion:

Before concluding, an important qualifier needs to be made here. Along with many liberal denominations, some churches which are conservative otherwise also believe in the ordination of women. But difficult passages relating to this subject cannot be evaded by rewriting them or by translating them in such a way as to "fix" the meaning to the desired interpretation. An honest evaluation of the Scriptural evidence is required when making a decision on a difficult issue like this one.

But since the NRSV does rewrite difficult verses or fixes the meaning to the desired interpretation, it is obvious why this version is favored by liberal churches and others that ordain women.

Bibliography:

The KJV/ NKJV Parallel Reference Bible. Nashville: Thomas Nelson, 1991.

Baur, Walter. *Greek - English Lexicon of the New Testament*. trans. Arndt & Gingrich. Chicago: The University of Chicago Press, 1979.

Brown, Driver, Briggs, Gesenius. *Hebrew & English Lexicon*. Peabody, MA: Hendrickson, 1979.

Erickson, Millard. *A Concise Dictionary of Christian Theology*. Grand Rapids: Baker Book House, 1986.

Friberg, Timothy and Barbara. *Analytical Lexicon to the Greek New Testament*. Copyright © 1994. As found on *BibleWorks™ for Windows™*. Copyright © 1992-1997 Michael S. Bushell. Big Fork, MT: Hermeneutika.

Harris, R. Lard. et.al. eds. *Theological Wordbook of the Old Testament. Vol.II*. Chicago: Moody Press, 1980.

Kittel, Gerhard & Gerhard Friedrich. *Theological Dictionary of the Old Testament*: Abridged in One Volume. by G.

Bromiley. Grand Rapids: William B. Eerdmans Publishing Co., 1985.

Martin, R.P. "Apaugasma" in *New International Dictionary of New Testament Theology*. Vol.2, ed. by Colin Brown. Grand Rapids: Zondervan, 1971.

New Revised Standard Version. Grand Rapids: Zondervan, 1989.

Revised Standard Version. Grand Rapids: Zondervan, 1971.

Seow, C.L. *A Grammar for Biblical Hebrew*. Nashville, Abingdon Press, 1987.

Torbet, Robert. "The Ecumenical Movement" in *Christianity in America: A Handbook*. Grand Rapids: William B. Eerdmans Publishing Company, 1983.

Chapter Nineteen
Review of the New Living Translation

The *New Living Translation* (NLT) is an update of the *Living Bible* (LB). The LB is a paraphrase, but the NLT claims to use a dynamic equivalence method of translation. A few representative verses will be looked at to evaluate whether this claim is true.

Matthew 16:18
KJV: And I say also unto thee, That thou art Peter, and upon this rock I will build my church; and the gates of hell shall not prevail against it.

NKJV: "And I also say to you that you are Peter, and on this rock I will build My church, and the gates of Hades shall not prevail against it.

NIV: And I tell you that you are Peter, and on this rock I will build my church, and the gates of Hades will not overcome it.

NLT: Now I say to you that you are Peter, and upon this rock I will build my church, and all the powers of hell will not conquer it.

The first three versions all have "gates" in the last clause. This is the literal meaning of the Greek word (Friberg). However, for some reason the NLT felt it was necessary to change this word to "powers." Does this matter?

In ancient times walls were put around cities to defend them against attackers, but the gates in the walls were the weak points in the defense. So it was against the gates that attackers generally focused their assaults.

The main point of this historical background is that gates are defensive, not offensive, weapons. So Jesus is saying in this verse that *Hades* will not be able to defend itself against the onslaught of His Church.

But with the NLT changing "gates" to "powers," along with translating the following verb as "conquer," the NLT turns the situation around and makes the Church having to defend itself against *Hades.* Not even the dynamic equivalence NIV considered such a change to be necessary.

Luke 4:30
KJV: But he passing through the midst of them went his way,
NKJV: Then passing through the midst of them, He went His way.
NIV: But he walked right through the crowd and went on his way.
NLT: but he slipped away through the crowd and left them.

The context of this verse is when the people had forced Jesus to the edge of a cliff in order to throw Him off. But note how the text reads in the first three versions: while they are trying to kill Jesus, He passes right through the lynch mob! This could only be a miracle. When people are tying to lynch someone he generally doesn't just walk by them!

However, note that the NLT says Jesus simply "slipped away." This rendering eliminates the miraculous from this verse. Again, not even the NIV makes such a change.

The Greek word means:
(1) *go through, pass through* a place (AC 13.6); of a sword *pierce, penetrate* (fig[uratively] in LU 2.35); (2) of travel fr[om] place to place *go about, travel throughout* (LU 9.6); (3) of death *extend to, come to* (RO 5.12); (4) fig[uratively] of a report *spread, be told everywhere* (LU 5.15).

So the Greek word means to go through something. There is no connotation of "slip" to it.

John 3:21

KJV: But he that doeth truth cometh to the light, that his deeds may be made manifest, that they are wrought in God.

NKJV: "But he who does the truth comes to the light, that his deeds may be clearly seen, that they have been done in God."

NIV: "But whoever lives by the truth comes into the light, so that it may be seen plainly that what he has done has been done through God."

NLT: "But those who do what is right come to the light gladly, so everyone can see that they are doing what God wants."

The KJV says that our good words are "wrought in God," the NKJV that they are "done in God," and the NIV that they are "done through God." Each of these renderings show that we cannot do any good works on our own, it is only "in" or "through" God that we can do good.

The NLT, however, says that we can "do what is right" and are able to be "doing what God wants." All of these words (except for "do" and "God") are not in the Greek text. And by adding these words, our need to be "in God" in order to be able to do good works is eliminated. So the NLT clearly denies the Calvinist doctrine of total depravity and is bordering on teaching salvation by works.

Acts 13:48

KJV: And when the Gentiles heard this, they were glad, and glorified the word of the Lord: and as many as were ordained to eternal life believed.

NKJV: Now when the Gentiles heard this, they were glad and glorified the word of the Lord. And as many as had been appointed to eternal life believed.

NIV: When the Gentiles heard this, they were glad and honored the word of the Lord; and all who were appointed for eternal life believed.

NLT: When the Gentiles heard this, they were very glad and thanked the Lord for his message; and all who were appointed to eternal life became believers.

It is to the NLT's credit that it corrected the mistranslation of the original *Living Bible* in this verse. As was discussed in Chapter Three, instead of, "as many as had been appointed to eternal life believed" (NKJV), the LB had, "as many as wanted eternal life, believed." This change moved the basis of salvation from God's previous "appointment" to human "wants," and thus eliminated the Calvinistic overtones of this verse. But the NLT's rendering is now similar to the NKJV and other versions.

However, the second phrase has been significantly altered. Rather than, "and glorified the word of the Lord" (NKJV), the NLT has, "and thanked the Lord for his message."

But the Greek word rendered "glorified" in the NKJV means:
(1) as giving or sharing a high status *glorify, make great* (RO 8.30); (2) as enhancing the reputation of God or man *praise, honor, magnify* (MK 2.12); (3) as putting into a position of power and great honor, esp[ecially] in the future life *glorify* (JN 7.39); (4) pass[ive] (a) of things greatly valued and excellent *be wonderful, glorious* (1P 1.8); (b) of pers[ons] receiving great honor *be glorified, praised* (LU 4.15).

So the Greek word has a much stronger connotation than just to "thank someone." And the English word "glorify" captures the meaning of the Greek word very well.

Glorify means:

1. to cause to be or treat as being more splendid, excellent, etc., than would normally be considered: to glorify military life. 2. to honor with praise, admiration, or worship; extol: to glorify a hero. 3. to make glorious; invest with glory. 4. to praise the glory of (God), esp[ecially] as an act of worship (*Webster's*).

Ephesians 1:5

KJV: Having predestinated us unto the adoption of children by Jesus Christ to himself, according to the good pleasure of his will,

NKJV: having predestined us to adoption as sons by Jesus Christ to Himself, according to the good pleasure of His will,

NIV: he predestined us to be adopted as his sons through Jesus Christ, in accordance with his pleasure and will

NLT: His unchanging plan has always been to adopt us into his own family by bringing us to himself through Jesus Christ. And this gave him great pleasure.

The first three versions all say we were "predestined" to be adopted. Friberg defines the Greek word as, "*decide on beforehand, determine in advance.*" Lidell and Scott have, "*to determine beforehand, to predetermine, pre-ordain,* N.T.

So the word includes the idea of a determining in advance what will happen. And the English word "predestine" means, "to destine in advance; foreordain; predetermine" (*Webster's*). So "predestine" captures the meaning of the Greek word rather well.

However, the NLT only says it was God's "unchanging plan." The difference here is that something that is predestined will definitely happen, while a "plan" (whether unchanging or not), can be thwarted. Now it is true that no one can thwart God's plan, but that is because His plans have been predestined by Him to occur. But someone reading the NLT would not know that God predestines His plans as the word does not occur in the NLT.

Secondly, the first three versions all say that the reason God predestined our adoption is because it was "according to the good pleasure of His will." But the NLT has our adoption giving God "great pleasure."

> The Greek word rendered "will" in the first three versions means:
> Gener[ally], as the result of what one has decided *will;* (1) objectively *will, design, purpose, what is willed;* (a) used predom[innately] of what God has willed; creation (RV 4.11); redemption (EP 1.5); callings (CO 1.9), etc.; (b) of what a pers[on] intends to bring about by his own action *purpose* (LU 22.42); (c) of one's sensual or sexual impulse *desire* (JN 1.13; EP 2.3); (d) of what a pers]on] intends to bring about through the action of another *purpose* (LU 12.47); (2) subjectively, *the act of willing* or *wishing;* (a) predom[innately] of the exercise of God's *will* (GA 1.4); (b) of the exercise of the human will *desire, wish* (2P 1.21).

So the word refers to God's "will" or "purpose." But rather than our adoption being dependent on God's will as the Greek text has it, the NLT, by not translating this word, makes God's pleasure dependent on our adoption. With both of these changes, the NLT has eliminated the Calvinistic theology that is in these verses.

Galatians 3:20

KJV: Now a mediator is not a *mediator* of one, but God is one.

NKJV: Now a mediator does not *mediate* for one *only,* but God is one.

277

NIV: A mediator, however, does not represent just one party; but God is one.

NLT: Now a mediator is needed if two people enter into an agreement, but God acted on his own when he made his promise to Abraham.

A strictly literal translation of this verse would be, "But the mediator is not of one, but the God is one." But note how different the NLT is from this literal translation. The literal translation has only 12 words whereas the NLT has 26 words. Now admittedly, especially when taken out of context, the literal translation is rather difficult to understand. A.T. Robertson says, "Over 400 interpretations of this verse have been made!"

So what has the NLT done? It has picked from among these over 400 possible interpretations and has given what it believes is the one correct INTERPRETATION. But it most definitely has not TRANSLATED this verse.

Is the NLT correct in its interpretation of this verse? Maybe, maybe not. That is not the point. The point is, the purpose of a translation is to translate the Hebrew and Greek text into English. It is not the job of a translation to interpret the text.

Now some of these other versions have added some words to the literal translation to try to make it easier to understand. However, the first two have italicized or bracketed the added words so the reader knows that the words have in fact been added.

And note that the NIV, although not italicizing the words, has only added two words to the text, "represent just." This is a far cry from the NLT's many additions.

Hebrews 2:9

KJV: But we see Jesus, who was made a little lower than the angels for the suffering of death, crowned with glory and honour; that he by the grace of God should taste death for every man.

NKJV: But we see Jesus, who was made a little lower than the angels, for the suffering of death crowned with glory and honor, that He, by the grace of God, might taste death for everyone.

NIV: But we see Jesus, who was made a little lower than the angels, now crowned with glory and honor because he suffered death, so that by the grace of God he might taste death for everyone.

NLT: What we do see is Jesus, who "for a little while was made lower than the angels" and now is "crowned with glory and honor" because he suffered death for us. Yes, by God's grace, Jesus tasted death for everyone in all the world.

This verse is controversial due to its theological implications. Calvinists believe that Jesus only died for His elect. Arminians believe Jesus died for all people, and this verse is one which Arminians will point to in order to support their doctrine.

The verse ends in the KJV with "every man" and in the NKJV and NIV with "everyone." However, the word "man" or "one" is added. They are not in the Greek text. But, unfortunately, none of these versions italicize this added word.

However, notice how the NLT deals with this verse. The verse ends with "everyone in all the world." These additions really force an Arminian perspective into the text. But again, none of the words after "every" are actually in the text, and the NLT gives no indication that they are added.

So how should a translator deal with such a controversial text? In this writer's opinion, it is best for translators not to interject their own interpretations into the text if at all possible. Now the reason why each of these versions, and most others, add word(s) to the end of this verse is because ending the verse with "every" would leave the verse "hanging."

However, along with "every," the Greek word can also mean "all" (Friberg). And using "for all" would leave the text ambiguous (as the Greek text is) as to who the "all" is: all people or all the elect.

Similar to this verse is John 12:32:

KJV: And I, if I be lifted up from the earth, will draw all *men* unto me.

NKJV: "And I, if I am lifted up from the earth, will draw all *peoples* to Myself."

NIV: "But I, when I am lifted up from the earth, will draw all men to myself."

NLT: "And when I am lifted up on the cross, I will draw everyone to myself."

Note again, the NLT renders the same Greek word as "everyone." But again, the word means simply "all" or "every." In this case, the KJV and NIV add "men" and the NKJV, "peoples." But at least the KJV and NKJV italicize these words, only the NIV does not indicate the word is added. And the NLT has followed the NIV's lead by adding "one" to "every" without any indication it has done so.

Note also, the NLT (along with the NIV) has also changed "if" (a condition of the third class, indicating some degree of uncertainty) to "when," which indicates a much more "certain" condition than the third class condition warrants.

In addition, the NLT has rendered "from the earth" as "on the cross." This is one possible interpretation of Jesus' statement, but not the only one. Jesus could also be referring to being "lifted up" in the sense of being exalted in evangelism and worship.

This latter interpretation is somewhat more likely given the third class condition preceding it. It is only "if" believers exalt Jesus that people are drawn to Him. The NLT's interpretation is less likely given that Jesus' crucifixion was a certainty (Matt 26:54; Luke 18:32-33). But the important point is, "on the cross" is an interpretation, not a translation. The word means "earth" not "cross" (Friberg). And again, not even the NIV makes this extreme of a change.

Conclusion

The NLT is slightly more accurate than its predecessor, the LB, and it corrects some of the LB worse renderings. However, the NLT is still not as accurate as a dynamic equivalence version, such as the NIV. So the NLT is a little more accurate than a true paraphrase, but it is not really accurate enough to be a true dynamic equivalence version either. It is somewhere in between these two principles.

But however it is classified, the NLT is simply not a true translation of the original texts, despite the word "Translation" being in its title. It is actually a commentary, with an Arminian bias. If one wants to write a commentary from an Arminian perspective, that is their choice, but it is not okay to insert Arminian or any other kind of interpretations into what is called a "translation" of the Bible.

Bibliography:

BibleWorks™ for Windows™. Copyright © 1992-1999 *BibleWorks*, L.C.C. Big Fork, MT: Hermeneutika. Programmed by Michael S. Bushell and Michael D. Tan.

Friberg, Timothy and Barbara. *Analytical Greek New Testament*. Copyright © 1994 and *Analytical Lexicon to the Greek New Testament*. Copyright © 1994. Both as found on *BibleWorks™ for Windows™*.

New International Version (NIV). Grand Rapids: Zondervan, 1984.

King James Version (KJV).

New King James Version (NKJV). Nashville: Thomas Nelson Publisher, 1982.

New Living Translation (NLT). Tyndale Charitable Trust. 1996.

Robertson, A.T. Word Pictures in the Greek New Testament, as found on *BibleWorks for Windows™*. Copyright © 1992-1999 BibleWorks, L.C.C. Big Fork, MT: Hermeneutika. Programmed by Michael S. Bushell and Michael D. Tan.

Gary Zeolla

Webster's Talking Dictionary/ Thesaurus. Licensed property of
Parson's Technology, Inc. v. 1.0b. Software Copyright 1996
by Exceller Software Corp. Based on Random House
Webster's College Dictionary. Copyright 1995 by Random
House, Inc.

Chapter Twenty
Review of the NET Bible

Part One

The *New English Translation*, also know as *The NET Bible*, is an Internet Bible translation project. The full text of the translation is posted at www.netbible.org/netbible/, so it is freely available to anyone with an Internet connection. But what is this translation like? Part One of this review will look at the Background Pages for the NET. Part Two will then study some sample verses from the NET.

Background Pages

Below are some quotes from the background pages for the NET, along with my comments. The quotes are indented.

New versus Updated Translation:

Quoting from the "Preface" first:
> The NEW ENGLISH TRANSLATION, also known as THE NET BIBLE, is a complctcly new translation of the Bible, not a revision or an update of a previous English version. It was completed by more than twenty biblical scholars who worked directly from the best currently available Hebrew, Aramaic, and Greek texts.

In several other places the background pages make a big deal about the NET not being an update of a previous translation but a "completely new translation." As this book makes clear, currently my preferred Bible version is the *New King James Version* (NKJV). Prior to that I used the *New American Standard Bible* (NASB). Both of these versions updated previous versions (the *King James Version* and *American Standard Version*, respectively).

Also, my own translation, the *Analytical-Literal Translation* (ALT), was initially an updating of *Young's Literal Translation*. So I obviously do not consider an update of a previous Bible version to be somehow inferior to a "new" translation.

On the other hand, another favorite translation of mine is the *Literal Translation of the Bible* (LITV), which is a new translation. So the bottom line is, a good Bible version can be produced either starting "fresh" from the Hebrew and Greek texts or by updating a previous version. But whichever method is used, the final recourse has to be to the Hebrew and Greek texts. This is done whether one is starting a new translation or updating a previous one.

Freely Distributed:

An interesting point in regards to the NET is it can be attained freely:

Anyone anywhere in the world with an Internet connection will be able to use and print out the NET Bible without cost for personal study. In addition anyone who wants to share the Bible with others can print up to 1,000 copies and give them away free without the need for written permission.

The original authors of the Bible made the books and letters they had written available for free. That is what we're doing electronically.

This is a plus. Most new Bible versions require extensive royalty payments for distribution. However, the Bible does say, "The laborer is worthy of his wages" (Luke 10:7; 1Tim 5:17; NKJV). So this writer does not believe it is wrong for a person or company to profit from the effort put into producing and distributing a Bible version. And it should be noted, a hardcopy edition of the NET Bible is now available for purchase from the NET's Web site. So someone is profiting from it.

The situation is similar for the *Analytical-Literal Translation* (ALT). The full text is posted on Darkness to Light's Web site (www.dtl.org/alt/), and it is available for purchase in hardcopy format. However, both versions are copyrighted, and there are limits as to how much they can be distributed without written permission.

Study notes:

The NET has extensive study notes. The notes window says, "These are explanations of different possible translations and rationale for the preferred translation as well as study notes on selected passages."

This review will not evaluate the quality of the "study notes" which involve giving possible interpretations of the text, but the comments in the footnotes concerning the translation seen in the text of the NET will be discussed in the next chapter. Here, a couple of comments will be made on a couple of the ways the notes are utilized in the NET Bible.

> ...the translators and editors used the notes to show major interpretive options and/ or textual options for difficult or disputed passages, so that the user knows at a glance what the alternatives are.

So the notes are supposed to indicate when there are textual variants for a passage. However, one verse will be looked at in the next chapter where an important textual variant is not even mentioned in the note.

> ...the translators and editors used the notes to give a translation that was formally equivalent, while placing a somewhat more dynamically equivalent translation in the text itself to promote better readability and understandability.

285

The bottom line of this quote is that a more "free" translation is given in the text while a literal translation of God's actual words are relegated to a footnote. This "feature" will be seen in the sample verses in the next chapter.

Process of production:

> Finally, the use of electronic media gives the translators and editors of the NET Bible the possibility of continually updating and improving the translation and notes.
>
> By publishing every working draft of the NET Bible on the Internet from the very beginning of the project, more people have previewed the NET Bible than any translation in history.

The NET Bible is now finished, but this is how it was produced. And these two points were a plus. It is helpful to allow readers a chance to review and make input into a translation while it is in progress. However, the NET is not the only Bible version that did so. The ALT was posted on the Web from its earliest stage. So people had a chance to review and comment on it while it was being produced. And in fact, this writer received many helpful comments from readers while working on the ALT. In addition, the *World English Bible* (WEB) is following the same pattern (www.ebible.org).

Interesting claim:

> The NET Bible truly is the first English translation for the next millennium.

This was written in 1999, but the idea remains the same. There are several Bible versions that were finished or were in progress around the turn of the millennium. And every one seemed to be making this claim. But which was truly "first" is hard to say, and rather irrelevant. The quality of a translation is what matters, not its timing.

Literal Translation not Possible?

Next, the NET translators make an interesting, and disturbing claim.

Although one of the general principles of this translation is to indicate in the footnotes a more literal rendering, not every departure from such is noted. For one thing, Greek and English are sufficiently different that to document every departure would be an exercise in futility. No translation is completely literal, nor should that be a desirable goal.

A completely word-for-word literal translation would be unreadable. John 4:15, for example, would be rendered: "Says to him the woman, 'Sir, give to me this the water that not I thirst nor I come here to draw." Matthew 1:18 would say, "Of the but Jesus Christ the birth thus was. Being betrothed the mother of him, Mary, to Joseph, before or to come together them she was found in belly having from Spirit Holy." Such examples are not isolated, but are the norm. Claims for a literal translation must necessarily have a lot of fine print.

Since this writer translated a Bible version with the word "Literal" in its title, it's a little hard not to take offense at these bold pronouncements. This writer believes that a literal translation is not only the most appropriate method of translating but can also produce a rather readable text. There is no doubt that by re-writing the text one can produce a more readable version. But is a re-written version of God's Word still God's Word? That is the important question.

Moreover, the above "examples" as to the awkwardness of a literal translation are highly exaggerated. Furthermore, no "fine print" is required but simply an explanation of the principles used in translation. This is done in the Background Pages for the ALT, which are posted on the ALT section of Darkness to Light's Web site (www.dtl.org/alt/). That said, a comparison will be made of the claimed "literal" translations in the quote above with the ALT and the NET.

John 4:15:

"lit": Says to him the woman, "Sir, give to me this the water that not I thirst nor I come here to draw."

ALT: The woman says to Him, "Lord, give this water to me so that I shall not be thirsting nor coming to this place to be drawing."

NET: The woman said to him, "Sir, give me this water, so that I will not be thirsty or have to come here to draw water."

Note first that the awkwardness of the first phrase is reduced in the ALT by simply changing the word order. It is mentioned in the ALT Background Pages that word order changes will be made for readability sake but kept to a minimum.

Second, the definitive article ("the") before water is omitted. Again, the ALT Background Pages mention that the definite article is often omitted as Greek frequently uses the article when it is awkward or unneeded in English. In this case, the "this" does the function of the article by making the noun definitive. The woman is not referring to just any water, but the kind of water Jesus referred to in the previous verse.

Third, "that" (Gr., *ina*) can also be translated as "so that" (Friberg). And in this context it makes more sense. So there is no movement from literal here.

Fourth, the verbs "thirst" and "come" are present tense, subjunctive mood. As explained on the ALT: Background Pages, these forms together mean the text is best translated using a "progressive" sense and, as context warrants, with "shall" or "should" (Dana and Mantey, pp. 181, 171). So the ALT is actually more literal than the supposed literal translation given.

Fifth, the word "here" can also be translated "to this place" (Friberg). So again, there is no movement from literal here. And finally, "to draw" is a present tense infinitive, which again indicates a progressive sense (Dana and Mantey, p. 181). So again, the ALT is more literal in rendering it as it does.

So putting the above together, the only movement from literal in the ALT is a minor word order change and the omission of one article. Otherwise, the rest of the ALT is actually just as if not more "literal" than the claimed literal translation. And all of this is explained in clear, not fine, print on the ALT Background Pages.

But as for the NET, it adds the words "have to" and "water" without any warrant from the Greek text and without indicating the words are added. So it has, in this writer's opinion, gone further from literal than is needed to make the sense clear.

Now, the second example is more difficult. But it will first be said, despite the NET's claim, this is an "isolated" difficult verse and not the norm.

Matt 1:18:

"lit": Of the but Jesus Christ the birth thus was. Being betrothed the mother of him, Mary, to Joseph, before or to come together them she was found in belly having from Spirit Holy.

ALT: Now the birth of Jesus Christ was in this manner: For His mother Mary, having been promised in marriage to Joseph, before they came together [fig., had sexual relations] was found having in [the] womb [fig., to have become pregnant] by [the] Holy Spirit.

NET: Now the birth of Jesus Christ happened this way. While his mother Mary was engaged to Joseph, but before they came together, she was found to be pregnant through the Holy Spirit.

First, there is some word order change in the ALT, but again, only as much as is needed to make the text clear. Moreover, "But" (gr. *de*) is always consider a "postpositive," meaning in the Greek text it is usually the second word but is always translated first. This is standard.

Second, the word "thus" can legitimately be translated as "in this manner."

Third, the phase "Being betrothed" is actually more accurately rendered in the ALT by "having been promised in marriage." First, "betroth" at this time meant, "to promised in marriage" (*Webster's*). They are simply two different ways of saying the same thing. Either would be legitimate translations of the Greek. But "betrothed" is archaic, so it is not used in the ALT.

Further, the verb is an aorist, passive participial. Hence "having been" is an accurate translation as explained in the ALT: Background Pages (and see Dana and Mantey, pp. 161, 193).

Fourth, "before or to come together them" is a literal rendering of each word, and using "to" is the normal way an infinitive is translated. However, Friberg specifically says that the phrase "before or" (Gr. *prin e*) simply means "before." Also, as clearly explained in the ALT: Background Pages, it is not always necessary to use "to" in translating an infinitive. In addition, Dana and Mantey specifically state, "The infinitive with *prin* or *prin e* is used to express *antecedent* time" (p.215, emphasis in original).

And finally, "them" is an accusative (i.e., a direct object), so "them" would be the most literal rendering of the word form. However, the reason for the use of this form is simply the word order in the Greek, placing the pronoun after the verb rather than before as in English. So changing it to the nominative (i.e. subject) "they" is simply due to changing the word order.

So on every point, "before they came together" is a perfectly legitimate and accurate translation. It only deviates from a strictly literal translation in very minor ways, but all of which are justified on lexical and grammatical grounds.

And finally, the hard part: "she was found in belly having from Spirit Holy" vs. "she was found [to be] having in [the] womb [i.e. to have become pregnant] by the Holy Spirit."

Translating such "delicate" issues as pregnancy, sexual acts, bodily functions, and like is difficult. The reason is, each culture has their own "socially acceptable" ways of describing such things, and ways that are not so socially acceptable. And what is often seen in the Bible are "idioms" for such things.

However, even in such cases, it is this writer's opinion that the literal translation of the idiom should be given first, and then in an explanatory note the meaning of the idiom expressed, or at least, if the meaning is given in the text, then the literal translation should be given in a footnote. The reason for having the literal rendering somewhere is simple: the meaning of the idiom just might be debatable. So readers should be given the literal translation so they can decide for themselves if the given explanation is correct. But giving an explanation is also helpful as sometimes it might be hard for readers to understand the idiom.

In this case, first it should be noted, every lexicon I checked gives a possible meaning for the Greek word as "womb" along with "belly" (e.g. Friberg). So the NET is exaggerating the difficulty in saying the "literal" translation is "she was found in belly."

So using the perfectly legitimate translation of "womb," the ALT renders the phrase "having in [the] womb." The use of "having" is due to the verb being a participle. But the important question here is, would the average person know what "having in [the] womb" means?

In this writer's mind, to say a woman is having in the womb, though awkward, would clearly indicate pregnancy is meant. And I would think most readers of average intelligence would be able to figure this out. But to be sure, the ALT gives the explanatory note of "to have become pregnant."

And finally, the word "from" can also be translated as "by" (Friberg). [And with a minor word order change and adding "the", the ALT's "by [the] Holy Spirit" is just as literalas, but much more readable than, the NET's claimed literal "from Spirit Holy." So again, the NET, at every point, simply seems to be trying to make a "literal" translation seem more difficult than it really is.

Conjunctions:

The NET Preface writes:

A major category of non-literal translation involves certain conjunctions. For example, the Greek word *kaiv* (*kai*), meaning generally "and, even, also, yet, but, indeed," is often left untranslated at the beginning of a sentence. When such is the case, there is usually no note given. However, if the possibility exists that an interpretive issue is involved, a note is given.

In this translator's mind, conjunctions are very important. They show there is a relationship between the verse in question and the preceding or following verse. In other words, if the reader is studying a verse and it begins with a conjunction, the preceding verse should always be checked.

Similarly, the following verse should also always be checked to see if it begins with a conjunction. If a conjunction occurs in one or both places, then the reader knows the verse in question does not "stand alone" but must be interpreted in the light of the related verses. Such a practice would go a long way in preventing the very common practice of taking verses out of context.

Given this importance of conjunctions, this translator would not like to take it upon himself to decide when a conjunction is "important" and when it is not. So conjunctions are always translated in the ALT. The NET translators, however, appear to feel they are qualified to make such decisions for their readers.

On one point though, the Preface is correct, conjunctions like *kai* do have a range of meanings. Although, in this case, the most basic meaning is "and," depending on context, alternative translations can and should be utilized. So the ALT does use different, though a limited number of renderings, to translate conjunctions.

Inclusive language:

> With the NET Bible our concern was to be gender-accurate rather than gender-inclusive, striving for faithfulness to the original biblical texts while at the same time seeking to attain accuracy in terms of Modern English.
>
> At the same time, we do not employ "Ideological Gender Inclusivity," since we do not believe the Bible should be rewritten to incorporate gender-inclusive language foreign to the original.

With this basic philosophy, this writer is in agreement. If the text can be accurately translated in an inclusive manner then it should be. But under no circumstances should the text be altered to make it inclusive where it is not.

However, when it comes to the translation of specific terms, the ALT does differ from the NET in several translation decisions. At times the ALT would be less inclusive but at other times more inclusive than the NET.

Greek text used:

> The following quote is taken from the page, "Introduction to the NET Bible New Testament."
>
> As for the Greek text used in the NET New Testament 1.0, an eclectic text was followed, differing in a number of places from the standard critical text as

represented by the Nestle-Aland 27th edition and the United Bible Societies' 4th edition.

Where there are significant variant readings, these are normally indicated in a text critical note, along with a few of the principal witnesses (manuscripts) supporting the variants.

So the Greek text being used to translate the NT from is basically the Critical Text (CT). As discussed elsewhere in this book, this writer strongly believes the *Textus Receptus* (TR) or even better the Majority Text (MT) are much to be preferred over the CT.

In the verses to be looked at in the next chapter, a couple of places where there are "significant variant readings" between these texts will be seen. It will also be seen whether the NET keeps it promise to footnote such significant variants.

Idioms and Pronouns:

The following quotes are taken from the page "Appendix A: NET Bible Principles of Translation."

Idiomatic expressions and figurative language in the original languages have been changed when they make no sense to a typical modern English reader or are likely to lead to misunderstanding by a typical modern English reader. The literal reading has been placed in a note giving a brief explanation (translator's note).

Nouns have been used for pronouns where the English pronoun would be obscure or ambiguous. This has been indicated in a note.

So again, it is seen the NET relegates God's actual words to a footnote, while giving its interpretation of the words in the text.

Now it is true that sometimes idiomatic expression can be hard to understand or that the antecedent to a pronoun can be ambiguous. And an explanatory note would be helpful to a make such things clear. But again, this writer believes God's actual words should be given first (i.e. in the text) and then the explanation in a note, rather than vice-a-versa. But at least the NET says it will give God's words in a footnote rather than omitting them altogether.

Miscellaneous translation decisions:

Questions expecting a negative answer have been phrased to indicate this to the English reader.

Indicating the expected answer to a question, as shown by the Greek grammar, is helpful. Such a practice is utilized in the ALT. Along with when a negative answer is expected, the ALT also shows when a positive answer is expected.

Clearly redundant expressions such as "answered and said" have been avoided unless they have special rhetorical force in context. The literal reading is frequently indicated in a note.

Again, this writer would not like to take it upon himself to decide when God was "clearly redundant" versus when such a phrase is being used for a reason. So the ALT always translates the text as God inspired it.

Introductory expressions like "verily, verily" have been translated idiomatically, the single amen as "I tell you the truth" and the double amen (peculiar to John's Gospel) as "I tell you the solemn truth."

Any method of translating this phrase that indicates the speaker is declaring what he believes is positively true is acceptable. The ALT uses "Positively" and "Most positively" for these terms respectively.

In places where passive constructions create ambiguity, obscurity, or awkwardness in modern English, either the agent has been specified from context or the construction changed to active in the English translation, with an explanatory note.

The particular "voice" (active, passive, or middle) has been inspired for a reason. So again, the voices are translated as what they are in the ALT. As throughout this review, this writer simply does not feel it is necessary or prudent to "second-guess" God and change the grammatical forms God chose to use.

This review is continued in the next chapter.

Bibliography:
See end of Chapter Twenty-one.

Chapter Twenty-one
NET Bible Review

Part Two

This review is continued from the previous chapter.

Verses

In this second half of this review, an evaluation will be made of how the principles discussed in the previous chapter play out in actual translation of a few sample verses as they appear in the NET Bible and in the ALT. For comparison, verses will also be quoted from the NKJV and LITV.

Matthew 2:10
NET: When they saw the star they shouted joyfully. (fn: Grk "they rejoiced with very great joy.")

ALT: And having seen the star, they rejoiced exceedingly [with] great joy.

NKJV: When they saw the star, they rejoiced with exceedingly great joy.

LITV: And seeing the star, they rejoiced exceedingly [with] a great joy.

This verse is again a rather simple verse to translate. There are only a couple of decisions that a translator needs to make. The first is how to render the participle in the first half of the verse. And each of the decisions seen above are possible ("When they saw," "having seen," and "seeing").

The second is whether the word "exceedingly" is an adjective modifying the noun "joy" or if it is an adverb modifying the verb "rejoiced." Either is grammatically possible, but the latter is more likely. And such simple differences

Gary Zeolla

between Bible versions are not significant. But they do show why even literal versions can differ.

However, there are also differences between these verses that go beyond simple decisions on how to translate a grammatical form. The first is whether to even translate the conjunction *kai* at the beginning of the verse. A literal translation would simply translate it. But both the NET and NKJV have deemed the word "unimportant" and have left it untranslated.

Now this is a rare example as the NKJV does generally translate conjunctions. But as the above background information for the NET indicated, it is common for the NET not to translate this conjunction.

But the more important differences appear in the second half of the verse. First is a point somewhat opposite to the above: in the ALT and LITV the word "with" is bracketed whereas in the NET and NKJV it is not. The reason for bracketing the word in the former two versions is the word "with" is not actually in the Greek text but is added for clarity.

Now again, this is a rare example for the NKJV as it generally does offset words added for clarity (using italics). But the NET never does so. Again, is this important? Is it OK for translators to add words to the text which have no basis in the original Hebrew or Greek without somehow offsetting them so that readers know they are added?

Again, this writer does not believe so. To mix the translators' added words with God's words without leaving the reader any way to distinguish between the two is misguided. In this case, the word is not significant. But an example will be seen later where it is. And to prevent a reader from basing an interpretation of a verse on a word that is not actually God-breathed, this writer feels strongly such added words should be offset in some way.

Furthermore, on the question of omitting and adding words to the text, there are several Biblical verses which warn against adding or subtracting from God's words (see Deut 4:2; 12:32; Prov 30:5,6; Rev 22:18,19).

Finally on this verse is the last phrase. The only difference between the last three versions is again, the different decision on the word "exceedingly" and whether to offset the added word "with." But the NET has "solved" both of these questions by simply re-writing the phrase to "they shouted joyfully."

As the NET's own footnote indicates, the Greek verb means "rejoiced" not "shouted." And the final word is a noun ("joy") not an adverb ("joyfully"). So why does the NET not just translate the verb and noun? The answer would be that the translators deemed the phrase, "they rejoiced [with] very great joy" either too difficult for the average person to understand, or maybe, they just thought it was too awkward.

But this writer has never found this phrase to be difficult or awkward. Now maybe someone else out there has, but it really is not that difficult. Maybe it is a little awkward, with the redundancy and all. But this redundancy is for a reason.

The Greek text contains what is called a "cognate accusative." This means the noun in the accusative case is a "cognate" (has the same root) as the verb (i.e. "joy" and "rejoiced"). And this Greek construction is used to emphasize the text. And that is what the redundancy does: it emphasizes the strong emotion felt. So not translating this "redundancy" leaves the text less forceful than it is in the Greek.

John 3:13

NET: "No one has ascended into heaven except the one who descended from heaven—the Son of Man." (lengthy interpretive comments, but no mention of a textual variant)

ALT: "And no one has ascended into heaven, except the One having descended from heaven—the Son of Humanity, the One being in heaven.

NKJV: "No one has ascended to heaven but He who came down from heaven, that is, the Son of Man who is in heaven.

LITV: And no one has gone up into Heaven, except He having come down out of Heaven, the Son of Man who is in Heaven.

This verse again shows the loss of the conjunction at the beginning of the verse in the NET and in the NKJV, while being retained in the ALT and LITV.

A noticeable difference is then seen in the use of "the Son of Humanity" in the ALT rather than the traditional "the Son of Man." So this is one case where the ALT is more inclusive than the NET. The word in question does mean "man," but it more generally refers to humanity as a whole (Friberg).

But the most important difference is seen in the last phase, or more specifically, is seen in the NET not including the final phase, "who is in heaven."

The reason the NET does not include this phrase is because the phrase is not include in the Critical Text which the NET is based on. However, the phrase is included in the *Textus Receptus* and in the Majority Text, one or the other of which the other versions follow. The textual evidence for including this phrase is discussed in Chapter Nine, so it will not be pursued here.

But here, it will be pointed out that the NET, despite the promise in its background pages, does not even indicate this textual variant in a footnote. The verse has lengthy interpretive comments but no mention of this very significant textual variant.

The reason this variant is important is because, with the phrase, this verse is saying that Jesus, while He was on the earth talking to Nicodemus, was also in heaven. As such, this verse demonstrates Jesus was omnipresent even during His incarnation. And thus, this verse is a proof-text for His deity.

Acts 13:48

NET: When the Gentiles heard this, they began to rejoice and praise the word of the Lord, and all who had been appointed for eternal life believed. (fn: The imperfect verb *echairon* (*ecairon*) and the following *ejdovchazon* (*edochazon*) are translated as ingressive imperfects.)

ALT: Now the Gentiles hearing [this], they began rejoicing and glorifying the word of the Lord, and as many as had been appointed to eternal life believed.

NKJV: Now when the Gentiles heard this, they were glad and glorified the word of the Lord. And as many as had been appointed to eternal life believed.

LITV: And hearing, the nations rejoiced and glorified the Word of the Lord. And as many as had been appointed to eternal life believed.

The main reason I use this verses as a "test verse" is to see if the version tries to evade the rather strong "Calvinistic" sense of the verse. The key word in this regard is "appointed." The Greek word can also be translated as "ordained" (Friberg). Furthermore, the verb is in the perfect tense and passive voice. This construction indicates a previous action with ongoing results done to the subject by another (in this case the other One most likely is God). Hence the use of "had been" in all versions.

With the correct translation being "had been appointed" this verse appears to be teaching that those, and only those, who had previously been "appointed" to eternal life believed. Such an interpretation has strong implications for the doctrine of predestination.

Since all four versions, including the NET, use "had been appointed" there is no difficulty with these translation trying to evade this interpretation by translation. Of course, Arminians would want to interpret the verse differently. But any interpretation must be based on a proper translation.

That said, there are other elements worth looking at in this verse. First is the conjunction at the beginning of the verse. The Greek word is *de* and can be translated variously as "but," "now," or "and." So the "Now" in the ALT and NKJV and the "And" in the LITV are both accurate. But the important point is, the NET does not translate the conjunction at all.

The next notable difference is "When the Gentiles heard" (NET and NKJV) vs. "hearing [this], the nations" (ALT) or "hearing, the nations" (LITV). Again, a participle is involved, which can be rendered in either of these fashions. Also, "Gentiles" or "nations" are both possible translations of the Greek word (Friberg). So either way of rendering is legitimate.

The next important difference is seen in the phrase "they began to rejoice" as it is rendered in the NET. As the NET's footnote correctly points out, this verb is an imperfect, which both the NET and the ALT are taking as being in the "ingressive" sense. This means the verb is describing the beginning of a past action.

However, a significant difference is that the NET has "they began to rejoice" while the ALT has "began rejoicing." This difference is important as the most basic meaning of the imperfect is an action that was ongoing in the past. And the English participle is the best way of indicating this ongoing sense. So the ALT brings out all points of the Greek grammar.

However, both the NKJV and LITV miss both of these points of the Greek grammar. They both use a simple English past ("were glad" and "rejoiced," respectively). So the ALT shows both the "ingressive" and the ongoing sense of the verb, the NET only the ingressive sense, while the NKJV and LITV neither.

The next difference is rather simple. The NET has "all who" while the other versions have "as many as." It will just be said the latter is a more literal translation of the Greek text (Friberg).

So overall, the differences in this verse between these four versions are not that significant. But this will change with the next verse.

1Corinthians 7:1

NET: Now with regard to the issues you wrote about: "It is good for a man not to have sexual relations with a woman." (fn: *Grk* "It is good for a man not to

> touch a woman," a euphemism for sexual relations.
> [plus additional interpretive comments])

ALT: Now concerning [the things] of which you* wrote
to me: [it is] good for a man not to be touching a
woman [sexually].

NKJV: Now concerning the things of which you wrote
to me: *It is* good for a man not to touch a woman.

LITV: But concerning what you wrote to me, [it is] good
for a man not to touch a woman;

First on this verse, for the first time all four versions translate the conjunction at the beginning of the verse. Again, it is *de* which can be legitimately translated as "but" or "now." But the important point is, it would be nice if the NET, and even the NKJV, were more consistent in this regard.

There are minor differences in the next phrase which won't be pursued here. The important differences in this verse usually occur in the second clause. This is a case where an idiom (or "euphemism" as the NET footnote calls it) is being used. And most versions just can't resist interpreting this idiom for their readers.

The second clause has two minor differences between the versions, and one important one. The first minor one is the last three versions correctly offset the words "it is" as being added for clarity while the NET does not.

The second minor difference is the ALT has "to be touching" while the rest have "to touch." The reason for this is that the infinite is in the present tense, which the ALT generally renders with its most basic "progressive" sense. This means Paul it not talking about merely a one-time simple "touch" but an ongoing behavior of "touching" a woman.

But the important question is, what does Paul mean by "to touch a woman?" What is the figurative meaning of the idiom? There are two main interpretations.

The first is that this phrase is an idiom for getting married; the second is that it refers to engaging in sexual relations with a woman. The NET rewrites the verse to indicate the latter interpretation, and it waits for a footnote to let readers know that the text has in fact been interpreted.

However, as was seen in Chapter Four, this writer believes the verse is referring to touching a woman in a such sexual manner that it ignites the man's or the women's sexual passions (see verse 9). And the ALT indicates this possible interpretation by adding "sexually" in brackets to the end of the verse.

But an interesting point is that this writer got the idea to add this word from the NET. At one time it had, "It is good for a man not to touch a woman sexually," but for some reason this rendering was changed to the above at a later date.

This writer believes the initial reading was better. The NET did not have the word "sexually" bracketed as it should be, but at least it was only one added word to what was otherwise a literal translation of the text. But the new reading involves entirely rewriting the last phrase.

Galatians 3:20

NET: Now an intermediary is not for one party alone, but God is one. (fn: interpretive)

ALT: But the mediator is not for one, but God is one.

NKJV: Now a mediator does not *mediate* for one *only,* but God is one.

LITV: But the Mediator is not of one, but God is one.

This verse is easy to translate, but very difficult to understand. The literal rendering can be seen in the ALT and LITV. However, most versions add words to help the reader understand the passage, and both the NET and NKJV have done so in this passage.

However, there is a big difference between how these two have done so. The NKJV has italicized its added words while the NET has not. So the reader of the NKJV knows which words are original and which are interpretive, but the reader of the NET has no way of making this distinction.

The NET does have a lengthy footnote giving a possible interpretation of this verse, which is fine. Footnotes are a good place to include interpretation, but the text itself is not. It would have been best if the NET kept interpretation in footnotes rather inserting interpretive words into the text without indicating in the text it has done so.

1Timothy 3:16

NET: And we all agree (fn: Grk "confessedly, admittedly, most certainly."), our religion contains amazing revelation (fn: Grk "great is the mystery of our religion" or "great is the mystery of godliness" [plus interpretive comments]):

He (fn: Grk, "who" [extended textual variant comments]) was revealed in the flesh,

Vindicated by the Spirit,
Seen by angels,
Proclaimed among Gentiles,
Believed on in the world,
Taken up in glory.

ALT: And confessedly, great is the secret [or, mystery] of godliness: God was revealed in flesh, justified [or, shown to be righteous] in spirit [or, by [the] Spirit], seen by angels, preached among [the] nations [or, Gentiles], believed on in [the] world, taken up in glory!

NKJV: And without controversy great is the mystery of godliness:

God was manifested in the flesh,
Justified in the Spirit,
Seen by angels,
Preached among the Gentiles,
Believed on in the world,
Received up in glory.

LITV: And confessedly, great is the mystery of godliness: God was manifested in flesh, was

> justified in Spirit, was seen by angels, was
> proclaimed among nations, was believed on in the
> world, was taken up in glory.

Throughout this book I have not retained any special formatting when quoting verses from various Bible versions. But I wanted to do so here as the difference is important. The NET and NKJV format the verse in the same manner in which they format poetic portions of the Bible (like the Psalms). The reason for this format is based on the theory that Paul is quoting from an early Christian hymn or creed in this verse.

However, this idea is just that, an idea. It has not been proven. The only way it could ever actually be proven would be to find an ancient manuscript with the full hymn or creed that Paul is supposedly quoting from. But until such a magnificent discovery should be made, the idea will remain an unproven theory.

So the question is, should a Bible version format its pages so as to include an unproven theory in its format? J.P. Green, the translator of the LITV, strongly believes it is inappropriate to do so and this writer agrees. Hence why the LITV and the ALT are not formatted in such a way.

But questions of format aside, it will be said this passage is rather difficult to translate, hence why there is considerable difference between the versions. However, there are limits to which a translation can go and still be an actual translation. And as the NET's own footnotes show, the NET has gone far from a literal translation in the first "stanza."

But most importantly in this verse is the textual variant. The ALT, NKJV, and LITV all begin the second "stanza" with the word "God" while the NET has "He." In this case, the NET does footnote the variant. In fact, as indicated, it has a lengthy textual footnote defending the reading of "who" instead of the word "God."

I present the reasons why I believe "God" is the appropriate reading in Chapter Nine. So the textual debate will not be pursued here. But two points will be mentioned.

First, as with John 3:13, by using "He" rather than "God," the NET again eliminates a proof-text for the deity of Christ. Second, notice I said the NET's footnote defends the reading of "who" yet in its text it uses "He." Why? Simple: "who" simply makes no sense in the passage. It makes it sound like a question when it is not. But "God" makes perfect sense.

Now in its note, the NET tries to utilize the idea of this passage being an excerpt from a creed or hymn to support the reading of "who." The claim is that the "original" text Paul was quoting from used "who" and he quoted it verbatim without adjusting the grammar, hence the seemingly nonsensical wording. But this writer does not find combining an unproven theory and limited manuscript support to be convincing, especially when the vast majority of the manuscript evidence is against it.

Conclusion

Despite the NET's bold claims in its background pages, a "literal" translation is possible, readable, and understandable. But because of its animosity towards a literal translation, the NET translators have produced a Bible version that is far from a literal translation. Not only does it out-right paraphrase at times, but the translators also insert their interpretations into the text without any indication in the text that they have done so.

On top of this, the NT is based on the CT. So just in the verses evaluated above, there was a loss of two proof-texts for the deity of Christ. And there are other significant differences between the CT and the TR/ MT.

So being a "dynamic equivalence" version bordering on being a paraphrase at times and being based on the CT means the NET Bible simply is not the type of version I would recommend to anyone. At best it could be used for comparison purposes with a more literal version.

Along with its notes, the NET could also be used as one uses a commentary. But the use of a literal or formal equivalence translation and a real commentary would be preferable.

Bibliography for chapters twenty and twenty-one:

Dana, H.E. and Julius Mantey. *A Manual Grammar of the Greek New Testament*. New York: Macmillan, 1955.

Friberg, Timothy and Barbara. *Analytical Greek New Testament*. Copyright © 1994 and *Analytical Lexicon to the Greek New Testament*. Copyright © 1994. as found on *BibleWorks™ for Windows™*. Copyright © 1992-1999 *BibleWorks*, L.C.C. Big Fork, MT: Hermeneutika. Programmed by Michael S. Bushell and Michael D. Tan.

Rienecker, Fritz. *A Linguistic Key to the Greek New Testament*. Trans. and ed. by Cleon Rogers. Grand Rapids, MI: Zondervan, 1980.

Webster's Talking Dictionary/ Thesaurus. Licensed property of Parson's Technology, Inc. v. 1.0b. Software Copyright 1996 by Exceller Software Corp. Based on Random House *Webster's College Dictionary*. Copyright 1995 by Random House, Inc.

Chapter Twenty-two
Recommended Bible Versions:
Sample Passages

To aid in choosing a Bible version, below are sample passages from the seven versions most recommended in this book. Passages have been reformatted so all have the same formatting.

At the end of the passages, is a list of the abbreviations and notations seen in the ALT, along with the corresponding entries from the appendix in the ALT for textual variants.

Matthew 6:9-13

YLT: 9 thus therefore pray ye: 'Our Father who {art} in the heavens! hallowed be Thy name. 10 'Thy reign come: Thy will come to pass, as in heaven also on the earth. 11 'Our appointed bread give us to-day. 12 'And forgive us our debts, as also we forgive our debtors. 13 'And mayest Thou not lead us to temptation, but deliver us from the evil, because Thine is the reign, and the power, and the glory—to the ages. Amen.'"

LITV: 9 So, then, you should pray this way: Our Father [who is] in Heaven, Hallowed be Your name. 10 Your kingdom come; Your will be done, as [it is] in Heaven, also on the earth. 11 Give us today our daily bread, 12 and forgive us our debts as we also forgive our debtors. 13 And do not lead us into temptation, but deliver us from the evil, for Yours is the kingdom and the power and the glory to the ages. Amen.

ALT: 9 "Therefore, _you*_, be praying like this: 'Our Father, the [One] in the heavens, let Your name be regarded as holy. 10 'Let Your kingdom come; let Your will be done, as in heaven, [so] also on the earth. 11 'Give us today the bread sufficient for the day. 12 'And forgive us our debts [fig., sins], in the same way as _we _ also forgive our debtors [fig., the ones having sinned against us]. 13   'And do not lead us into temptation, _but_ deliver us from evil [or, from the evil [one]]. Because Yours is the kingdom and the power and the glory into the ages [fig., forever]! So be it [Gr. *amen*]!'"

KJV: 9 After this manner therefore pray ye: Our Father which art in heaven, Hallowed be thy name. 10 Thy kingdom come. Thy will be done in earth, as *it is* in heaven. 11 Give us this day our daily bread. 12 And forgive us our debts, as we forgive our debtors. 13 And lead us not into temptation, but deliver us from evil: For thine is the kingdom, and the power, and the glory, for ever. Amen.

NKJV: 9 "In this manner, therefore, pray: Our Father in heaven, Hallowed be Your name. 10 Your kingdom come. Your will be done On earth as *it is* in heaven. 11 Give us this day our daily bread. 12 And forgive us our debts, As we forgive our debtors. 13 And do not lead us into temptation, But deliver us from the evil one. ^aFor Yours is the kingdom and the power and the glory forever. Amen."
^a NU omits the rest of v. 13.

MKJV: 9 Therefore pray in this way: Our Father, [who is] in Heaven, Hallowed be Your name. 10 Your kingdom come, Your will be done, on earth as [it is] in Heaven. 11 Give us this day our daily bread; 12 and forgive us our debts as we also forgive our debtors. 13 And lead us not into temptation, but deliver us from the evil. For Yours is the kingdom, and the power, and the glory, forever. Amen.

WEB: 9 "Pray like this: 'Our Father in heaven, may your name be kept holy. 10 Let your kingdom come. Let your will be done, as in heaven, so on earth. 11 Give us today our daily bread. 12 Forgive us our debts, as we also forgive our debtors. 13 Bring us not into temptation, but deliver us from the evil one. For yours is the kingdom, the power, and the glory forever. Amen.'"

John 15:1-3

YLT: 1 'I am the true vine, and my Father is the husbandman; 2 every branch in me not bearing fruit, He doth take it away, and every one bearing fruit, He doth cleanse by pruning it, that it may bear more fruit; 3 already ye are clean, because of the word that I have spoken to you;'

LITV: 1 I am the True Vine, and My Father is the Vinedresser. 2 Every branch in Me not bearing fruit, He takes it away; and each one bearing fruit, He prunes, so that it may bear more fruit. 3 You are already pruned because of the Word which I have spoken to you.

ALT: 1 "_I_ am the true grapevine, and My Father is the vineyard keeper. 2 "Every branch in Me not bearing fruit, He takes it away [or, lifts it up]; and every [branch] bearing fruit, He prunes clean, so that it shall be bearing more fruit. 3 "Already you* are pruned clean because of the word which I have spoken to you*."

KJV: 1 I am the true vine, and my Father is the husbandman. 2 Every branch in me that beareth not fruit he taketh away: and every *branch* that beareth fruit, he purgeth it, that it may bring forth more fruit. 3 Now ye are clean through the word which I have spoken unto you.

NKJV: 1 "I am the true vine, and My Father is the vinedresser. 2 "Every branch in Me that does not bear fruit He takes away[a]; and every *branch* that bears fruit He prunes, that it may bear more fruit. 3 "You are already clean because of the word which I have spoken to you."
    [a] Or *lifts up*

Gary Zeolla

MKJV: 1 I am the True Vine, and My Father is the Vinedresser. 2 Every branch in Me that does not bear fruit, He takes away. And every one that bears fruit, He prunes it so that it may bring forth more fruit. 3 Now you are clean through the Word which I have spoken to you.

WEB: 1 "I am the true vine, and my Father is the farmer. 2 Every branch in me that doesn't bear fruit, he takes away. Every branch that bears fruit, he prunes, that it may bear more fruit. 3 You are already pruned clean because of the word which I have spoken to you."

Romans 12:1-2

YLT: 1 I call upon you, therefore, brethren, through the compassions of God, to present your bodies a sacrifice—living, sanctified, acceptable to God—your intelligent service; 2 and be not conformed to this age, but be transformed by the renewing of your mind, for your proving what {is} the will of God—the good, and acceptable, and perfect.

LITV: 1 Therefore, brothers, I call on you through the compassions of God to present your bodies a living sacrifice, holy, pleasing to God, [which] is your reasonable service. 2 And be not conformed to this age, but be transformed by the renewing of your mind, in order to prove by you what [is] the good and pleasing and perfect will of God.

ALT: 1 Therefore, I call on [or, plead with] you*, brothers [and sisters], through the compassions of God, to present your* bodies a living sacrifice, holy, acceptable to God [which is] your* intelligent, sacred service. 2 And [you* are] to stop conforming yourselves to this age, _but_ [are] to continue being transformed by the renewal of your* mind, in order for you* to be proving what [is] the good and acceptable and perfect will of God.

312

KJV: 1 I beseech you therefore, brethren, by the mercies of God, that ye present your bodies a living sacrifice, holy, acceptable unto God, *which is* your reasonable service. 2 And be not conformed to this world: but be ye transformed by the renewing of your mind, that ye may prove what *is* that good, and acceptable, and perfect, will of God.

NKJV: 1 I beseech[a] you therefore, brethren, by the mercies of God, that you present your bodies a living sacrifice, holy, acceptable to God, *which is* your [b]reasonable service. 2 And do not be conformed to this world, but be transformed by the renewing of your mind, that you may prove what *is* that good and acceptable and perfect will of God.

[a] urge
[b] rational

MKJV: 1 I beseech you therefore, brothers, by the mercies of God to present your bodies a living sacrifice, holy, pleasing to God, [which is] your reasonable service. 2 And do not be conformed to this world, but be transformed by the renewing of your mind, in order to prove by you what [is] that good and pleasing and perfect will of God.

WEB: 1 Therefore I urge you, brothers, by the mercies of God, to present your bodies a living sacrifice, holy, acceptable to God, which is your spiritual service. 2 Don't be conformed to this world, but be transformed by the renewing of your mind, so that you may prove what is the good, well-pleasing, and perfect will of God.

Galatians 3:19-21

YLT: 9 Why, then, the law? on account of the transgressions it was added, till the seed might come to which the promise hath been made, having been set in order through messengers in the hand of a mediator—20 and the mediator is not of one, and God is one—21 the law, then, {is} against the promises of God?—let it not be! for if a law was given that was able to make alive, truly by law there would have been the righteousness,

LITV: 19 Why the Law then? It was added because of transgressions, until the Seed should come, to whom it had been promised, being ordained through angels in a mediator's hand. 20 But the Mediator is not of one, but God is one. 21 Then [is] the Law against the promises of God? Let it not be! For if a law had been given which had been able to make alive, indeed righteousness would have been out of law.

ALT: 19 Why then the Law? It was added on account of transgressions, until the Seed should come to whom it had been promised, having been set in order [or, ordained] by means of angels by [the] hand of a mediator [i.e. Moses]. 20 But the mediator is not for one, but God is one. 21 Therefore, [is] the Law against the promises of God? Absolutely not! For if a law was given which was able to make alive, [then] righteousness would indeed be by law.

KJV: 9 Wherefore then *serveth* the law? It was added because of transgressions, till the seed should come to whom the promise was made; *and it was* ordained by angels in the hand of a mediator. 20 Now a mediator is not *a mediator* of one, but God is one. 21 *Is* the law then against the promises of God? God forbid: for if there had been a law given which could have given life, verily righteousness should have been by the law.

NKJV: 19 What purpose then *does* the law *serve?* It was added because of transgressions, till the Seed should come to whom the promise was made; *and it was* appointed through angels by the hand of a mediator. 20 Now a mediator does not *mediate* for one *only,* but God is one. 21 *Is* the law then against the promises of God? Certainly not! For if there had been a law given which could have given life, truly righteousness would have been by the law.

MKJV: 19 Why then the Law? It was added because of transgressions, until the Seed should come to those to whom it had been promised, being ordained through angels in [the] Mediator's hand. 20 But the Mediator is not [a mediator] of one, but God is one. 21 [Is] the Law then against the promises of God? Let it not be [said]! For if a law had been given which could have given life, indeed righteousness would have been out of Law.

WEB: 19 What then is the law? It was added because of transgressions, until the seed should come to whom the promise has been made. It was ordained through angels by the hand of a mediator. 20 Now a mediator is not between one, but God is one. 21 Is the law then against the promises of God? Certainly not! For if there had been a law given which could make alive, most assuredly righteousness would have been of the law.

1John 3:7-9

YLT: 7 Little children, let no one lead you astray; he who is doing the righteousness is righteous, even as he is righteous, 8 he who is doing the sin, of the devil he is, because from the beginning the devil doth sin; for this was the Son of God manifested, that he may break up the works of the devil; 9 every one who hath been begotten of God, sin he doth not, because his seed in him doth remain, and he is not able to sin, because of God he hath been begotten.

LITV: 7 Little children, let no one lead you astray; the one practicing righteousness is righteous, even as that One is righteous. 8 The one practicing sin is of the Devil, because the Devil sins from the beginning. For this the Son of God was revealed, that He undo the works of the Devil. 9 Everyone who has been begotten of God does not sin, because His seed abides in him, and he is not able to sin, because he has been born of God.

ALT: 7 Little children [or, [My] dear children], let no one be leading you* astray [fig., be deceiving you*]; the one practicing righteousness is righteous, just as He is righteous. 8 The one practicing sin is from the Devil, because the Devil [has been] sinning from [the] beginning. For this [reason] the Son of God was revealed, so that He should destroy the works of the Devil. 9 Every one having been begotten from God is not practicing sin, because His seed abides in him, and he is not able to be sinning, because he has been begotten from God.

KJV: 7 Little children, let no man deceive you: he that doeth righteousness is righteous, even as he is righteous. 8 He that committeth sin is of the devil; for the devil sinneth from the beginning. For this purpose the Son of God was manifested, that he might destroy the works of the devil. 9 Whosoever is born of God doth not commit sin; for his seed remaineth in him: and he cannot sin, because he is born of God.

NKJV: 7 Little children, let no one deceive you. He who practices righteousness is righteous, just as He is righteous. 8 He who sins is of the devil, for the devil has sinned from the beginning. For this purpose the Son of God was manifested, that He might destroy the works of the devil. 9 Whoever has been born of God does not sin, for His seed remains in him; and he cannot sin, because he has been born of God.

MKJV: 7 Little children, let no one deceive you. He who does righteousness is righteous, even as that One is righteous. 8 He who practices sin is of the Devil, for the Devil sins from the beginning. For this purpose the Son of God was revealed, that He might undo the works of the Devil. 9 Everyone who has been born of God does not commit sin, because His seed remains in him, and he cannot sin, because he has been born of God.

WEB: 7 Little children, let no one lead you astray. He who does righteousness is righteous, even as he is righteous. 8 He who sins is of the devil, for the devil has been sinning from the beginning. To this end the Son of God was revealed, that he might destroy the works of the devil. 9 Whoever is born of God doesn't commit sin, because his seed remains in him; and he can't sin, because he is born of God.

ALT: Abbreviations and Notations

In Brackets:

[the] – Words added for clarity are bracketed. Within bracketed alternative translations, bracketed words indicate words added for clarity, i.e. [or, [My] dear children] (1John 3:7) indicates the word "My" is added.
fig., – Possible figurative meaning of preceding literal translation.
Gr. – Transliteration of the Greek word previously translated.
i.e., – Explanatory note ("that is" or "in explanation").
or, – Alternative translation of the preceding word or phrase.

Miscellaneous:
but – Indicates the use of the Greek strong adversative (*alla*) instead of the weak adversative (*de*, translated as "but" when used in an adversative sense).
you* – Indicates the original is plural (also, your*). With no asterisk the second person pronoun is singular.
you – Indicates the pronoun is emphasized in the Greek text (also, _I_, _he_ , _she_ , etc.).

ALT: Appendix Entries for Textual Variants

Note: The TR and CT variants are translated as they would appear in the ALT if it was based on these texts.

Matt 6:13 MT/ TR: Because Yours is the kingdom and the power and the glory into the ages! So be it! – CT: omits

Rom 12:2 MT: [you* are] to stop conforming yourselves to this age, _but_ [are] to continue being transformed – TR/ CT: stop conforming yourselves to this age, _but_ continue being transformed (See the end of Chapter Eleven for details on this variant.)

Rom 12:2 MT/ TR: for you* – CT: for

Bibliography:

Analytical-Literal Translation of the New Testament of the Holy Bible (ALT). Copyright © 1999-2001 by Gary F. Zeolla of Darkness to Light ministry (www.dtl.org).

King James Version (KJV). Public domain.

Literal Translation of the Bible (LITV). Copyright 1976 - 1999. Used by permission of the copyright holder, Jay P. Green, Sr.

Modern King James Version (MKJV). Copyright 1962 - 1999. Used by the permission of the copyright holder, Jay P. Green, Sr.

New King James Version. Nashville, TN: Thomas Nelson Publishers, 1982

World English Bible (WEB). Longmont, CO: Rainbow Missions, Inc., copyright-free.

Young, Robert. *Young's Literal Translation* (YLT). Public Domain, 1898.

Appendixes

Appendix #1
Summary Outlines on Bible Versions

The following outlines summarize the information presented in this book.

Different Translation Principles

I.   Literal translation (YLT, LITV, ALT).
    A. EVERY WORD in the Hebrew and Greek texts translated.
    B. Words added for clarity are italicized or bracketed.
    C. Best concurs with the doctrine of verbal inspiration and the commands and warnings of Scripture (Deut 4:2; Prov 30:5,6; Rev 22:18,19).

II. Formal or complete equivalence (KJV, NKJV, MKJV, WEB, NASB).
    A. Hebrew and Greek texts translated as WORD FOR WORD as possible.
    B. Minor deviations from a literal translation to improve readability.
    C. Words added for clarity are italicized or bracketed.
    D. Concurs very well with the doctrine of verbal inspiration and the commands and warnings of Scripture.

III. Expanded (*Amplified Bible*; Wuest).
    A. One author attempts to bring out NUANCES of the original languages.
    B. Amplifications are helpful, but can also be questionable.
    C. The text tends to be awkward to read.
    D. The ALT also contains expanded features.

IV. Dynamic equivalence (NIV, *God's Word*, and most other modern versions).
  A. Attempts to express the MEANING of the Hebrew or Greek texts.
  B. Produces very readable versions.
  C. Words often added without any indication in the translation.
  D. Hebrew and Greek words frequently left untranslated.
  E. Grammar of words and phrases altered.
  F. Tendency to interpret rather than just translate.

V. Paraphrase (*Living Bible*; *The Message*).
  A. The text is REWORDED by one author.
  B. Produces very expressive and readable versions.
  C. Little regard for original vocabulary, syntax, and grammar.
  D. Author's theological biases can infiltrate the text.
  E. Significant portions and points of a verse can be left out.

Different Greek Text-Types

I. Textus Receptus (LITV, KJV, NKJV, MKJV).
  A. Based on handful of manuscripts available in 1500's, but these manuscripts:
    1. Reflected the text type seen in the vast majority of later discovered manuscripts.
    2. Reflected the text type widely distributed and accepted in early centuries.
    3. Reflected the text-type used in most early translations.
  B. Text used by Bible translators from the Reformation until 1881.
  C. Recognizes Gnostics and other heretics produced corrupted manuscripts.

II. Majority Text (ALT, WEB).
   A. Based on belief God has "providentially preserved" His words:
      1. Based on the now over 5000 manuscripts available.
      2. Text type seen in the vast majority of manuscripts (4000+).
      3. Text type widely distributed and accepted in early centuries.
      4. Text type used in most early translations.
   B. Recognizes Gnostics and other heretics produced corrupted manuscripts.
   C. Corrects readings in the TR with little manuscript support.

III. Critical Text (NASB, NIV, and most other modern-day versions).
   A. Primary premise: Bible should be treated just like any other book.
   B. Based on handful of early, Alexandrian texts.
   C. Developed by making decisions on "Transcriptional Probabilities."
      1. These rules and decisions can be subjective and questionable.
      2. Assumes Christian scribes deliberately altered "difficult" readings.
   D. Ignores that Gnostics and other early heretics produced corrupted manuscripts.

IV. Comparison of Greek texts.
   A. The three texts are in substantial agreement.
   B. Most differences are insignificant, but some significant variants.
   C. MT and TR are very similar.
   D. Most differences and significant differences between the MT/ TR and CT.

E. TR/ MT tradition best concurs with God's promise to preserve His words: Psalm 12:6,7; Matt 24:35; Luke 16:17.

Appendix #2
Additional Books by the Author

Gary F. Zeolla is also the author of the following books.

Scripture Workbook: For Personal Bible Study and Teaching the Bible:

This book contains twenty-two individual Scripture Studies. Each study focuses on one general area of study. These studies enable individuals to do in-depth, topical studies of the Bible. They are also invaluable to the Bible study teacher preparing lessons for Sunday School or a home Bible study.

The range of topics covered in the different studies is broad: from what the Bible teaches about itself to what the Bible teaches about divorce and remarriage. Contained in each study are hundreds of Scripture references. So there will be no lack of material from which to begin your studies. ISBN: 1-58721-893-3

Creationist Diet: Nutrition and God-given Foods According to the Bible:

This book answers such questions as: What did God give to human beings for food? What does the Bible teach about diet and nutrition? How do the Biblical teachings on foods compare to scientific research on nutrition and degenerative disease like heart disease, cancer, and stroke?

In answering these questions, the book starts with God's decrees about foods at Creation, in the Garden of Eden, after the Fall, and after the Flood, and gleans nutrition information from the rest of the Bible, while correlating this information with scientific research. ISBN: 1-58721-852-6

In addition, Gary F. Zeolla is the translator of the following Bible version:

The Analytical-Literal Translation of the New Testament of the Holy Bible (ALT):

The purpose of the ALT is provide a translation of the Greek New Testament that will enable the reader to come as close to the Greek text as possible without actually having to be proficient in Greek. And the name of the ALT reflects this purpose.

"Literal" refers to the fact that the ALT is a word for word translation. Every word in the original text is translated—nothing is omitted. The original grammar of the text is retained as much as possible. And any words added for clarity are bracketed, so nothing is added without it being indicated as such.

"Analytical" refers to the detailed "analysis" done on the grammar of the text. The grammar is then translated in way which brings out "nuances" of the original text that are often missed in traditional translations.

In addition, "analytical" refers to aids that are included within the text which enable the reader to "analyze" and understand the text. Such information is bracketed. It includes the following:

1. Alternative translations for words and phrases.
2. The figurative meanings of words and phrases.
3. Modern-day equivalents for measurement and monetary units and time designations.
4. Explanatory notes.
5. References for Old Testament quotations and other cross-references.

The Greek text used for the ALT is the *Byzantine Majority Text*, specifically: *The Greek New Testament According to the Byzantine Textform*. As edited by Maurice A. Robinson and William G. Pierpont. Revised edition, 2001. The ALT is one of the first translations of the New Testament to be based on this newest and most accurate Greek text. To aid in comparing the

ALT with other Bible versions, significant textual variants are listed in an appendix.

The above items are available from the publisher 1stBooks (www.1stbooks.com) and from conventional and online bookstores.

Appendix #3:
About Darkness to Light

Gary F. Zeolla is the founder and director of Darkness to Light ministry (www.dtl.org). Darkness to Light is dedicated to explaining and defending the Christian faith. It is written from a Reformed-Baptist perspective, but the focus is on the "essentials of the faith." The subjects of theology, apologetics, cults, ethics, and many others are discussed using articles, e-mail exchanges, and other items.

There is also an extensive section on the Bible versions controversy. But unlike most such sites on the Internet, there is no harsh language used in the discussions. The same is true for all other sections of the site. Controversial issues are discussed in a logical and straightforward manner, without any harsh language.

In addition, posted on the site is the full text of the *Analytical-Literal Translation of the New Testament of the Holy Bible*. As the name implies, this is a very literal translation. It also includes aids within the text to help readers better understand the text. It is one of only two current versions that are based on the Majority Greek Text. So it is a very unique version.

Overall, there is much information posted on the site dealing with just about every aspect of the Christian faith.

The name for the ministry is taken from the following verse:

"...to open their eyes, in order to turn them from DARKNESS TO LIGHT, and from the power of Satan to God, that they may receive forgiveness of sins and an inheritance among those who are sanctified by faith in [Christ]" (Acts 26:18).

The words "darkness" and "light" have a wide range of meanings when used metaphorically in Scripture, but basically, "darkness" refers to falsehood and unrighteousness while "light" refers to truth and righteousness. People turn from darkness to light when they come to believe the teachings of the Bible and live in accordance with them.

Appendix #4
Contacting the Author

The author can be contacted at: gary@dtl.org, but please note the following:

1. I generally use my handheld PC to check and answer e-mail. It can only receive "text only" messages. So please do not send me "rich text" or HTML formatted e-mails or attached files.

2. All e-mails are read and taken under consideration. But I regret I simply do not have the time to respond to everyone personally.

3. E-mails of general interest will be published, edited, and commented upon as I deem appropriate. Published e-mails will only include the e-mailer's first name or initials, unless otherwise requested. If you do not want your e-mail published, write "Confidential" at the top of the message.

4. Comments can also be sent via "snail mail" to: Gary F. Zeolla ~ c/o Darkness to Light ~ PO Box 138 ~ Natrona Heights, PA 15065.

About the Author

Gary F. Zeolla is the founder and director of Darkness to Light ministry, which is dedicated to explaining and defending the Christian faith (www.dtl.org). In addition to *Differences Between Bible Versions*, Gary Zeolla is the author of the following books:

Creationist Diet: Nutrition and God-given Foods According to the Bible.
Scripture Workbook: For Personal Bible Study and Teaching the Bible

He is also the translator of the *Analytical-Literal Translation of the New Testament of the Holy Bible*.

All three of these books are available from the publisher 1stBooks (www.1stbooks.com) and from most conventional and online bookstores.

Printed in the United States
1197200001B/13-15

9 780759 625013